"Social networking to land a job is nothing new, but Miriam's book offers plenty of advice I've never even thought of before—and I write about this on a daily basis! *Social Networking for Career Success* is broken into easily digestible chunks of information that will benefit everyone from college students to experienced professionals. It's a whole new world of job hunting out there!"

—Heather R. Huhman,
Founder and President, comerecommended.com

"Miriam has assembled the ultimate go-to-guide for the modern job seeker. The advice is clear and concise, the tools easy to understand and the value undeniable. You need to read this book."

—Mark Stelzner, Founder of JobAngels

"This is a crucial book for anybody—regardless of age, education level, industry, or function—to gain a career edge and succeed in a world where social media has become as essential as the printed resume used to be. *Social Networking for Career Success* shows you how to gain access to the best opportunities, before they are posted to the general public, and is a resource that you will refer to again and again."

—Andrew Neitlich,
Co-Author of *Guerrilla Marketing for a Bulletproof Career*

"Miriam Salpeter is a true leader in the social networking world and in her book, "Social Networking for Career Success," she shares her expert advice for social media users of all levels and career goals. This book should be on the shelf or e-reader of anyone who is serious about career success in today's hyper-connected world. Highly recommended."

—Lindsey Pollak, Author of *Getting from College to Career: 90 Things to Do Before You Join the Real World*

"*Social Networking for Career Success* is the modern job seeker's insider guide to job search and career management success. Miriam shares all the secrets, sites, and strategies to put anyone, including a web novice, at home in confidently navigating the otherwise complex web of social media job search to identify and win the job."

—Laura DeCarlo, President of the global association,
Career Directors International; creator of the Certified Professional
in Online Job Search & Reputation Management; and Author of
*Interviewing: The Gold Standard, Job Search Bloopers,
and Interview Pocket RX*

"Miriam Salpeter is a job seeker's best friend. Her business is helping others use social media to land their next job . . . and she does so beautifully! Now, there are others out there who 'get' social media, but can't teach it, and even more who can teach it, but don't have anything unique to say. Miriam is one of the only social media gurus who consistently and clearly shares a simple, yet unique, strategy for using social media to land your next gig. Read this book if you are still unsure how to really maximize your time on the various, emerging social media platforms available; I assure you, you will emerge much more knowledgeable and armed for your job search. This book is well worth the money, and highly recommended!!"

—Laura M. Labovich, Founder,
The Career Strategy Group

"*Social Networking for Career Success* is a head above other social media resources. Miriam is a respected blogger and experienced social media pro who provides strategic insights and technical guidance. She anticipates her readers' questions, deftly transitioning from the high view to the essential details. This is the must read guide for anyone who wants to use social networking to access new career opportunities."

—Debra Feldman,
Executive Talent Agent, JobWhiz

"Miriam has successfully used social networks to advance her personal brand. This book will show you how you can do the same!"

—Dan Schawbel, author of *Me 2.0* and founder of Millennial Branding

"Today more than ever it's critical to know how to navigate the digital ecosystem. This book provides readers with real world stories and advice on how to leverage social networking to find a job or simply advance their career."

—Robyn Cobb, VP Digital Influence, Ogilvy Public Relations

"This really—seriously!—is a must-read book for everyone, unemployed or not! Excellent, landmark book—the best I've read on this topic! Social media and social networks are dramatically impacting the job search/recruiting landscape for all of us, and the velocity of change is picking up. So, smart people will read and implement Miriam's suggestions before they need to job search, because to ignore this technological revolution is to be left behind—waaaayyyy behind. And, very few of us can afford that!"

—Susan P. Joyce, Editor/Publisher, Job-Hunt.org

"*Social Networking for Career Success* is a comprehensive, well-organized guide for any professional or job-seeker to advance his or her career. Whether you are a passive candidate or engaged in an active job search, this book will prove to be a valuable resource in managing your online presence and creating a positive brand that will attract employers."

—Andrea Santiago, Guide to Health Careers at About.com

"We use social networking sites everyday to check-in, update our friends and share ideas with the world. But what if you need to find a job or establish a new career? Miriam's book offers practical and strategic advice to build your online brand along with examples of people doing it right."

—Tim Tyrell-Smith, Founder of Tim's Strategy and
Author of *30 Ideas: The Ideas of Successful Job Search*

"*Social Networking for Career Success* is basic enough for those who are clueless about social media, yet rich enough to offer social media pros information they likely don't already know."

—Vivian Steir Rabin and Carol Fishman Cohen,
Co-Authors, Back on the Career Track

"No one knows the intersection of social media and careers better than Miriam Salpeter. I am always learning something new from her, and thanks to Social Networking for Career Success, you will too! The best thing about this book is its substantial detail—by the time you're finished, you'll be ready to take advantage of dozens of social networking strategies you didn't even know existed."

—Alexandra Levit, Author of *New Job, New You:*
A Guide to Reinventing Yourself in a Bright New Career

"Miriam not only shows you how to efficiently and effectively use social media tools to land your dream career, she also gives you some valuable insight into how you can make it easy for employers to find you. And she does it with a little bit of humor and spunk!"

—Heather McGough, Microsoft Recruiter since 2000

SOCIAL NETWORKING FOR CAREER SUCCESS

Second Edition

SOCIAL NETWORKING FOR CAREER SUCCESS

Second Edition

Miriam Salpeter

NEW YORK

Library of Congress Cataloging-in-Publication Data

Salpeter, Miriam.
  Social networking for career success : using online tools to create a personal
brand / Miriam Salpeter. -- Second edition.
    pages cm
  ISBN 978-1-57685-932-2
  1. Business networks. 2. Online social networks. 3. Career development. 4.
Branding (Marketing) I. Title.
  HD69.S8S253 2013
  650.140285'4678--dc23
                        2013027025

Printed in the United States of America

9 8 7 6 5 4 3 2 1

Second Edition

ISBN 978-1-57685-932-2

For information or to place an order, contact LearningExpress at:
  80 Broad Street
  Suite 400
  New York, NY 10004

About the Author

MIRIAM SALPETER MA, is owner of Keppie Careers, a coaching and consulting firm helping entrepreneurs and job seekers leverage social media and traditional tools to achieve their business and career goals. Miriam is in demand as a social media and job search strategist, consultant, and speaker. She has co-authored two other highly acclaimed and award-winning books published by Learning-Express: *100 Conversations for Career Success* and *Social Networking for Business Success: Turn Your Ideas into Income.* Traditional media outlets, such *The Wall Street Journal, The New York Times*, and Forbes.com, frequently cite Miriam's advice regarding how to leverage social media and CNN named her to its list of "top 10 job tweeters you should be following." Miriam contributes weekly to *U.S. News & World Report* and to AOL Jobs.com and shares cutting-edge strategies for business owners and job seekers via her own site, KeppieCareers.com.

A vice president for a Wall Street firm prior to earning a master's degree from Columbia University, Miriam headed the Career Action Center at the Rollins School of Public Health of Emory University before launching her own business. She has been helping to empower job seekers and small-business owners for more than 17 years.

Miriam lives in Atlanta with her husband, Mike, and their three boys. She invites you to connect with her on Twitter @Keppie_Careers and to touch base via her blog:

www.keppiecareers.com.

Acknowledgments ▶

A special thank you to my colleagues and good friends who have collaborated with me on two books since *Social Networking for Career Success* first came out: Laura Labovich and Hannah Morgan. I'm so glad to have had the chance to work with each of you and am grateful for your friendship and continuing collaborations.

Another special shout out to the members of a group we affectionately refer to as the "masterminds": Pamela Gottfried, Corey-Jan Albert, Rochelle Nation, and Jennifer Willhoite. This team of "in person" colleagues and friends from a variety of backgrounds proves how useful it is to combine online networking with "in real life" meetings.

Thanks to all of my wonderful colleagues and friends who generously contributed their expertise and advice; this book is richer because of their input. A special thank you to my colleague Jacqui Barrett-Poindexter for her friendship, and to Laurie Ruettimann for connecting me to this opportunity. Thanks to John Youngblood, who hired me for my first career advising job and, after I left Emory, helped launch me on the social media path by suggesting I start a blog. It was a pleasure working with the great team at LearningExpress, especially Sheryl Posnick, Director of the Book Program.

Most importantly, I appreciate my family, especially my amazing husband Mike, and wonderful boys, for all of their support and encouragement. I dedicate this book in memory of my mom, Stephanie Cohen, who demonstrated how to be a great communicator and leader, and always taught me that I could do anything.

CONTENTS ▶

CONTENTS

Foreword

When the economy hit the skids several years ago and people started losing their jobs right and left, I was astounded by the number of people who had no clue about how to find a job.

One man told me the last time he had looked for work he had simply picked up a copy of *The New York Times*, circled a few ads, made some phone calls and voila! He had a job. But looking for a job through Twitter? Facebook? LinkedIn? He admitted he didn't know the first thing about social networking.

As the bad times stretched on, I talked to dozens of unemployed people for my USA Today syndicated workplace column who were beginning to panic, and began lurching into the social networking arena with all the grace of Bambi on ice. They sent out mass LinkedIn requests to people they didn't know, looking more like online stalkers than qualified professionals with valuable skills to offer.

The employed were just as worried. They fretted about losing their jobs, so they decided to make some equally clumsy forays into the online world. There were half-hearted attempts to update LinkedIn profiles and sometimes idiotic tweets where they called the boss an ass and shared the fact they had a hangover from too many Jell-O shooters the night before.

For the jobless and the employed, venturing into the online social scene wasn't always pretty.

Unfortunately, things haven't improved all that much since the economy went in the toilet. Yes, employers are hiring again—slowly—and fewer employees feel like they'll get a pink slip any day now. But that doesn't mean all the important lessons have been learned.

Job seekers still tweet about the bad breath of an interviewer and don't expect to be caught doing it (they get caught—they always get caught). Workers, exhausted by the daily grind, haven't added anyone new to their online networks for the last eight months.

In writing about workplace and career issues for more than 20 years, I've heard just about every excuse in the book as to why people mess up in their careers and job searches. But one thing I know for sure—excuses won't get you a job or a promotion, and employers have even less patience than before for the ones who can't get their act together.

That's why Miriam's book is a goldmine. She not only gives you all the information and resources you need to enter the social networking world and thrive in it, but she's also going to keep you from making a fool of yourself. She knows what works and what doesn't, because she lives these practices every day.

Miriam first commented on my blog several years ago. She never asked for anything in return, just left thoughtful ideas again and again. She directed sources my way. She retweeted requests for information I needed for stories.

Over the years, I've used her as a source, laughed with her over the antics of our boys and appreciated how hard she has worked to learn the online networking world and develop her expertise.

So, when she asked me to write the forward for this book, I was happy to oblige. Miriam is someone who has done her homework, who has walked the talk and now offers others this wonderful resource. She's done a lot of the hard work—now it's time for you to take advantage of it.

Anita Bruzzese
Syndicated columnist for *USA Today*

Introduction

Maybe you are looking for a job. Or, you are planning to keep doing exactly what you have been doing for years. You may be thinking about a completely new career and need to smooth the transition to your next big opportunity. Perhaps you are seeing the writing on the wall and deciding that starting a business—and hanging your own virtual shingle—is in the cards. You are a new graduate, an experienced professional, or somewhere in between. Whatever your current situation, and job goals, this book is for you. Social networking is also for you—and it can profoundly impact your career in many positive ways. It's not a surprise that a lot has changed since this book came out two years ago; social media is a fast-moving target. This edition includes countless updates, including information about two networks that did not exist when the first edition was published (Google+ and Pinterest). I've also added details about many new, useful tools, tips, and tricks to help you leverage your time online.

One thing has not changed: my advice about how to set your goals and approach your time online. The most successful social media users generously share their expertise with online communities and grow their networks of people who know, like, and trust them. When you take this approach, you'll learn a lot and benefit from a supportive, helpful, and accommodating team of new friends and colleagues online.

If you have not yet dived into the world of social networking and experienced how powerful it can be, you don't know what you are missing. If you think LinkedIn is only for job seekers and Twitter for stalking celebrities, I have great news—these and other networks can change your life in ways you will never understand until you jump in with both feet and try them out.

You may be skeptical. I meet people who are all the time. Perhaps you don't think sharing your personal or professional information online is going to help your career or business. Maybe you don't have time and think social networking is for people who have nothing better to do all day. The truth is, social networking gets some bad press. Many consider it a way to lose a job, not a tool for getting one! If this sounds like you, you are not alone. I challenge you to read this book, and to really engage in these online communities. After doing so, I challenge you to tell me it's not worth it.

I've leveraged my own social network to write this book. It includes expert advice and opinions from over 100 of my colleagues and friends, other coaches, recruiters, human resource professionals, and others, all of whom I've met via Twitter or by reading their blogs. I share stories from people who have used social networking to get them where they want to go—and their advice can help you do the same.

This book is different from many you may have seen about social networking; I actively work with the tools I devote chapters to telling you about. I tell you that Twitter can keep you connected while I am watching my Twitter stream, which keeps me up-to-date regarding resources and information for this book. I am not researching this topic—I am living it! As a job search and social media coach, I teach entrepreneurs and job seekers how to optimize these tools, as I have done myself, for success.

When I started in social media, I was just one needle in a haystack, working alongside hundreds of thousands of career coaches. Today, reporters for major national newspapers and media outlets regularly contact me to provide expert advice. I created my online reputation and distinguished myself as a subject matter expert, and this book tells you how you can do the same thing (no, you don't need to be a technical whiz to do it—I am certainly not one).

Recent economic changes have proven that everyone—whether they know it or not—is a job seeker. You can no longer count on doing the same work, in the same field, for the long term. However, you can take control of your career and reputation in a way that was not possible just a few years ago.

Social networking can empower you to grow your reputation beyond your office, and to create a cohort of people who know and respect you from all over the globe. The power of that exponential network—and having people who take an interest in your professional expertise and insight—is invaluable when you need to decide on a next step. Whether it's by your own choice (you decide to make a move) or someone else's (maybe you were laid off), creating a network of colleagues online can prove invaluable.

This book includes how-tos for beginners as well as tips and tricks that even some of the most experienced social networkers don't know. It's filled with expert advice and first-hand knowledge about these topics, from me and others who use these tools every day and know what you need to make this all worth your time.

Social networking is not a magic wand. You need to be able to bring the expertise to share. It's important to listen first and learn the rules of engagement. Just as you wouldn't approach a stranger on the street to ask for help landing an opportunity, you cannot expect strangers online to raise their hands to help you until you have joined their community. But once you do, you won't be sorry.

Are you ready to learn how to take advantage of today's networking tools, so you can stop looking for a job and instead let opportunities find you? Are you prepared to try something new? If so, then this book is for you!

RESOURCE

Visit www.socialnetworkingforcareersuccess.com for information, updates, advice, and resources, including links to contributor's sites.

SOCIAL
NETWORKING
FOR CAREER
SUCCESS

Second Edition

1 Leveraging Social Networking for Success

Have you ever planned and hosted a dinner party? If so, and you're not a master entertainer, party planner, or chef, it was probably a challenge. Depending on the complexity of your event, there were likely a lot of details to consider:

- time and date
- whom to invite
- what to serve
- how to set the table
- where everyone will sit

Individually, none of these tasks are impossible, but when you examine them as a group, they may seem overwhelming. The same is true about job hunting. If you are not a master resume writer, networker, interviewee, and online marketing expert, successfully landing a job may seem as difficult as hosting a Hollywood dinner party.

Take this analogy a step further: Would you want to host a big party without modern conveniences? For some, this includes sending E-vites and grocery shopping online; for others, it means being able to search for recipes and menus on the Internet, or using the latest in dishwasher and convection oven technology. Maybe you remember when planning simply involved thumbing through a pile of cookbooks, scraping food off plates, and spending hours up to your elbows in soapy water? Even if these are familiar rituals, modern conveniences allow you to meet your guests' expectations more efficiently and with less work.

When it comes to your job hunt, there are tools and resources now available that no one dreamed of just two decades ago. Instead of waiting for the Sunday classified ads, the Internet offers constant access to job leads. Today, you no longer need to visit the library to conduct basic research about organizations—company data and information flood the Web. Networking no longer requires getting dressed to mingle in person with a bunch of strangers while balancing a drink and appetizer plate. Job seekers can take advantage of terrific networking opportunities from home, balancing nothing but a laptop on their knees.

However, along with all of these conveniences come new challenges. Just as easy access to amazing recipes and unique ingredients raises the bar for your dinner parties, today's hiring managers have higher expectations of job seekers than in the past. This is not your parents' job hunt, and you should understand how to use online tools to propel your plans forward. Once you tap into the power of social media, and understand how much easier it makes your job hunt, you will not know how you ever got by without it.

The Old-Fashioned Job Search

Years ago, the newspaper and telephone were a job seeker's key tools. You may remember trying to decipher a four- or five-line want ad to decide if you were a good fit for a position. You might have had to send away for materials to research an organization, or hope your local librarian could help you review some microfiche with company data. Applying for jobs meant sending a resume by snail mail, on bond paper and in a matching envelope with a postage stamp. No one talked about *keywords* or *applicant tracking systems*, which digitally read your resume or online application before human eyes ever see it. In those days, networking meant hoping that your brother-in-law or neighbor might be able to put you in touch with a great job lead.

Back then, most people did not think much about building a large network; you looked for a job when you needed one and didn't concern yourself with expanding your reputation beyond your company. Top-level executives may have relied on job opportunities to come to them (via recruiters or headhunters), but most people focused on the *push* strategy—pushing a resume out when in search mode. Typical job seekers couldn't easily find or attract opportunities beyond their immediate networks. In some ways, this made career management simpler. No one expected you to maintain a *personal brand*—a reputation beyond your organization or circle of colleagues—since there were no easily available mechanisms to enhance your reputation on a broad scale. However, when you consider the hoops you needed to jump through to even find out about opportunities (especially if you were conducting a long-distance search or hoping to relocate), it was hardly easy to find a job.

Today's Job Hunt

Today, things are different. Successful professionals don't sit back and wait until it's time to find a new opportunity to build a network or demonstrate their expertise. Savvy careerists create a personal brand, build their reputations, and weave networks of colleagues far in advance of ever needing a job. Instead of pushing out their resumes, they *pull* in the people who matter—including the ones who might eventually hire them or lead to a key connection.

⮩ TIP

Picture the modern job seeker as a magnet, constantly attracting opportunities by using social media to raise his or her profile in a way that draws in people—and jobs.

PERSONAL BRANDING

Dan Schawbel, personal branding guru and author of *Promote Yourself* (St. Martins, 2013), defines personal branding as:

"The process by which individuals and entrepreneurs differentiate themselves and stand out from a crowd by identifying and articulating their unique value proposition . . . and then leverage it across platforms with a consistent message and image to achieve a specific goal. In this way, individuals may be recognized as experts in their field, establish their reputation and credibility, advance their careers, and build self-confidence."

While personal branding must be about *your* authentic self, it is also important to consider your target audience to define and put forth a great brand.

The good news? You too can harness the Internet's power to fuel your job hunt and help position yourself as an expert in your industry. You do not need to be a computer genius to leverage online tools, find information to expand your network, research organizations, and attract job leads. There are many different approaches to online and social networking, and this book highlights the ones most important for job seekers. Once you have the right information, you will be able to negotiate the Web effectively and integrate these strategies into your routine, even if you are managing a very busy schedule.

What is a Social Network?

Most people understand that LinkedIn, Facebook, Twitter, Google+, and Pinterest are social networks, and are considered a subset of social media.

What exactly is social media and why is it important? SearchEngineWatch.com defines it as the following:

"A category of sites that is based on user participation and user-generated content. They include social networking sites like LinkedIn or Facebook . . . social news sites like Digg or Reddit, and other sites that are centered on user interaction."

OnlineMatters.com suggests:

"Social media is any form of online publication or presence that allows end users to engage in multi-directional conversations in or around the content on the website."

DuctTapeMarketing.com agrees, defining social media as:

" . . . the use of technology combined with social interaction to create or co-create value."

Keep that last definition in mind—it's important to focus on the fact that *you* will be creating and adding value to the social network you choose. Social networking focuses on two-way interactions, between the site (or the person running the site) and the people reading or using it. A blog that allows comments is a two-way interaction between the author and anyone who comments; an online bookmarking site that encourages you to share your preferences with your cohort is social.

It's important to know how to leverage these networks to make the most of them for your career success. This chapter will help you learn how to use online tools, including social networks, to effectively research target markets, position yourself as an expert, and attract potential employers. Chapters 2 and 3 aim to convince you why you should bother with social media (especially if you are skeptical), and Chapter 4 will help you put it all together before you get started creating your own online identity, the subject of the rest of the book!

Your Personal Brand and Your Network

To a certain degree, the cliché, "the more things change, the more they stay the same," applies to job seeking. At a very basic level, job seeking still involves the same elements:

- identifying opportunities
- connecting your skills with an employer's needs
- making a strong case for the *touch points*—the overlap between what hiring managers want and what you offer.

The difference today is that the tools for expanding networks and making those initial connections have changed dramatically. For years, career coaches have advised that networking is the most important element of the job search. Malcolm Gladwell's book, *The Tipping Point* (Little Brown, 2000), outlines how important it is to broaden your network—to meet and connect with *weak ties*, people who previously had no direct relationship to you.

A *New York Times* article, "The Brave New World of Digital Intimacy," highlighted Gladwell's premise and emphasized the importance of expanding your network beyond your immediate circle:

> *"This rapid growth of weak ties can be a very good thing. Sociologists have long found that 'weak ties' greatly expand your ability to solve problems. For example, if you're looking for a job and ask your friends, they won't be much help; they're too similar to you, and thus probably won't have any leads that you don't already have yourself. Remote acquaintances will be much more useful, because they're farther afield, yet still socially intimate enough to want to help you out."*

Successful job searching today relies on the ability to exponentially extend your circle via multiple channels, and building a strong personal brand is an important first step. Creating your personal brand is like setting the table when planning to eat a meal. You would not eat dinner without a fork and knife—do not plan your career without identifying your value proposition and researching the marketplace.

⇨ TIP

Remember—you should *always* consider your target audience. Your personal brand is not only about you!

Do Your Research

Just as you would not shop for dinner ingredients without survey-ing your guests to find out their preferences and aversions before deciding what to cook, don't plan your online presence without first exploring the terrain. Luckily, there are many great tools to help you identify and target organizations, people, and actual job descriptions.

Find Companies

It might seem strange advice for a job search coach to offer, but I never advise people to spend a lot of time actually searching for a positions. In fact, the best advice I can give job seekers who are researching jobs is this: Don't look for a *job*; look for a *company*. If you focus on job descriptions (targeting only job boards or posted listings), you will miss out on unadvertised opportunities.

Seeking a specific organization will help you find your niche. Learning as much as possible about the companies that interest you allows you to sound like an expert during informational interviews (informal talks with people who work in targeted companies or jobs) and actual interviews (when being prepared with company data and information is a crucial element of success). Most impor-tantly, effective and thorough research helps you position yourself as the industry expert your targeted organizations seek.

Finding information about companies online is easy; filtering it to identify what is most useful is the real challenge. For a good over-view of material available online, simply entering keywords in Google or your favorite search engine may yield useful results. For example, if you want to learn more about energy companies in Den-ver, simply enter {*energy company, Denver*} into a search engine's field. It will yield a list of links to companies matching that descrip-tion. Depending on the company, you may have access to news releases, presentations, fact sheets, SEC filings, annual reports, job descriptions, and much more. More importantly, you will get a good sense of the company's culture.

Things to consider:

1. Is there information about people who work at the organization? Some companies highlight bios and provide extensive information about their people; others seem to function as if there is no one behind the scenes.
2. Are there links to social networks? Does the company maintain a blog or Twitter account? Do they invite you to "like" them on Facebook or maintain a YouTube channel? If companies are active on social networks, connecting with them may give you an edge.
3. Is the site corporate or fun?
4. Does the company seem to emphasize teamwork and/or highlight the importance of volunteerism?
5. Are there links such as "Career Opportunities" or "Jobs?" Click these to see if any match your interests and skill set.

⇨ TIP

Never let the fact that a company may not currently list an appropriate job deter you from pursuing more information and leads. Remember that looking up actual job leads on a website is the last step—do not simply search for a job, search for a company!

SOCIAL NETWORKING TERMINOLOGY

If you're new to social networking, take some time to learn the following essential terms:

- **Social networking** happens online, where people create communities—to share ideas, suggestions, and experiences. On social networking websites, each user has a profile and may contribute and engage in conversations with other members. Think of social networking as an ongoing communication with a broad audience through a variety of platforms or sites.

continued from page 9

- **Blog** comes from the term *web log*. It is a constantly changing website that includes information, commentary, opinions, and advice about a topic. A blog is usually updated regularly with new posts and information. Some people maintain personal blogs, which resemble journals or diaries. Other blogs are professional in nature, where a writer shares expertise about a subject area. There are also corporate blogs, which are aimed at connecting customers with new information on a daily or weekly basis. For example, Newell Rubbermaid, a global marketer of consumer and commercial products, maintains a blog highlighting Sharpie writing products. You may also encounter blogs on major media sites, such as *The New York Times*, which are updated with opinions on major news events in real time. Blogs may include writing, video, graphics, and audio.

- **LinkedIn** is a professional network that allows you to post the equivalent of your resume, share information and links via updates, and connect and engage with people you may want in your network. LinkedIn's Groups feature allows you to meet and learn from new people you wouldn't otherwise know, and they provide news aggregation services (via LinkedIn Today) to help keep you up-to-date with what's going on in industries that interest you. LinkedIn also allows people to post jobs, and offers a useful interface to help you connect with opportunities where you have contacts.

- **Twitter** is a service that allows users to send and read messages, known as *tweets*. **Tweets** are short posts of up to 140 characters displayed on the author's profile page. This type of messaging and sharing information in brief spurts is known as **microblogging**.

- **Facebook** is a social network that allows users to find and add friends to a personal network. Once someone is your Facebook friend, he or she will see whenever you update your profile. You can let people know what you are doing, share personal news and gossip, or just comment on current events. You can also send private and public messages to any of your friends. Many companies use Facebook to connect with customers, prospective clients, and potential hires.

- **Google+** is Google's social network, and while you won't see it mentioned on the nightly news or in magazine ads, it's important to keep on your radar because Google+ will help you get noticed online. If you use their network, you will have a better chance of being indexed and found for the expertise you offer.

continued from page 10

If a company that interests you maintains a presence on social networks, you have a golden opportunity to learn more about the organization and easily connect with people who work there. Once you have a strong presence on these networks, you will be able to use them as bridges to reach the people with the authority to hire you.

Tools to Research Targeted Companies

Simple queries powered by your favorite search engine are great ways to uncover information and help propel your search, but there are other resources designed to help you learn about organizations that you may not have considered. Add these time-tested tools to your job search arsenal.

Best Lists
- *Fortune Magazine* runs an annual list of the top 500 companies and the best 100 companies.
- *Working Mother* publishes lists of best places for mothers to work, best companies for hourly workers and multicultural women, and best law firms for women, among others.
- *The Great Place to Work Institute* oversees several lists, including the best small and medium companies to work for. Enter {*Best Companies, lists*} in Google's search field to find up-to-date information from these and other sources.

Sites Providing Company Information
- **Job-Hunt.org**, run by Susan Joyce, offers a directory of over 8,000 links to employer sites, as well as a plethora of useful resources for job seekers at any stage of the hunt.
- **Quintcareers.com**, published by Randall and Kathy Hansen, is another terrific site with a lot of useful research links.
- **Vault.com** provides information on more than 10,000 companies and 180 industries, jobs, careers, employers, and

education programs. You'll also find job search advice, salary info, job listings, employee message boards, and surveys.

- **Hoovers.com** offers access to more than 65 million company profiles and 85 million key people, allowing you to build focused company and contact lists and to organize and track your conversations.
- **Glassdoor.com** touts a free inside look at over 80,000 companies, including salaries, reviews, and interviews, all posted anonymously by employees.
- **WetFeet.com** helps job seekers make smart career decisions through expert career advice, company rankings, information about top MBA programs, and sample resumes.
- **eBossWatch.com** allows you to search for the boss or company that you are interviewing with or considering working for, to see how other employees have rated them.
- **ReferenceUSA.com** provides contact information for specific companies, and performs general searches (e.g., all the florists in the Atlanta area, using such limiters as *county* and *employee size*). Many public libraries offer access to this database from their homepage, free with a library card. Otherwise, this is an online subscription service.
- *Social networks* including LinkedIn, Facebook, Twitter, Google+, and others are good places to research organizations. I describe their usefulness and how to leverage what they offer throughout the book.

Find People

Once you identify and target organizations that are good matches for you, start searching for individuals in those companies who might be good candidates to approach for informational interviews. Remember, an **informational interview** or **informational meeting** is an informal get-together with someone—maybe over coffee or lunch. The meeting provides an opportunity to share your expertise and insights, and to ask specific questions about a company, field, person, etc.

Sometimes, it is very easy to find people to target for these meetings. Many companies list this information on their websites. Other times, additional research is needed. Luckily, online resources make it easier. Consider using these tools to find what you need:

1. **Google** a job title or person's name. It is much easier to find useful results when someone's name or title is unique.

2. **LinkedIn** is a very useful, first-line resource. In fact, my personal experience when I first started using LinkedIn was that I located two long-lost high school friends I had not been able to find anywhere else. Many people include e-mail addresses and other contact information in their LinkedIn profiles, so you may actually be able to e-mail people directly, rather than via LinkedIn's introductions mechanism. You can also search by company, title, and/or name. (Read much more about using LinkedIn in Chapters 5, 6, and 7.)

3. **Twitter** is a terrific place to find and connect with people. Find people on Twitter using tools such as Wefollow.com, Twellow.com, and Followerwonk.com. Note that you do not need to be a Twitter user to take advantage of these directories. (Learn more about leveraging Twitter in Chapters 8, 9, and 10.)

4. **Facebook** is a great way to learn what people are doing, even if you have not seen or heard from them in years. You may be surprised to learn how this network, which never touted itself as being professionally useful, may actually connect you with just the person you need. (Read more about how to leverage Facebook in Chapter 11.)

5. **FourSquare.com** encourages you to "check in" when you visit various locations and businesses. It is a *geo-location* service (it tracks where you are via mobile devices, such

as smart phones). How can this help? If you are trying to identify people who work in a particular organization or company, FourSquare allows you to search places, people, and tags. Enter the name of the company, find the correct location, and you may be able to find people who work there and connect with them either on FourSquare or Twitter.

6. **Pipl.com** searches the *deep web* for information. The site explains, "Also known as 'invisible web,' the term 'deep web' refers to a vast repository of underlying content, such as documents in online databases that general-purpose web crawlers cannot reach." Try searching for your own name on this site to understand how it works. It may display results for other people with your name, but I have found it to be a very useful resource. Be careful to only use business contact information to reach people. Mailing a letter to a home address (even when you can easily find it) is not appropriate.

7. **Meta-search engines**, such as polymeta.com, can also prove useful. If the person whose name you are searching has any online presence, this site will find it. Be aware that if other people share your contact's name, information about those individuals will be mixed in.

Be sure to always search your own name in these search engines. This way, you will understand how these searches work and learn what people searching for your name may find. If you do not have an online presence yet, you may be surprised to learn that the only information online about you is that you volunteered for community day in your town three years ago or that you participated in a local golf charity tournament. If that is the case, hopefully you will be motivated to take action and create content online, so you have input as to what people learn about you when they Google your name.

Recruiters

Before you think about identifying recruiters as part of your job and information search, it is important to determine if a recruiter would be interested in you. In this section, my friend and colleague, Stephanie Lloyd Schnick, Executive Search Consultant and Owner of Calibre Search Group, shared some important points for job seekers who are considering using recruiters. She states:

> *"If you have a stable, upwardly mobile career track in a particular field, are not a job hopper, and demonstrate unique and specific experiences and skills, you may be a good candidate to work with a recruiter."*

It is easy to address the question of who should not use a recruiter. If you are a job hopper, are trying to break into a new field, or are not particularly experienced or unique in your skill set, a recruiter probably will not be interested in working with you. Recruiters do not tend to work with entry-level candidates, recent college graduates, or professionals transitioning from one field to another. These are Stephanie's answers to common jobseeker questions about recruiters.

What should job seekers know about recruiters? Why do companies use them?

The first thing to understand is that third-party recruiters (i.e., executive search consultants) are paid by companies to fill a particular position or role. According to Stephanie, "Our job is not to find people jobs; it is to find the right people for clients' jobs."

Many times, the reason a company chooses to go outside their own recruiting organization and use an outside recruiter to fill a job is that it's a particularly difficult position to fill, or maybe they are overloaded and need assistance. Perhaps the need to fill the position is extremely urgent and speed is a factor, or that the company's recruiting strategy is to stay lean internally and use outside firms as needed.

How do third-party recruiters differ from internal/corporate recruiters?

Third-party recruiters don't work for an employer; therefore, they spend nearly 100 percent of their time on targeted search and sourcing efforts. Third-party recruiters also tend to specialize in a particular niche.

What should I expect to gain from working with a recruiter?

As mentioned, a recruiter's job is to help employers by filling specific openings. If they think that you might be a good candidate, there are advantages to working with a recruiter, as compared to trying to get into a company blindly on your own.

First of all, they have relationships with client companies. Most recruiters have placed other job seekers with the company and therefore have additional insight from those individuals. They have clients they've been working with for many years and they can help candidates:

- prepare for interviews with specific clients
- know what to expect in terms of corporate culture
- learn specifics about the group and/or person they'll be talking to

Another advantage is that they'll typically present just two or three individuals for a given opening, and those candidates will have the opportunity to be thoroughly reviewed and considered. In contrast, the HR departments of most companies are dealing with potentially hundreds of applicants for each open position every single day, many of whom may or may not even get so much as a glance.

When I first met Stephanie, she used the term *purple squirrel* to identify the type of candidate she targets when recruiting—someone so unique and specific that it is almost impossible to replicate him or her.

> **⤸ TIP**
>
> CareerXRoads, a company that researches and tracks hiring trends, found that only 9.1 percent of jobs are filled through recruiters. Remember, networking is still considered the number-one way to find new employment opportunities. Only seek out a recruiter when appropriate.

How Can I Find a Recruiter?

Clearly, some people do benefit from partnering with recruiters. Mike Ramer, President, Founder, and Industry Trainer at Ramer Search Consultants, Inc., suggests the following strategies for finding recruiters:

1. **Do an online search with parameters.** For example: {*Recruiter, Job Field* and/or *Industry, Geography*}; {*Recruiter, Marketing, Atlanta*}; or {*Recruiter, Banking, New York*}.

2. **Look for recruiter directories or staffing associations**. A few to consider include www.i-recruit.com and www.searchfirm.com. You can look up recruiters by geography, industry, or recruiting specialization.

3. **Use local recruiting/staffing associations with membership directories.** For example, visit their online sites and search using such parameters as: {*California, Staffing, Association*} or {*Phoenix, Recruiter, Directory*}. Most associations allow member searches by recruiting field or industry specialization.

4. **Use social media.** Ask for referrals on LinkedIn, Twitter, and Facebook. Send a tweet or post a message: "I'm looking for a new job in field/location, and I want to connect with a good recruiter in this area. Do you know someone I can contact?"

5. **Referrals.** Request referrals from work colleagues or friends who have found jobs through a recruiter, or have been contacted by recruiters.

6. **Attend industry trade shows.** Often, recruiters who specialize in specific fields attend these shows, and may even have a booth. Ask trade show participants if they know a good recruiter.
7. **Network with other recruiters.** Ask if they can refer you to good recruiters in your industry and/or location.

Other Places to Connect With Recruiters

Consider the following sources:

- **LinkedIn.** Every recruiter I have ever met agrees that LinkedIn is a big part of his or her efforts. Since it provides a database of *passive* job seekers (those not necessarily in an active job hunt), it naturally appeals to those trying to fill jobs that require very unique qualifications. A search for *recruiter* from my LinkedIn profile yields over 536,000 contacts.

- **Wefollow.com.** This site is a compilation of Twitter users who choose keywords to identify their niche. Search *recruiter* to find a list of the most influential recruiters on Twitter. While you do not need a Twitter profile to search Wefollow, if you do have one, you may follow recruiters of interest to access a wealth of information. Twitter also provides a very easy way to connect and demonstrate your interest and expertise to people who can help you land an opportunity.

- **HeadhuntersDirectory.com.** This site lists headhunters, executive recruiters, executive search firms, employment agencies, staffing, and personnel agencies.

- **RecruitersDirectory.com.** A database of recruiters, headhunters, staffing firms and recruiting agencies is located here.

Mike Ramer offers advice from a recruiter's perspective:

"Once you identify the right recruiter, don't simply send an e-mail; instead, call the recruiter. Recruiters do most of their work by phone and appreciate a call from proactive jobseekers. The best time to call a recruiter is early morning or late afternoon."

Find Job Descriptions Online

The Internet is a great tool for finding job descriptions in every field imaginable. Make the most of the powerful tools available online.

Job Boards

While job boards are not considered social media sites, I am including information about them because they do provide useful information and resources that you can leverage as part of your social media strategy. While CareerXRoads' 2012 study says 20.1 percent of jobs come via job boards, job seekers should not apply for 15 or 20 jobs a day through online job postings. That is *not* a good approach for most people, especially more experienced professionals. However, knowing how to properly evaluate job boards will help you use them as resources to gather information and propel your plans forward.

All job seekers should take advantage of the vast amount of information that job boards provide, for initial research purposes. Once you identify positions of interest, it is easy to conduct broad-based online searches for details about the organizations advertising those jobs. Job board searching is also useful for those in exploratory career stages. These searches can help job explorers learn about new fields, companies, and opportunities that are well suited to their skills.

Even if you would not consider applying for a particular job you find—maybe it is located in Omaha and you don't plan to relocate from Boston—you may still learn a lot about the types of skills needed and what accomplishments your desired employers seek. Then, you can leverage that information in your online profiles (and in your resume) to help attract the attention of the types of employers you are targeting.

NAVIGATING JOB BOARDS

Job search expert Susan P. Joyce has been observing the online job search world and teaching online job search skills since 1995. Susan has been editor and publisher of Job-Hunt.org, an extremely useful and information-rich site for job seekers since 1998. The following is her advice for evaluating job boards.

- ❏ Have you heard of the site?
- ❏ Do you have to register before you can search for jobs?
- ❏ Does the site have a comprehensive privacy policy?
- ❏ Who has access to the database of resumes?
- ❏ Can you limit access to your personal contact information?
- ❏ Does the site charge you for access to job opportunities?
- ❏ Is the site easy to use?
- ❏ Are the jobs fresh or old?
- ❏ Are most of the jobs posted by employers or by agencies acting on behalf of employers?
- ❏ Can you set up one or more e-mail agents that will send matching jobs to you?
- ❏ Can you store more than one version of your resume so that you can customize it for specific kinds of jobs?
- ❏ Will you be able to delete your resume after you have found a job?

Chris Russell is the CEO & Founder of CareerCloud, LLC and a veteran of the online job board industry. Chris suggests job seekers consider the following when deciding what job boards to visit:

- ❏ Know what you want to do.
- ❏ Which industry are you targeting?
- ❏ Which level of job are you seeking?
- ❏ Are you at the beginning of your career or an experienced pro?

Chris reminds job seekers that having a clear idea of employment goals is key before searching for the right job boards to use. He suggests the following online resources to help identify job boards:

- **AllStarJobs.com:** www.allstarjobs.com
- **Job-hunt.org:** www.job-hunt.org/jobs/states.shtml
- **RileyGuide.com:** www.rileyguide.com/jobs.html
- **Jobtarget.com:** www.jobtarget.com
- **CareerCast.com:** www.careercast.com/jobs
- **AIRS job board directory:** www.airsdirectory.com/mc/forms_jobboard.guid
- **JobBoardReviews.com:** www.jobboardreviews.com

When selecting job boards, Chris suggests that you visit each job board to conduct additional research and determine the site's viability, keeping the following in mind:

- Take a careful look at the "About Us" page. Does the site maintain a blog and/or social networking tools? Are there recent news clippings?
- How many jobs does it have?
- Do they advertise?
- Does the site have memberships in such organizations as the International Association of Employment Websites?
- Does the site offer job alerts? These are great time savers. This way, the jobs come to you and you don't have to remember to visit the site every day.

Job boards that are recommended for niche job seekers include the following:

- **Idealist.org.** More than just a job board, this is also an interactive site for sharing resources, events, and opportunities. This is a good site to find volunteer opportunities as well as jobs in nonprofit organizations.
- **SnagAJob.com.** A good site to search for hourly jobs.
- **USAJobs.gov.** A good site to locate government jobs.

Chris reminds job seekers to follow employers' posted instructions to get the most from job boards. For example, if the job description says you should only apply via e-mail, only e-mail your resume. Additionally, recognize that hiring cycles are long. Even if the posting is several weeks old, when in doubt, *always* apply. He notes:

"The major job search engines don't crawl every niche job board online, so to truly maximize your job search, you have to incorporate all the niche boards that are relevant to you."

Jobs Directly from Company Sites—LinkUp.com

When researching companies and job descriptions, you will want to search job descriptions posted directly on company websites. One good place to look is Linkup.com. Linkup.com aggregates jobs from company websites, giving job seekers direct access to a variety of current position descriptions.

Use Google to Search for Job Descriptions

Did you know that Google, or any search engine, can easily serve as your gateway to job descriptions? You don't need to directly visit a job board to cull through positions. Just enter the job title of interest, location (if relevant), and the word *job* into a search field and you will find a variety of position descriptions from various sites. If you want to work in marketing, for example, conduct searches including {*marketing jobs*} or {*marketing jobs, Charlotte*} and check out the relevant job boards with listings in that area.

Indeed.com and SimplyHired.com

Indeed.com and SimplyHired.com are great one-stop tools for job seekers. They search and aggregate positions posted on thousands of company career sites and job boards. When you search these sites, you can easily set parameters and gather information targeted directly to your needs.

You may also view opportunities posted on various sites from just one portal. Refer to the list of ways to evaluate job boards when you land on a posting, as each position will be from a different source and you will want to ensure you know something about that website before posting your resume or applying online. SimplyHired.com offers the option to interface with your Facebook profile, which helps you identify jobs in companies where your Facebook friends may work.

Twitter—a Source for Job Descriptions

Twitter offers a whole new way for employers to reach job seekers, both one-on-one and by streaming feeds of position descriptions. You never know when a direct connection via Twitter may lead to a job.

Polly Pearson (@pollypearson on Twitter), who described herself as VP of Employment Brand and Strategy Engagement at EMC, once tweeted:

> "*1 Tweet. 1 Hire. That was easy. I sent a tweet mentioning I was looking for an admin. A follower DM'd it to a candidate. Interview. Done.*"

DM'd means that the person following Polly's Twitter messages forwarded the information as a private message to the candidate. In the chapters dedicated to Twitter, I will share how using that tool for networking, information seeking, and building connections can propel your search and help connect you to a terrific expanded network.

In addition to one-to-one connections, Twitter has become a well-known replacement for job boards. The following are some popular Twitter feeds that send job descriptions to their followers. Consider following them on Twitter—typically, they tweet a brief description of the job and location and provide a link to the details:

- **@jobshouts/jobshouts.com:** Cofounded by recruiter Robin Eads in 2009, JobShouts! provides job listings that are moderated, 100 percent real, and listed by company name or recruiter (not scam jobs). Job seekers can login using their Google, Yahoo, Twitter, Facebook, LinkedIn, MySpace, AOL ID, or a number of other logins, to create a free and private user profile. Doing so allows you to receive instant notification, via direct private message, on Twitter whenever a job is posted that matches your profile.

- **@JobThread/jobthread.com:** Since 2006, JobThread has provided an online recruitment advertising platform that powers job boards for leading publishers, blogs, and niche sites. JobThread focuses on helping employers and recruiters reach candidates where they spend their time online, and on helping hiring managers connect with their target audiences. They do this by bringing jobs to the right niche audiences, from techies to designers and everyone in between.

- **@TweetMyJOBS/tweetmyjobs.com:** Founded in 2009, with 10,000+ job channels segmented by geography, job type, and industry, TweetMyJOBS has open positions from thousands of companies worldwide, and tweets more than 50,000 new jobs a day to targeted job seekers. TweetMyJOBS offers instant job ad notification and offers individuals the ability to respond immediately to open positions, free of charge. They also allow job seekers to upload their resume, and will tweet it out for them automatically.

- **@twitjobsearch/twitjobsearch.com:** TwitJobSearch scours Twitter; indexes tweets that are jobs, and filters out the rest.

Additional Resources for Job Opportunities

LinkedIn

Don't overlook job listings on LinkedIn—find them along the top navigation bar, labeled "Jobs." LinkedIn offers some distinct advantages and tools for job seekers. Every opportunity is linked directly to an individual who posted the job. In addition, LinkedIn points out how you are connected to that person by suggesting who may help make an introduction. It also allows you to apply or request a referral, and suggests how to forward job descriptions if you are not interested, but know someone else in your network who may be.

Texting

Michael Hanson, formerly of jobs2web, an interactive recruitment marketing company, has noted that some major consumer electronics retailers and large companies are experimenting with texting as part of their recruitment and marketing efforts. For example, companies will advertise in their stores, asking you to text them if you're interested in learning about job opportunities. They collect your e-mail address and provide links to their applicant tracking systems, where you must apply if you want to be considered for a job.

Michael noted that these are usually targeted, short-term campaigns that companies run to help them fill part-time and seasonal positions that are typically aimed at teenagers (a segment of jobseekers who are most actively engaged in texting).

Texting provides a way for organizations to interact with prospective candidates and for job seekers to alert companies that they may be willing to apply for a job. If you are interested in connecting with employers via text, visit their online job sites to learn if they are running a campaign. According to Michael:

"If you are an active jobseeker, you need to submit your information to a company's online career site or apply process to be considered for opportunities."

Applications for mobile devices

Job seekers who use mobile devices should be aware that there are new opportunities every day to add applications to your phone that will help you learn about and track job openings. Be sure to investigate available apps for your smart phone or tablet regularly, so you will be among the first to learn about new opportunities.

Takeaways

There is no question that today's job seekers have more opportunities to access and share information than they did years ago, and consequently, more responsibility for steering their own careers. This chapter suggests many resources to find information that will help you with your research.

Things to Remember

Old-fashioned job searches required that people push resumes out when they were actively looking for new opportunities. Today, by creating and sharing a personal brand that differentiates you from your colleagues, you have the opportunity to magnetically attract employers' interest—even when you are not actually looking for a job!

While not under the headline of social media, online job searching is an important part of many job seekers' daily routines. Key points to remember include:

- Don't look for a job—look for a company. This chapter suggested various ways to leverage the Internet's resources to identify and research target companies.
- Identify people (and recruiters, if you are a good candidate)

to meet and network with, in person and online, using the various tips and tricks in this chapter.

- There are a lot of places to find job descriptions online and via digital mediums. Be sure to use the resources described here to evaluate which arenas are best for you and to help inform how to create your online presence.

Today, networking is the most effective way to find a job. Your best use of online job descriptions (via job boards, Twitter, or other resources) is to learn about different types of jobs, investigate skills employers are seeking, uncover potential new fields or companies, and use that data to create an attractive profile and brand.

Craft your brand with your target audience in mind. Use the resources outlined in this chapter to learn about and understand potential employers (through careful research). If you follow this approach, you will be well prepared to begin articulating your value proposition across social networks.

CHAPTER

Using Social Media for Professional Development

Wouldn't it be great to have a panel of experts at your disposal, to help you keep on top of the latest trends and industry advancements? Who couldn't use an instant advisory board, a posse of professionals at the ready, prepared to answer random questions at any hour of the day or night? With social networking tools, this scenario doesn't have to be a dream—it is the reality for anyone who has developed a strong online community. I can personally attest to the fact that social networking can offer access to expert advice, opinions, and information at any hour. It allows you to gather and take advantage of information that improves your ability to excel at work, and at your job hunt.

Social networks provide a constant stream of relevant data, research, opinions, and information. The difference in access to resources before and after using social media is akin to the difference between living where the local grocery store is an hour away and only open at certain times and having a giant grocery store within walking distance that never closes. Once you enjoy the convenience of easy access to information, you will never know how you managed without it.

Capture Information via Twitter

You may not yet have considered the professional development aspects of social networking. However, Twitter is particularly useful in this regard. If you follow the right people, your Twitter stream can become the equivalent of an online university (with some fun and frivolity thrown in for good measure). Once you connect with the right community of professionals and colleagues, the amount of information available to you is limited only by your ability to process it.

Twitter Chats

A Twitter chat occurs when like-minded people trade messages on Twitter. There are active Twitter chats covering a wide array of topics. Since it is an open forum, anyone can participate and follow the conversation via a search term designated by a **hashtag**, represented by the # sign. Try Tweetchat.com to help you follow and participate in active chats.

> ↪ **TIP**
>
> A hashtag (the # symbol) is a way to identify or *tag* a topic or event on Twitter. Attaching the # makes events, or anything mentioned on Twitter, easier to search. Learn more about how to use hashtags in the chapters covering Twitter in this book.

Search {Twitter chats, Keppie careers} on Google to find a link to a list of chats that run at various times during the week. You may also send messages to chat leaders (listed on the Google document) if you have questions or want to plug in to communities between chats. You may be surprised by the diversity of topics available. For example:

- An open dialogue between various people in the agriculture, farming, and ranching worlds, including those in the business of producing food, feed, fuel, and fiber.
- A community of architecture professionals connecting to share ideas, debate, and collaborate.
- An informal art discussion among artists, critics, historians, gallery owners, imaginary historical figures, and friends of art everywhere.
- A weekly discussion for summer camp professionals to share and discuss marketing and promotional trends, topics, and related ideas.
- A collaborative tool for educators to debate and evaluate solutions to various problems.
- A weekly chat for job seekers and experts.

Clearly, there is a very diverse and varied group of people active on Twitter, allowing you to easily connect and trade advice and information from around the world. Creating and running a chat is as easy as promoting it and being online to make it happen. You can even update the Twitter chat directory with your own group's information. (Learn more about how to use Twitter chats and the benefits of starting a chat, in Chapter 10.)

Crowd Source and Gather Information

Once you connect to an active and vibrant Twitter community, you will be able to use Twitter as a resource for any question or inquiry that may cross your mind. In fact, I helped a writer for a major media outlet connect with expert sources for her story by simply sending a few tweets (and one or two private *direct messages*) to my Twitter friends. The reporter was astonished at how quickly I gathered the resources she needed.

While writing this book, I relied on my varied and diverse Twitter community from all over the world to offer suggestions and insights and to respond to inquiries for information.

Several authors I follow on Twitter crowd source information and advice while writing their manuscripts. When I first joined Twitter, I remember that Pam Slim, author of *Escape from Cubicle Nation* (Portfolio Hardcover, 2009), often asked questions and requested suggestions from her Twitter followers while she was writing that book. It amazed me how many people responded! She always took the time to reply, thanking everyone for their generosity and insights, which inspired her writing and helped her move forward with her book. She started tweeting about plans for a new book, and continues to benefit from an enthusiastic and creative community. Pam explains:

"Writing a book, like looking for a job, can be lonely. While writing my book, I not only got fantastic feedback about content to include, but also received tons of personal support. The last month writing, I barely slept, and I am convinced that 3 a.m. tweets of encouragement from my Twitter family around the globe anchored my sanity and allowed me to finish the book. Twitter is a really useful tool, but more than that, it is the bridge to build real, meaningful, and supportive relationships."

Building relationships is a key benefit of these networks; and connections and crowd sourcing does not have to be in pursuit of advice for a big project. People ask for information about vacation spots, restaurants, job postings, and just about any topic imaginable. I recently asked for recipes to use a bunch of blueberries I had just picked, and a Twitter friend with a recipe business sent me a great suggestion for a delicious blueberry pie.

Attend Conferences Virtually via Live Tweets

It's not always easy to keep up with all the local and national events that might interest you. You can't attend every conference or hear every interesting speech. However, with a well selected stream of Twitter friends and resources you have an opportunity to follow professional conferences and events from the comfort of your own home through *live tweeting*. During live tweeting, conference attendees forward notes and information from speaker sessions to people who are following them. More and more conferences are encouraging their attendees to tweet information from speakers and workshops, to generate buzz about an organization, event, or program.

You may benefit by following or reading live tweets, but it is also useful to position yourself as the person who does the tweeting. Mark Stelzner, founder of Inflexion Advisors, a respected and active thought leader in the HR community and primary author of the popular Infexion Point blog, notes that:

> *"More PR and media relations staff are treating bloggers and tweeters as new media press."*

LIVE TWEETING YIELDS CAREER SUCCESS

Alexandra Janvey, an avid social media user and librarian, responded to my tweet asking for information from people whose careers have been impacted as a result of live tweeting. She describes a virtual professional conference with over 300 participants that she recently tweeted:

> *"Through tweeting the conference, answering tweets, and looking at what people had to say, I met so many great individuals in my profession I would have never known about otherwise. It's a great method to make connections in your field and keep up with the trends."*

She notes that she encountered two significant new contacts via tweeting the conference, one who invited her to volunteer for a social media project that helped her enhance and develop her skills. Alexandra asserted:

> *"I believe Twitter helps you gain more out of a conference, make yourself known, and network. You never know where a connection might lead—to a volunteer opportunity, an internship, or maybe even a job."*

Mark suggests that those with active followings try to secure free media passes to various events. Once you establish yourself as well-connected with a loyal audience, you may be able to enhance your professional profile as someone who shares conference insights and information with your community.

Live Tweeting Guidelines

If live tweeting interests you, Mark Stelzner suggests the following guidelines.

Pre-Event Planning

The keynote is about to begin and it's time to get to work. What's the best way to cover the event?

- **Be a wallflower.** Like it or not, most traditional conference attendees will think you're being extremely rude by clicking away during the presentation. Instead, choose a spot toward the back of the room. You're also more likely to find power plugs there, and less likely to disturb those around you.
- **Set the stage.** Your followers may tune in to your Twitter stream at various points throughout the day. Level set with a tweet or two every few hours that describes the event's purpose, location, and name.
- **Attribute the speaker.** If someone says something interesting, be sure to explicitly state the source. Use quotation marks, a real or Twitter name, and/or a company reference. For example: {Metrics are key for community management, per @teresabasich.} If you don't state the source, your followers will be confused and may take the statement out of context.
- **Follow others.** Check the hashtag with some level of frequency, to determine if anyone else in the room is covering the event as well. This is a good way to connect in real life and potentially divide and conquer across simultaneous tracks.

- **Continue the conversation.** Although this can be difficult, watch for those statements that triggered interest among your followers. To the extent possible, reply to their comments, retweets, and thoughts.

Mark further notes:

"For the past three events I covered, nearly every cogent thought and worthwhile nugget was tweeted. Upon my return, I used tools like Twitter search to revisit the hashtag-driven content as source material for my blog posts."

While not everyone live tweets as well as Mark (I have virtually attended several conferences and learned a lot that I would have otherwise missed as a result of his well-written tweets), when you are a part of an active and vibrant Twitter community, it is easy to learn what thought leaders in your field are talking about.

Everyday Twitter Fodder

Chats and live tweets are great ways to learn what is going on in your industry, and having a community to crowd source questions on Twitter is terrific. Also, once you follow the right group of people, just watching your daily *Twitter stream* (the flow of tweets from people you track on Twitter) will provide updates and resources that are not easily available anyplace else. Twitter is an open network; you may follow people who know you and who may have never heard of you—from rock stars in your field (potential mentors) as well as peers and colleagues just like you—to keep up to date on news you can use with relatively little effort.

Social Media—A Skill Employers Seek

For those of you who think that using social media for professional development is only for those in communications, technical, and public relations industries, think again! Social Media is on Indeed

.com's top 10 job trends list. This indicates that the number of companies who are either using social media to share job openings or seeking candidates with experience using these tools is growing.

The skills social media users invoke with every post, such as knowing how to communicate succinctly and clearly, are useful. According to TheNextWeb.com:

> *"Using Twitter trains people to be succinct in their writing, leading to interesting, eye-catching, and short CVs which appeal to recruiters."*

It is possible that being able to use social media well may make it more likely for you to get hired, regardless of your target field.

LinkedIn—Broaden Your Knowledge

Twitter does not have the corner on the market when it comes to gathering information on what is new in your field. LinkedIn is well known as a professional social network and place to connect with colleagues, clients, and targeted employers. LinkedIn is also a favorite among recruiters who are seeking candidates who may or may not be in active job hunt mode. It also provides resources to help users connect with others about specific topics and to share advice and resources.

LinkedIn's Groups

Look at LinkedIn's top toolbar. Click on *Groups* and navigate to *Groups Directory* to discover a plethora of potential information and contacts. Group designations are incredibly diverse. For example, a quick search using the keyword *trucking* led to over 300 results in groups, including one with over 28,000 members. Anyone seeking real estate contacts and connections for advice and information will find over 17,800 groups.

Tim Puyleart, an environmental, health, and safety professional who is committed to mentoring and giving back to others, manages a very successful group on LinkedIn—the MN Safety, Health and Environmental Professionals. With over 900 members, the group has resulted in a number of jobs for its members. Tim began the group to help Minnesotans who wanted to network locally with other health and safety professionals, and did not find a lot of value in the very large, global groups that were popular but did not yield useful results for those looking for opportunities in the state.

Tim offers the following suggestions for anyone thinking of starting a LinkedIn group:

- Talk to people and ask what they would like to see in a group.
- Establish objectives. Why are you designing this group? What do you hope to accomplish?
- Post group rules to avoid spam or excessive promotion.
- Monitor content and stick to the rules.
- Connect with potential group members who are active on LinkedIn via other, similar groups. Explain that you hope to offer and gain their buy-in by cross-promoting their events or programs, and ask them to help grow your group.
- Tie online networking to in-person meetings (especially for a local group). Tim hosts happy hours that draw over 40 people to meet and talk.
- Work behind the scenes to help people network. Keep tabs on what people are looking for and serve as a connector to help them achieve their goals.
- Never dominate discussions or make the group about you. If you are the only one posting discussions and asking questions, collaborate with others and encourage them to participate.

Tim gladly spends about five hours per week managing his group and connecting people with resources and potential opportunities. While he does not use the group to purposely promote himself or his services, he notes that when he found himself without a job after managing the group for 18 months, alerting his network resulted in meetings that kept him busy nearly 40 hours per week for over six weeks—and did provide opportunities for employment.

continued from page 37

He also explains that recruiters often contact him to ask if they can share opportunities with group members. Tim is proud of the fact that some members ask to stay in the group even after they move away from Minnesota. He says:

"When I started this group, I had no idea of the potential it had for everyone involved. I am constantly reminded of the positive impact it has had among my peers who work in the Minnesota community. The time and energy spent to keep the group moving forward is well worth it."

Just like Twitter, LinkedIn's members are from diverse backgrounds; most anyone will be able to find colleagues to share advice and ask questions. All it takes is a quick keyword search. Of course, you can also begin your own group if you don't find just what you are looking for.

LinkedIn's groups provide a lot of rich resources. You can begin and engage in discussions, join subgroups, view and post jobs, and share and read news from members. The depth of discussions and usefulness of information from these groups will depend on how much activity members generate.

If you plan to use LinkedIn groups to generate information and advice, as well as to help you demonstrate your expertise on a broader scale, I would suggest including some large groups (with more than several thousand members). The more participants in a group, the more likely it is that you will be able to achieve your goals. However, a small but very active group can also be a good option for some people. Read more about how to leverage groups in Chapter 7.

Use Google+ to Extend Your Network

While not all of your friends or colleagues are on Google+, and you aren't hearing it mentioned on every major television awards show and sports broadcast, do not ignore Google+'s benefits.

Like Twitter, it's an open network, and you can find, follow, and connect with people you don't already know without needing an introduction.

The most important reasons to use Google+ for professional development:

- **Learn what thought leaders in your industry are thinking and writing about.** Once you identify people to include in your circles on Google+, it's easy to keep up with their posts and to learn information that will help you look "plugged in" to the information you need to know.

- **Meet new people and expand your network.** The same principles apply here as apply to Twitter—there are no boundaries to connecting with people you do not know. You can communicate directly to people by using their Google+ name. For example, if you want to reach me, you can use +MiriamSalpeter in your Google+ update, or for my business page, +KeppieCareers.

- **Demonstrate your expertise.** Similar to LinkedIn and Twitter, Google+ allows you to demonstrate your expertise by posting updates. If you choose to make these messages public (which I recommend), you have an opportunity to reach exponential numbers of people. Your updates will be indexed and searchable on Google.

- **Be found.** Google uses various algorithms to determine how to tailor the results that come up when people search for a topic. (They call this "search plus your world.") The trend is to display results based on social search. This means that if Google can identify you as being connected to someone searching for information (via Google+, for example), it is possible that your information (your blog, Twitter, LinkedIn, or Google+ posts) will appear as search results. How does this help you? One reason to use social networking is to be found. If you create an effective Google+ profile, contribute regular content, and interact professionally via Google+, it could help someone find you or something you've written.

In other words, creating content and sharing it is all you will need to do for a chance to be indexed and potentially found when someone else uses Google search to find information about what you know.

Blogs

NM Incite, a Nielsen/McKinsey company, reports that there are currently over 181 million blogs. Blogs offer a myriad of chances to touch base with other people who may share your professional, academic, and social interests. When I joined the blogosphere, the first thing I did was identify well-written and frequently updated blogs in my niche (career advice and job seeking). I spent as much time reading and commenting on my colleagues' blogs as I did writing my own posts. This provided several benefits:

- Reading other blogs gave me insight into hot topics and what top bloggers thought about them, which helped inspire and focus my writing.
- Frequently commenting on blogs provided a personal connection to their authors, many of whom reached out to me and helped promote my work—by mentioning it on their blogs or inviting me to guest post. This helped me feel like a member of the career blogging community and fueled my desire to keep writing.
- Engaging with bloggers via their comments section exposed their readers to my information and advice, which resulted in increased traffic for my blog. I still have visitors to my blog who find me via comments I left on one very popular site years ago.

Whether or not you decide to actually create and author a blog, reading and commenting on other blogs is a great exercise in personal brand building and an excellent way to expand your network. Actively participating in the blogosphere provides an opportunity for you to enhance your professional development on a regular basis.

How to Identify Blogs to Read

When I surveyed my Twitter friends about their favorite ways to find new blogs to read, not surprisingly, many responded that they ask for referrals from friends and colleagues. However, if your friends don't know a blog from a log, here are some helpful resources:

- **Alltop.com**: A magazine rack of blogs, this site categorizes numerous topics and provides easy access to blogs in your targeted niche.
- **Google blog search (http://blogsearch.google.com/):** a site that searches blogs.
- **Set alerts:** Track subjects or key words and receive e-mail alerts when it indexes something relevant. Go to http://www.google.com/alerts to set up alerts that will no doubt include content from many blogs.
- **Twitter and Google+:** Many people who tweet and post on Google+ also maintain blogs. Follow the link from a person's Twitter or Google+ profile to learn about the blog. Most links your online friends share are to blogs you may find useful.
- **Google:** Enter {*best blogs, topic*} in Google, where the topic is your area of expertise. For example, {*best blogs, accounting*} yields several results, including the top 50 blogs for accountants.
- **Technorati.com:** Select *Blog* instead of *Post* at the top and type your search term topic. Technorati provides a list ordered by authority, a measure of a blog's standing and influence in the blogosphere.
- **StumbleUpon.com:** This site uses a ratings system to create a collaborative opinion about a site's value. StumbleUpon

provides a list of topics, and you can select your interests and potentially be matched with other people's suggestions.

Social Media—A Bridge for Career Advancement

One of the best things about participating in social media is that it can help level the playing field for people who are transitioning jobs or careers. The rest of this chapter outlines examples of the following:

- **Career changers** may have a difficult time proving that they have what it takes to succeed in their targeted positions. Social media can help them bridge the gap.
- **Self-employed entrepreneurs, freelancers**, and **new businesses** may have a difficult time distinguishing themselves in a crowded market. Many job seekers are deciding to create their own businesses instead of pursuing employment opportunities. Social networking can connect them to the right clients.
- **Experienced professionals** seeking a new career may face ageism in a youth-centric workplace, and can benefit from social media tools. When engaging in new technology, seasoned professionals demonstrate that their many years of experience do not prevent them from learning new things.

Career Changers

If you have been trying to switch careers, you may have encountered a lot of obstacles along the way. There is no surefire way to transition, but engaging in social media can certainly help you build a bridge between where you are now and where you want to be:

- **It allows you to extend your network to meet people you otherwise would never encounter.** Let's face it, if you have been working in one field for a while, your connections in a new industry are likely few and far between. Actively working on your social media profile and reaching out to potential colleagues gives you the opportunity to engage one-on-one with exactly the people you need to meet.

- **You have easy access to information and resources about your targeted profession.** If you have not worked in the field, you have some catching up to do. There is no easier way to get up to speed than by joining online communities and following key bloggers and leaders in the field.

- **Demonstrate your newfound expertise and make a name for yourself in a new industry.** If you are highly motivated and have the skills that it takes to do the job you're targeting, you should be able to leverage the information you gathered via social media sources to become a blogger (if you write well) or prolific poster on any network. As a result, you may be perceived as much more experienced than your resume suggests.

- **Your lack of experience may become less important once potential colleagues view you as an active contributor.** You may be surprised to find that once you make a name for yourself, it is possible to attract the attention of hiring managers.

- **Familiarity with social media tools may be just the differentiator you need.** Don't forget that social media is on Indeed.com's top trend list for job descriptions. While many people may know about social media or have accounts, fewer actually build a strong personal brand using it and other social media tools. Knowing how to leverage these tools may help bridge an experience gap.

- **Seeing your title or tagline online may help you overcome emotional hurdles.** Barbara Poole, management consultant, trainer, coaching veteran, and founder of Employaid.com, suggests that defining yourself online may help you believe that you are viable in a new field.

CAREER CHANGE SUCCESS STORY

Alexis Grant, an entrepreneurial writer and digital strategist (http://alexisgrant.com), remembers applying for journalism and other writing/editing jobs. She explains:

"Something different kept falling into my lap—social media gigs. I resisted it at first. I saw social media consulting and immediately thought, 'snake-oil salesman.' I mean, who really needs someone to help their company with social media? Everyone knows how to do this stuff!"

Eventually, she recognized that everybody doesn't know how to leverage these tools. She adds:

"[Social media] positions kept finding me. Here's one example: I applied for a writing/editing position with an international organization. The woman in charge of hiring wrote me an e-mail saying that I looked qualified for the Web writing position, but what they'd really noticed on my resume was my social media skills. Finally, I saw the light and began taking on clients, helping small businesses and organizations with Facebook, Twitter, FourSquare, blogging, etc."

USING SOCIAL MEDIA TO CHANGE CAREERS

Jessica Lewis transitioned to a nonprofit career after 10 years in a different field. She states:

"Social media had an amazing effect on my exploration of other careers. I had access to all kinds of people in my target jobs, many of whom were happy to answer my questions and converse with me. All I had to do was ask, and engaging in social media made that part simple. Social media allowed me to look into a different career with no commitment or pressure."

SOCIAL MEDIA TRANSFORMED MY LIFE

Kate-Madonna Hindes (known online as @girlmeetsgeek), a former corporate advertising and marketing writer, used blogging and Twitter to launch an entirely new career as a social marketer and career columnist. She attributes her success in part to the fact that she leveraged Twitter and her blog to create a presence that made it easy for people to find her—and to know what she had to offer.

> *"Social media changed my life . . . I had been blogging for eight years and on Twitter for three years, sharing information about myself and advice for others. I was known for using various, fun hashtags on Twitter, such as #gojobseekersgo, which got the attention of the Minneapolis Star Tribune. Just because they found me on Twitter, I am now writing the front page job section, providing career advice to our readers! Savvy Minnesota picked up my story as well, and the combination of social media and traditional media led to me being contacted by a recruiter for a pretty high-profile government opportunity. I'm a finalist for the job, and even if it doesn't work out, my story proves that you can influence your future using social media tools. The greatest advice I can give anyone is that social media and social networking should be treated like a platform to broadcast who you are, what your career values entail and the passion you have to offer. It's a win/win."*

Self-Employed, Freelancers, and Businesses

It wasn't too long ago that starting a business involved raising money, renting an office with a mailing address, hanging an actual shingle, advertising in the Yellow Pages, and hoping that people would come to your door to request your products or services. Creating buzz might have involved sponsoring a local event or sports team. In those days, a television, newspaper, or radio ad were the most effective ways to reach a lot of people at once.

Times have really changed! Today, businesses can open with nothing more than a few dollars and some online know-how.

Connecting with thousands of people through the click of a mouse is not unheard of, and creating buzz can be as easy as creating a YouTube video that goes viral and becomes extremely popular online.

If you watch advertisements on television, read magazines, or view print ads, you probably know that many large and small businesses have jumped on the social networking bandwagon.

Many job seekers become small business owners, and I want to share some ideas about how businesses are taking advantage of online social media. You never know when you may decide it is time to start working for yourself. The following stories offer useful lessons for all types of entrepreneurs.

COMPANIES SUCCEED BY ENGAGING CUSTOMERS

Tasti-D-Lite (tastidlite.com) is a low-calorie frozen dessert franchise that began in New York City, but has since expanded throughout the United States. The company has been using social media since early 2008 to reach their customers. I have been following @tastidlite on Twitter for several years. B. J. Emerson, their former Social Technology Officer, offered the following thoughts:

"Creative and effective listening provides a strategic advantage when it comes to engaging with customers online. Opportunities abound for those who listen actively and monitor the various channels for mentions and conversations related to the brand, product, or service. With more customers expecting companies to respond to customer service requests through these channels, those brands that are socially negligent will certainly lose."

Tasti D-Lite prides itself on regularly engaging in conversations that help expand brand awareness and encourage customer loyalty. Providing a strong presence and being known as a customer-friendly brand sets them apart from competitors. B. J. adds:

continued from page 46

"One of our favorite types of engagements is when we catch customers in the middle of making a decision and we have the opportunity to influence the outcome in real time. In one case, a Twitter user announced that she was waiting to meet her husband, to visit either Tasti D-Lite or Mr. Softee. Our gesture in response was to simply follow her on Twitter, which would send her an e-mail notification. Her public response was 'OMG, Tasti D-Lite is now following me on Twitter . . . Quick, where's Mr. Softee?' An exchange resulted in the user finding a link to some coupons. She later announced what flavor Tasti D-Lite she ended up getting that evening."

B. J. believes that when consumers know that brands are listening and actively engaging, they usually reciprocate. In another example, they thought it would be fun to have a scavenger hunt of sorts, and for two days communicated on Facebook and Twitter that they would reveal the location of a hidden $50 gift card by posting a video at a certain date and time. At the appointed hour, they uploaded the short video disclosing the exact location, and the first person to arrive on the scene and grab the card would be the winner. Seven minutes later, a Twitter follower entered the store and claimed the card. He asserts, "This type of engagement and response is just one of the many types of opportunities that businesses have within these social channels."

GROWING A BUSINESS

Pizzeria Venti, in the Atlanta area, is a family-run restaurant whose owners, Brian and Jaime Lackey, have leveraged social media to connect with the community and grow their business. I first met Jaime and Brian while attending a *tweet-up* at their restaurant. A tweet-up is an in-person networking opportunity for people who have a mutual interest in using Twitter. I would never have heard of @PVATL (the restaurant's Twitter handle/name) had it not been for their engagement on Twitter.

Jaime and Brian use Twitter to connect with potential customers and local media in several ways. For example, a reporter from the local NBC

continued from page 47

affiliate covered their "free slice day" in her Friday Freebies segment, resulting in a number of people who came in to the restaurant to tell them that they live just down the road and that they'd never heard of Pizzeria Venti until they saw the report on TV. Jaime notes that several bloggers have learned about the restaurant via Twitter and help get the word out.

The restaurant constantly uses Facebook and Twitter to connect with customers and locals. Jaime explained:

"We use Facebook as a medium to broadcast information about specials, events, and menu items. It is a huge compliment for people to allow us into their personal space by 'liking' us on Facebook. We owe those fans an easy way to receive information about specials and events—as well as an easy way for them to provide feedback for us."

Jaime has many stories about how using Twitter also makes it easy to connect with the community in a way that Facebook and e-mail marketing programs cannot. For example, she once saw a post that read "Anyone know a place near Lenox Mall with a TV and a private room?" She responded, "We have private dining rooms and large-screen TVs. How can we help?" Later that day, a local company reserved the dining room for a group of 25 to 30 people, all based on a couple of Twitter messages. Jaime explains:

"If you're doing your job well and providing a great place for an event, great food, and great service, you'll love having a group of Twitter users at your place of business, because they are likely to talk about the restaurant and the food, as well as post pictures while they are there!"

Jaime suggests the following to help find Twitter users who live and tweet from your area:

- Use Search on Twitter (http://search.twitter.com) to search for keywords and geographic locations. Many Twitter users create lists by city.
- If you collect e-mail addresses from customers, ask for Twitter handles as well.

Jaime also advises business owners to investigate social media to expand their businesses:

continued from page 48

"As restaurant owners, we believe social media is about accessibility and connecting with customers and the community. We tweet about community events and connect with individuals about topics that have nothing to do with the restaurant. The end goal is increasing sales at the restaurant; however, the social media game plan is much more fun than just sales. After a little while, you realize you are just talking to your friends."

Other resources to help you track local Twitter users include the following:

- Twellow.com/twellowhood
- LocalTweeps.com
- http://tweepz.com (white pages for Twitter)
- NearbyTweets.com
- WeFollow.com (use your city or location as the keyword)

Experienced Workers and those Transitioning to an Encore Career

Speak to any job seeker who is a member of the Baby Boomer generation, and you are bound to hear about ageism and the fact that hiring managers seem to get younger all of the time. I can't tell you how many people have insisted to me that they have been unemployed for an extended period of time because they are "too old" and the job market discriminates against them.

Age discrimination may play a role, but it seems that there may be other factors in play when experienced professionals have trouble landing jobs. Walter Akana, career and life strategist and founder of Threshold Consulting, believes that the issue of *relevance* may be a factor. He explains:

"In today's personally branded, free agent, social-media driven economy, work opportunities will result less and less from the traditional job search. As this new economy expands, employers with work opportunities will seek and find workers who are the

best fit for specific projects. And who will those workers be? They will be the ones who have gained the best visibility and credibility in their brand communities; they will be professionals with proven abilities who regularly exhibit thought leadership in ongoing conversations across a range of social media, as well as in-person situations. Social media goes well beyond the cosmetic appearance to imply more youthfulness. Social media is about being truly and actively engaged."

Lisa Johnson Mandell was a 49-year old entertainment reporter who remade her image by freshening up her appearance and wardrobe, and creating a hip online presence that made her seem more youthful. Her book *Career Comeback* (Hanchette Book Group, 2010) details her successful repackaging efforts, which included focusing on how her online presence portrayed her. She reminds her readers that just having experience is not enough—the experience needs to be presented in a way that target audiences will appreciate and value.

One of the nation's top experts on career issues and workplace trends, Marci Alboher, former blogger and columnist for *The New York Times* and author of *The Encore Career Handbook* (Workman, 2012) and *One Person/Multiple Careers: A New Model for Work/Life Success* (Business Plus, 2007), agrees that experienced workers can benefit by engaging in social media. Marci is currently a vice president for Encore.org, an organization that helps engage millions of baby boomers as a vital workforce for change via *encore careers*, a new stage of work after a primary career that offers continued income, personal meaning, and social impact.

Marci sees a few ways that social media can be helpful for experienced workers and those seeking an encore career:

- Finding information and trends in your targeted field
- Accessing experts and potential mentors
- Connecting with recruiters and learning about positions

Job seekers committed to work that benefits society (in fields such as education, health care, government, and nonprofits), should follow Marci (@heymarci) on Twitter and visit Encore.org, which has its own social networking site, LinkedIn group, and Facebook page. Marci suggests following some of her favorite sources for the latest news, trends, and job leads in the nonprofit and social venture world (choose your social network; most of them have a presence on Facebook, LinkedIn, and Twitter):

- Idealist: http://idealist.org (@idealist)
- Steve Joiner (@IdealistSteve)
- Nonprofit Professionals Advisory Group: Facebook and LinkedIn Groups; founder Laura Gassner Otting is also active on Twitter, @gassnerotting
- CommonGood Careers: @cgcareers; http://www.commongood careers.com (Facebook, LinkedIn)
- Dowser: http://dowser.org (Facebook, LinkedIn, @dowserdotorg)

Job seekers hoping to return to work may successfully target organizations or individuals who use social networks. For example, searching Twitter for a particular company name may yield people who either work for the organization or actually Tweet for it.

Finding businesses of interest on LinkedIn and Facebook and joining conversations there is a great way to connect. Review the chapters about LinkedIn, Twitter, Facebook, and Google+ to learn more about how to identify good contacts, no matter what type of work you seek.

If you think social networking is having a conversation across the picket fence, LinkedIn is the latest video game, Twitter is something that birds or gossips do, and you don't know a blog from a log, it will be difficult to be an attractive candidate for a job—no matter what your age. It's not only important to know what these resources are, it's crucial to know how to leverage them for a successful hunt. For all of the reasons listed in this chapter, social networking is a relevant and mandatory part of an active, engaged job hunt. Not only does using these tools help you, it also demonstrates that you are interested and willing to learn new skills.

If you haven't looked for a job in a while and/or aren't tuned in to managing your *digital footprint*—what comes up when someone Googles your name—it's time for a quick lesson in social media. An online presence is key to how people perceive you, and if you are active and engaged online, doors that seemed closed may open.

Things to Remember

It has always been important to keep up with trends and information— to stay current and to keep your professional skills on track. Experienced careerists may remember early resistance to transitioning away from typewriters, but you'd be hard pressed to find someone who does not believe computers make our lives much easier.

The way we communicate will continue to change. Nielsen's 2012 report shows people spend more time on social networks than any other category of sites—20% of time on computers and 30% of mobile time.

Today's technology not only makes it easier to access information, it also makes it possible to share resources on a large scale. When fully utilized, social media provides:

- An easy way to track and stay ahead of trends in your industry or field.
- Ongoing professional development opportunities in the form of following or sending live tweets from conferences and professional events.
- Resources to meet and engage with colleagues from all over the world; social networks make it easy to find information, as well as position yourself as a leader and expert in your field.

- Crowd sourcing opportunities. Once you join the right communities, you can ask any question imaginable and expect someone to reply.
- Great ways to access information and resources otherwise unavailable.
- Bridges to new opportunities for career changers, entrepreneurs, and retired people who plan to reenter the workforce. Being able to learn new information, interact and with networking contacts, and create content online all provide positive opportunities.

If you mobilize the information and ideas in this book, and are resourceful and aware, you may be surprised to learn that these tools can be a lot of fun and helpful. Clearly, social media is not just for a particular audience or useful only for technical professionals.

Since social networks are very fluid, expect that specific platforms may come and go, and that popularity may wax and wane. However, the flow of information, advice, and resources is ongoing, provides a consistent link to trends, and allows you to keep ahead of peers who are not using these networking tools. Social media is here to stay. The choice is yours—engage or be left behind?

CHAPTER 3

Social Media Basics

Why Should I Use Social Networks?

Erik Qualman, author of *Socialnomics*, creates a very popular, well-distributed, and consistently updated video stream that highlights reasons to be interested in social media. One point of the videos is to prove that social media is not a fad that will go away. One recent video made several interesting points:

- Social media is the #1 activity on the web.
- 93% of marketers use social media.
- If it were a country, Facebook would be the third largest in the world based on population, and two times the U.S. population.
- One of five couples married in the United States met via social media.

Data provided by *Socialnomics* shows that social media and social networking have been widely adopted around the world. The social web is an international destination. Embracing social media, in whatever form that makes the most sense for you, is very important to establishing your professional profile.

As a job seeker, someone managing his or her career, or an entrepreneur, the only way to influence results when someone uses a search engine to find out about you is to join the social web and to create indexable, searchable content. Some people believe that if Google doesn't have results for your name, you might as well not exist! Luckily, the choice is up to you—you can join the millions of others who are communicating with each other and producing online content, sit by and be defined by someone else, or get left behind.

Social Networks Are For Everyone

When managing your career, the most important thing to demonstrate is your uniqueness. This is important for career changers, freelancers seeking opportunities, and retirees looking to return to work. It is also imperative that students, recent graduates, and experienced workers (including middle managers, upper-level executives, and even CEOs) leverage social media.

SOCIAL NETWORKING IS NOT A FAD

Social networking sites are key tools for the overwhelming majority of organizations who hire. Jobvite's 2012 Social Recruiting Survey reports that 92 percent of U.S. companies use social networks to find candidates. CareerBuilder also found that one in three employers will reject applicants based on what they find on social sites.

One response to this research is to stay away from social media. After all, if you do not use social media, you have less chances of being eliminated from consideration as a result of something unsavory you share. This would be a rash, and potentially detrimental, reaction, considering the possible upside of using these tools well: CareerBuilder noted that

continued from page 56

nearly 30 percent of hiring managers used social media to find information that caused them to hire candidates.

The best lesson to learn: use social media tools to showcase what you know professionally, and you may attract a hiring manager's attention.

YOUR GOAL—BE FOUND

Keep in mind that being found is the main point of using social networks. It is not useful to engage online using an alias or pseudonym. You should make it easy for someone to contact you, and consider that everything you share is part of the public record.

Remember, this is not your parents' job search; being successful in today's competitive, ever-changing environment means being engaged online, where prospective companies, colleagues, and decision makers will be looking for you. If you are highly qualified and take full advantage of social networks, job opportunities will actually come to you instead of you having to find them. Once you set things in motion, you may be able to look for jobs in your sleep, as people read and respond to your information online.

What if You Are Not Looking For a Job?

Even if you are not looking for a new opportunity right now, it is likely that you will need to (or want to) look for an opportunity at some point. It is rare these days for people to spend their entire careers working at one place.

Jeanine Tanner "J. T." O'Donnell, career strategist, workplace consultant, and founder of Careerealism.com, notes:

> "... every job is temporary and Americans can expect to have as many as nine careers in a lifetime, with an average of three jobs in each one."

Building an online presence will help you create a platform that will support you during a job search, and help draw opportunities to you, without you needing to apply for each one. One of the trickiest job hunting situations to manage is looking for work while currently employed. Except for very unique circumstances, you do not want your current boss to be aware that you are looking for new opportunities.

Clearly, posting a resume to a job board that might be found by a colleague or supervisor is out of the question. However, social networks are not just for job seekers—they are for everyone with an interest in making a name for him or herself. Creating a LinkedIn profile and growing your network does not necessarily indicate that you are staring to look for a new job. Becoming active on Twitter is not a red flag to your boss that you are about to jump ship, and investigating networks such as Google+ is not the same as hanging an *I'm looking for a new job* sign around your neck.

This is one of the best things about these networks; they allow you to be the type of job seeker some employers prefer—the passive job seeker, or someone who is not outwardly and actively looking for a new opportunity. So, you get the best of both worlds. If you are an active job seeker, the social web provides a plethora of opportunities to find information and connect with decision makers. If you are not a job seeker, it allows you to get on peoples' radar screens, without knocking on their doors or mailing out resumes.

Choosing a Network and Setting Goals

Social networking is a very personal experience. Before you consider integrating any of these tools into your daily routine, select the social networks that make the most sense for your needs and goals.

Twitter, Facebook, and Google+, sites I recommend for job seekers, are destinations that may invite users to share personal details that are not necessarily appropriate for career networking, so having a focus is important.

Factors to Consider

When planning your online presence, consider these factors:

- ❑ How much time do you have to build and maintain your profiles?
- ❑ What are your goals and expectations for the social networks?
- ❑ Are you committed to using social networking for professional purposes, or purely as a way to connect with friends and family?
- ❑ Are you disciplined enough to manage your online time effectively?
- ❑ What tools help you optimize your best skills?
- ❑ Are you more adept at presenting your expertise using video or audio?
- ❑ Do you tend to be verbose, or do you communicate succinctly?
- ❑ Are you more comfortable in a network that is purely professional, or do you function better when there is a crossover between business and personal?
- ❑ Can you easily filter a lot of information at once, or do you prefer to manage information in small pieces?
- ❑ Are you disciplined enough to manage privacy settings when necessary, and to only share information you would not mind your boss (or prospective boss) to see?

After you read about the various types of social networking sites discussed in this book, review the list at the end of this chapter for suggestions of networks to use or avoid, based on your skills, interests, and needs.

A NOTE ABOUT PRIVACY

Be aware that any network that has information about you is fair game for anyone who wants to research your background. For example, even if you decide that your Facebook page will be a personal network that you do not open for professional use, it is still possible (even likely) that a professional contact may access your Facebook page when conducting an online search about you. Something you share with a designated circle in Google+ can easily be widely reshared, even if the network discourages it. When you post information online, assume it is public—even if it is intended for a closed network.

PRIVACY IS FLEETING ONLINE

Louise Fletcher, owner of Blue Sky Resumes, shared the story of Dave Weigel, a *Washington Post* rising star, on her blog. The Post hired him as a political reporter to expand their online coverage. Louise explains:

> *"Dave was also a member of a private listserv group named Journ-Olist, where 400 bloggers who trusted one another discussed the issues of the day in a private forum. Or should I say, a forum they thought was private.*
>
> *One anonymous member of the group, for reasons only known to them, decided to archive Dave's e-mails and release them to several conservative websites. They were not flattering. In a series of snarky comments, Dave revealed his apparent distaste for many of the people he was covering.*
>
> *The* Washington Post *fired him within a day of learning about the e-mails. Dave's friends and readers have mainly backed him, arguing that his private e-mails should never have been made public and that, in his reporting, Dave was always fair and even-handed."*

The important point to remember here is that all it takes is one breach of trust to expose information that you thought was private. Even if you are only sharing with friends and close colleagues, remember that e-mails and online fodder should always be considered public. The lesson here is that if it would destroy your career, credibility, or reputation if what you write is published in *The New York Times*, then don't share it online.

Types of Social Networks

To help focus on the wide variety of social sites, I will highlight the following in this section:

- Blogs
- Microblogs
- Social networking sites
- Social bookmarking/social news
- Video/photo/audio sharing mechanisms
- Slide and document sharing tools
- Additional social networks

Each type of site offers a different user experience. Depending on your needs, you will want to evaluate the best sites for an optimum return on your time investment.

Blogs

If you spend any time online, you have likely visited and read blogs without even knowing they were blog sites. Consider starting a blog to help you achieve your goals.

Pros

- You can set up a blog for free, with very little technical prowess, at Wordpress.com, Blogger.com, and Typepad.com, among other free blogging platforms. Be aware that using a free platform does limit you a bit in design and content.
- You can go one step further and create a site at www.yourname.com, which indexes well for Google and can serve as a hub for all of your online activity. You can also maintain complete control of the content.
- A motivated blog builder may also incorporate video and audio elements using a wide array of tools.
- A blog allows you to demonstrate your knowledge and expertise in an area.

When done well, a blog is among the best ways to build your personal brand online.

Cons

- Maintaining a blog requires more time and effort than simply joining a social network such as LinkedIn, Twitter, Facebook, or Google+.
- Blogging requires strong writing skills. If you do not write well, a blog may hurt more than help you.
- Gaining momentum and readership requires persistence and patience.

Microblogs

Twitter.com may be the best known microblogging platform, but there are others. These include Tumblr.com and Plurk.com. These sites encourage users to share short spurts of information, often including a link (URL) to a longer blog post or article. Microblogs also allow you to share songs and other audio. Erick Schonfeld from TechCrunch, a blog dedicated to highlighting Internet products, states that microblogs are "designed for quick hits but can support photos, themes, and other more blog-like features."

Pros

- It is very easy to begin sharing content via a microblogging platform; it does not require a lot of maintenance.
- Barriers to entry are very low; connecting to people you do not know via Twitter is as easy as sending them messages.
- Even someone who does not write well can learn to communicate effectively in short spurts. It does require some effort to share useful information in, for example, 140 characters or less on Twitter, but it is probably much less intimidating to most people than creating a 300-word blog post.
- Connecting and growing a community is not difficult, with the right set of tools and effort.

Cons

- It is easy to be overly casual in microblogs (especially Twitter), which could be detrimental to anyone who cannot filter what he or she shares.
- It is common for microbloggers to post random information without giving it much thought.
- Posts on microblogs tend to be ephemeral—unless a follower tracks your posts, is online at the same time as you, or the post includes his or her name, it is unlikely that it will be read (but since Google indexes it, negative posts may be found via search).

Social Networking Sites

LinkedIn, Facebook, Google+, Pinterest, Plaxo.com, Ryze.com, Ning.com, Hubpages.com, Squidoo.com, and Annotum (http://annotum.org/) are just a few of the larger social networking sites that may be helpful for job seekers developing an online presence.

Pros

- Social networking sites targeted at professionals, such as LinkedIn, Plaxo, and Ryze, can be useful places to reconnect with contacts from previous jobs and organizations. They are also useful for expanding your network organically.
- Recruiters spend a lot of time on LinkedIn, in particular. Many organizations turn to it as a go-to platform to source hires. Someone hoping to fill a position may update his or her LinkedIn status to let people know of a job available. Then, the person's network may pass along the information.
- It is relatively easy to create profiles on these sites.
- Many of the larger social networks rank well for Google search, and LinkedIn profiles tend to appear near the top results.
- Facebook is currently the largest social network, and it is very likely you will find people you want to meet or reconnect with there.

- You can create profiles and spend as much or as little time as you deem necessary to make them work for you.
- Pinterest is a fast-growing site for people who like to share visual images.

Cons

- It is tempting to create profiles and leave them stagnant, which does not help you develop your personal brand.
- Social networks such as Facebook invite you to engage in games and behavior that may not improve your personal brand.

Social Bookmarking and Social News Sites

These types of sites invite you to create a profile and share items you like with members of your community. Social bookmarking includes sites such as Technorati.com and Stumbleupon.com. Social news sites include Digg.com and Reddit.com.

Pros

- Using these sites well helps you keep up with news and information in your niche, and then share it through these and other networks—this demonstrates your thought leadership and knowledge, and bolsters your brand.
- Once you set up a profile it is easy to bookmark or tag a site to share, and easy to see what your contacts have shared.
- Focusing on common interests helps expand your network; you have the opportunity to meet people you otherwise would never know.
- Using these sites well can help you gain traction and traffic for your blog posts, or those of your social networking friends.

Cons

- These sites are mainly about sharing and commenting; they

are not as useful as microblogs, blogs, and social networking sites are when it comes to creating content.

- These sites are less likely to result in direct contact with a recruiter or hiring manager.

Video/Photo/Audio Sites

YouTube is currently the best known and most popular site for sharing video. YouTube notes that its users upload 72 hours of video every minute. Other visually based networks include Flickr.com and Instagram, which allow users to share video and photos. Twitter's Vine application allows you to capture and share brief, 6-second videos.

Audio is another powerful medium for some job seekers. A platform such as BlogTalkRadio.com allows you to create your own online radio program with nothing more than your telephone or microphone and a computer. Podcasting is another option; it requires a little more technical savvy, but can be a very effective mechanism for creating a community.

Pros

- These tools do not necessarily require strong writing skills. No one will be judging your spelling or noticing typos on a visual or audio platform.
- If you are an artist or in a visual field, a site such as Flickr or Instagram allows you to upload photos of your work, comment on others' photos, and join groups, which could lead to good networking opportunities.
- You can post a video resume or portfolio that has the potential to go *viral* (become popular online).

Cons

- Most videos from job seekers that go viral do so for the wrong reasons! Be sure that everything you share is professional and does not make you appear foolish.

- Strong presentation and speaking skills are crucial for success, and it is easy to produce a less than ideal result.

Slide and Document Sharing

Slideshare.net (with more than 60 million monthly visitors) and Scribd.com (with 90+ million monthly active users) allow you to share presentations, documents, and PDFs. You can then embed these slideshows in your own blog or site. Slideshare and Scribd entries can also be uploaded directly to LinkedIn and made viewable on your profile. Your goal when uploading should be to attract a new audience via quality presentations and documents, which can drive traffic to other social networking sites you use. Scribd is a good option to share e-books and other materials you want in the public realm.

Pros

- Presentations are a great way to demonstrate expertise and authority regarding a topic.
- Some people have created slide versions of their resumes, which is a bit unconventional, but for the right audience, may be effective.
- You can easily connect with others and seamlessly share information with colleagues and new contacts.

Cons

- Once you share your slides, it is possible others will use them without attributing credit to you.
- This is not commonly a well-known source for job leads or career specific networking, but certainly has the capacity to go viral. Be sure you share contact information so it is easy to reach you.

Additional Social Networks

FourSquare.com

This network once made *Time* magazine's list of 50 worst inventions, but it is still going strong. It is a location-based site that allows you to check in when you visit a place. You can then share your status with a select group or via Twitter. You can also win points and badges and become the mayor of places. At conferences for recruiters, speakers mention this tool as a useful resource to find candidates.

Some businesses (Starbucks, for example) are forming loyalty programs and providing discounts for frequent check-ins. For some, this can seem pretty frivolous, but at least one recruiter at Sirona Consulting, a company that helps and advises companies regarding recruitment strategies, has written about how recruiters can conduct searches (via Google and Twitter) to find potential candidates who are checking in at targeted companies. So, while this tool isn't as popular as LinkedIn with recruiters, it is possible for FourSquare to help you make useful connections. Learn more at http://foursquare.com. I share more details about how geolocation networks such as FourSquare may be useful for your job hunt in Chapter 15.

More is Not Always Better

Having a presence on one or more of these networks may make the difference between landing your dream job and continuing to look for it. Barbara Safani, career strategist and owner of Career Solvers, notes:

> *"People who don't think online networking is relevant to their job search may quickly become irrelevant to the hiring managers who think it is."*

Keep in mind that when it comes to managing your online presence, more is not always better. Carefully selecting networks that make sense for you, and focusing your time building and maintaining those profiles, is much more useful than starting a presence on all of them and hoping for the best.

Engage authentically. Share advice and information strategically and don't solely be focused on you and your needs. The most successful people in social media have reputations for helping others. Be the type of person who earns that reputation. When you optimize these tools, you may be surprised by how far they can propel your plans!

Things to Remember

Clearly, there are many possible social networks to consider joining. The list presented here is certainly not exhaustive—there are new networks popping up all the time, including local and niche networks that could be useful for job seekers. The most important thing to remember is to have a goal when you engage, and then stick to that goal.

These social networks do not function as magic wands, nor are they silver bullets that allow you to directly target and hit exactly what you want. These networks provide opportunities to meet and interact with people you would otherwise never know, and allow you to expand your opportunities for success.

Selected Networks
LinkedIn
Twitter
Facebook
Google+
Blogging
Pinterest
Tumblr/Plurk
Plaxo/Ecademy/Ryze/Ning/
Squidoo
Hubpages/Ezine
Technorati/StumbleUpon/
Digg/Reddit
YouTube
Vine
Instagram
Flickr
BlogTalkRadio
SlideShare/Scribd
FourSquare

Absolute Must-Have Networks
LinkedIn
Google+

Best ROI for time investment (potential connections, extending your brand)
LinkedIn
Twitter
Facebook
Google+
Blogging
Slideshare

Best for Google Rankings
LinkedIn
Twitter
Blogging
Google+

Best for Writers
Blogging
Twitter
Google+

Best if You Are Not a Writer
LinkedIn
Facebook
Technorati/StumbleUpon/
Digg/Reddit
YouTube
Instagram
Pinterest
Flickr
BlogTalkRadio
SlideShare/Scribd
FourSquare
Google+

Best for Speakers
YouTube
BlogTalkRadio

Most Interactive with Other People
LinkedIn
Twitter
Facebook
Google+
Blogging
Tumblr/Plurk
FourSquare

Most Interactive Between Other Social Networks
LinkedIn
Twitter
Facebook
Google+
Blogging
Tumblr/Plurk

Best for Artists
Pinterest
Flickr
YouTube
Instagram

Require Daily Time Commitment for Best Return
Twitter

Blogging
Tumblr/Plurk
Google+
Technorati/StumbleUpon/
Digg/Reddit
FourSquare

Don't Have a Lot of Time, but Still Need a Network
LinkedIn
Facebook
Technorati/StumbleUpon/
Delicious/Digg/Reddit
SlideShare
FourSquare
Google+

Easiest to Use
LinkedIn
Twitter
Google+
Pinterest
Plaxo/Ryze/Ning/Squidoo
Hubpages/Ezine
Flickr
BlogTalkRadio
SlideShare/Scribd
FourSquare

Probably Don't Need
Tumblr/Plurk
Plaxo/Ryze/Ning/Squidoo
Hubpages/Ezine
Technorati/StumbleUpon/
Digg/Reddit
Flickr
BlogTalkRadio
SlideShare/Scribd
FourSquare
Instagram

Creating and Tracking Your Online Personal Brand

I f you are convinced that social media can help you and you are beginning to identify what networks to target, it's important to take some time to hone in on what you have to offer—your *value proposition*—before you dive in. In this chapter you will:

- Learn more about personal branding and what you need to take into consideration when creating your profiles.
- Discover what to include and what NOT to include in your social networking platforms.
- Find out about people who have used social networking to successfully launch new careers.
- Learn about tools to help you monitor what people are saying about you or your business online.
- Find out how you can influence the results of online searches for your name, even if others share your name.

Personal Brand Buzz

In a competitive market, identifying and nurturing your brand allows you to share your value proposition—what makes you special and different from everyone else—with a broad audience.

Have you ever listened to someone else tell a story about something that involved both of you? Inevitably, they omit details you thought were important or mix up the specifics. It is always better to tell your own story. The same holds true when it comes to creating an online profile that supports your career objectives. A personal brand that you design and share, an online representation of your value proposition, will help you stand out in a crowd.

Origin of Personal Branding

Although it has become a buzzword, the term *personal branding* is not new. Tom Peters coined it in an article titled "The Brand Called You" for *Fast Company Magazine* in 1997. Back then, there was no YouTube and no slew of social networking applications, so one thing Peters suggested was to get out into the community to gain visibility.

In-person interactions still provide strong ways to share your personal brand, but I think that it is significant that Peters reminds his readers to leverage their best skills. He suggested:

> *"If you're a better writer than you are a teacher, try contributing a column or an opinion piece to your local newspaper . . . and if you're a better talker than you are teacher or writer, try to get yourself on a panel discussion at a conference or sign up to make a presentation at a workshop."*

Personal Branding Today

Just because there are so many online social networking options does not mean that all of them will suit you and highlight your best skills. It would be irresponsible to suggest that every social network will work for every individual. You are unique, and the ways that you will communicate your brand need to be unique as well.

Since so many people use social networks to create and extend their personal brands, it may seem that forming a visible online presence today is more challenging than ever. But access to and availability of a variety of social networks makes it that much easier to reach your target audience. If you leverage the networks well and have something valuable to offer, there is still plenty of room for strong branding.

Create a Helpful Online Brand

Although I had been successfully operating my career coaching and resume writing business locally for years, when I launched Keppie Careers online, the competition was intimidating. Then and now, there are almost 31 million results for *career coach* on Google. However, by leveraging my writing skills and joining the right networks to showcase my abilities, I defined my niche. Significant career experts recognize my blog as a top resource, and highly respected career resources, including *U.S. News and World Report*, AOLjobs.com, and others invited me to contribute on their pages. Additionally, writers for top traditional media sources, including *The Wall Street Journal*, *The New York Times*, Forbes.com, ABCNews. com, and other mainstream media writers contact me to comment on career search and social media topics because I have created an online brand that highlights my expertise in those areas. If you use the right tools and invest time and energy, you can create and propel a compelling brand that gets you noticed.

PERSONAL BRANDING FROM THE OTHER SIDE OF THE HIRING DESK

Karla Porter is a human capital management and workforce development consultant. She blogs about human capital and new media at karlaporter.com. These are her thoughts about why personal branding is important for job seekers:

Companies look for three things: customers or clients, vendors, and to employ solution providers. Solution providers have a unique role in the process of getting the company's service or product to market, and therefore benefit from marketing their talents and abilities on the same level as vendors.

Think of the marketing campaigns for the brands you know and love. What makes them stick in your mind? What encourages you to be loyal toward them? You wouldn't think of eating another type of cereal or wearing a different brand of athletic footwear, right? When a solution provider (job seeker) adapts the same thought process to market him or herself as a big brand does, he or she establishes unique key identifiers and a recognizable personal brand, which is important to stand out in a crowded job market.

When you employ a scaled and streamlined, branded personal marketing campaign (via social media channels), you link what you offer and who you are to your name. It's exactly what you strive for in your job search. To think of it in algebraic terms, employers look for a specific type of individual (X) to fill a specific need. $X = U$.

Becoming known by friends, family, co-workers, peers, professors, social networking contacts, and recruiters as X is what personal branding for the job search is all about. Create, live, and market your personal brand and make your professional dreams come true.

Getting Started With Your Personal Brand

Maybe you are still not convinced that focusing on your personal brand and finding ways to share it across the Internet is right for you. Maybe it sounds a little too self-centered. Or does it seem like such a big job that it's hard to imagine getting started?

If so, then consider this: Do you want someone else telling your story online? Or, do you want to maintain control of what people find out about you when they Google your name? Focusing on you and your brand is nothing more than identifying and propagating what you should be doing as a job seeker anyway. Know what you have to offer as it relates to your target market, and let your audience know it.

Considering what you have to offer while thinking of yourself as a brand should help you define yourself and establish your goals. This is the most important thing a job seeker can do. What you do with the insight (create a blog, share content via Twitter, or Google+, etc.) may be the difference between having job offers and opportunities come to you and you spending a lot of time sending resumes out to people who are advertising for opportunities that may or may not have already been filled.

REVERSE THE RECRUITING PROCESS AND ATTRACT OPPORTUNITIES

Social media allows job seekers to reverse the recruiting process. Job seeking used to involve submitting a resume. Today, you have the opportunity to use social networks like billboards working for you around the clock. Your profile can be distributed to hiring managers, searched, and shared. Create an online presence to allow recruiters, hiring managers, colleagues, and friends to know more about you, what you offer, and what you want. It's a way to draw jobs to you instead of spending your time searching for jobs.

Things to Consider When Creating Your Brand

Every social network offers you an opportunity to differentiate yourself, and each platform provides a place to highlight what you have to offer. Your brand must showcase what is different and unique about you. So, it makes sense to take some time to think about your pitch before you dive in. Before getting started, you need to identify your goals.

GETTING STARTED ON BRAND YOU

Meg Guiseppi, Reach Certified, C-level Executive Branding and Job Search Strategist and owner of Executive Career Brand (http://executiveresumebranding.com/), asserts that everyone already has a brand—whether they know it or not. She says:

"Your brand is your reputation—the perception of you held by the external world. Your brand is the unique combination of personal attributes, values, drivers, strengths, and passions that define you. Your brand helps those assessing you determine whether they should hire you or do business with you."

The following is an abbreviated version of the executive brand development process Meg uses to guide her clients. When you begin to think about how to promote your skills and accomplishments online, ask yourself these questions:

1. What is your vision and purpose?
2. What are your values and passions?
3. What are your top goals for the next year, two years, and five years?
4. What three or four adjectives best describe the value you offer?
5. What words do you use to define your personality?
6. What are your core skills? Get feedback from those who know you best—at work, at home, anywhere. A good option to accomplish this is the 360° Reach Personal Brand Assessment (http://www.reachcc.com/360reach), a confidential, web-based tool that collects anonymous feedback in real time from your choice of respondents.

continued from page 76

7. What are your strengths and weaknesses?
8. Who is your target audience? Determine where you want to fit in (industry and niche area of expertise). Learn what decision makers in that field are looking for when they're vetting candidates, and position yourself to capture their attention.
9. Who is your competition in the marketplace and what differentiates you from them?
10. What does your competition typically have to offer?
11. What value do you bring to the table that no one else does?

Remember the three Cs of personal branding. A strong personal brand communications plan embraces these three characteristics:

- **Clarity**—be clear about who you are and who you are not.
- **Consistency**—steadfastly express your brand across all communications channels, both online and offline.
- **Constancy**—strong brands are always visible to their target audiences.

Your Pitch

Consciously thinking about you and your personal and professional goals will help you create an effective personal pitch. Sometimes, this is called an *elevator pitch*, referring to the concept that you could share it with a contact during a quick elevator ride. Today's audiences have short attention spans, so now the focus is on a *twit pitch*, referencing Twitter's 140-character limit messages. It is important to be able to define what you have to offer succinctly and in a few words. Some points to consider when composing your personal pitch include:

- What is your goal/objective?
- What do you want to do? (Consider your target's needs.)
- What impact do you have?
- What results do you create?
- What problem(s) do you solve?
- How do you create positive results?

Consider using this template to help you craft your own pitch. Note that the information doesn't need to be in this exact order. For example:

I work with (target audience) to (what problem you solve). This is how (your impact/results).

This is the pitch I typically use:

As a social media strategist, new economy job search coach, consultant, speaker, and author, I provide practical tips and advice to help job seekers and business owners overcome obstacles and confidently achieve their goals.

My twit pitch could read:

A social media strategist & new economy coach, I help job seekers & small business owners leverage tools that help them achieve their goals. (139 characters and spaces)

Remember, your pitch is about you *and* your target. It is important to indicate how you can solve your target audience's problems. Make sure what you say resonates with your listener. (Use the suggestions in Chapter 1 to help you identify your targets' needs.)

What to Include In Your Online Profile

Think of your online profile as your *digital footprint*. When you create profiles and content on the Web, you expand your impact online. Your job is to deepen your digital footprint by including things you want people to know about you, and to provide information that will help make it easier for people you are trying to attract to find you.

Keywords

Keywords describe what you do and how you provide value; these are the words people hoping to hire someone with your skills will use to search for you online. For example, Ken Revenaugh, founder of Fast Track Tools (http://fasttracktools.com), a company offering solutions to help clients redesign their businesses and sales processes, suggests that a headhunter searching for someone to fill a sales leader role for a start-up technology firm may search for words such as: *sales, entrepreneur, director, manager, leader, innovator, rapid, change, custom, unique message* . . . the list goes on. Make a list of the top 10 terms someone might use if they were looking for someone with your expertise, and use those keywords in your profile.

E. Chandlee Bryan, co-author of *The Twitter Job Search Guide* (Jist, 2010) and a job search strategist and career coach at Best Fit Forward (http://www.bestfitforward.com), offers the following suggestions for identifying keywords that are relevant to your professional life:

- **Use LinkedIn's Advanced Search capabilities to search for people with a similar background to you.** Search by job function, field, employer, and keywords. Also review the Skills section in other complete profiles. Identify words they use to describe themselves, make a list of relevant keywords, and incorporate them into your own social media profiles.
- **Use job descriptions of interest to identify keywords that employers use.** To identify keywords visually, cut and paste the job description and position requirements into a visual tool, known as a tag cloud generator, such as Wordle (http://www.wordle.net/) or Tag Crowd (http://tagcrowd.com). These sites will translate the words into a visual, where the most prominent words will stand out from the background. Incorporate the biggest words in your profile or applications, and increase the likelihood that employers will find you. Figure 4.1 is a Wordle interpretation of a job at IBM for an

insurance specialist. You can see the words that stand out in the visual representation are most important to include in your materials.

Another suggestion to research keywords is to use Google's tool, which reports how many searches it records for each word or phrase you enter. Visit https://adwords.google.com/select/KeywordTool and test some words. It's best to incorporate the most often used search words into your profiles. For example, if you want to decide if you should label yourself a *secretary* (4,090,000 local monthly searches) or *administrative assistant* (2,740,000 local monthly searches), it might be wise to include the keyword *secretary* in your profile.

Manage Your Online Profile

Tom Peters made an important point in his *Fast Company* article when he said:

> *"When you're promoting brand You, everything you do—and everything you choose not to do—communicates the value and character of the brand."*

This is a crucial point to consider when constructing a professional profile online. It is important to remember that online privacy is a myth. With the click of a mouse, social networks can open the virtual doors to your profile, providing the key to your previously private information and photos to prospective employers, networking contacts, and others.

Is this a reason to stay off of these networks? Absolutely not. Is it a reason to carefully monitor what you share? Absolutely. Therefore, before we talk about things to be sure to include in your profile, it is important to focus on what *not* to include.

I cannot emphasize enough the fact that the companies who own these networks (such as Facebook) do not necessarily consider maintaining your personal and professional privacy as their primary goal. It is *your* responsibility to monitor your own activity (and that of your friends, insofar as it impacts your reputation). While it is certainly possible that off-color language or political commentary may be considered appropriate in some industries, and having a profile that suggests you complain an awful lot may not preclude you from every position, taking a *better safe than sorry* approach is prudent.

HIRING MANAGERS ARE LOOKING AT ONLINE PROFILES

Statistics should convince you to be careful. As mentioned, Jobvite's research shows that the overwhelming majority of employers are searching online for information about prospective hires. Microsoft also commissioned research, including interviews with over 1,200 hiring and recruitment managers in the United States, U.K., Germany, and France. They report:

"79 percent of United States hiring managers and job recruiters surveyed reviewed online information about job applicants. Additionally, 70 percent of United States hiring managers in the study said they have rejected candidates based on what they found."

It is up to you to decide how much personal information you share in your profiles. Remember, just because a network asks for information does not mean you are obligated to provide it. For example, LinkedIn now allows you to share your marital status as part of your professional profile, which I do not recommend. Google+ invites you to consider including tongue-in-cheek comments with a category called "Bragging Rights." Clearly, Facebook was intended to be a personal network, not necessarily for professional use. This is not to suggest that you should eliminate every personal aspect of your life from your Facebook profile. However, recognize that anything you post is public and can get you fired—or not hired.

Information to Eliminate from Your Profiles

Whether you are a 17-year-old high school student or a 65-year-old retiree looking to re-enter the workforce (either by traditional or entrepreneurial means), I would suggest eliminating the following from your online profiles:

- Anything illegal, racist, sexist, political, or that could be considered discriminatory (unless, of course, your field is politics, in which case, you clearly need to demonstrate your thoughts in that area)

- Descriptions of drinking too much/getting wasted
- Details regarding your sex life or pictures you would not share with your boss
- Complaints about your company, customers, interviewers, your boss, etc.
- Gossip about people
- Talk about stealing from your job
- Talk about anything considered inappropriate or impolite
- Profanity
- Talk about the fact that you are pretending to be sick and missing work
- Bragging about goofing off at work or being bored at work
- Announcing you are quitting your job if you have not told your boss
- Lies about anything
- Jokes about being fired
- Anything negative about a company, especially one where you might like to work

Privacy Concerns

I advise my clients to consider everything online to be public information, even if there are privacy settings available. It's also important to keep an eye on what your friends are posting or saying about you.

On Facebook, you should be notified when anyone tags a picture of you. If it is inappropriate, ask your friend to remove the photo, and immediately untag yourself, as your tagged pictures appear prominently on your Facebook profile. It is your job to police your wall for comments you don't want people to see. Remove them and remind your friends you are keeping your profiles professional.

Take a look at the applications on your profile and the groups you joined from the perspective of someone who might want to hire you. It's a good time to resign from such groups as, "So, I'm late again, what are you going to do about it?" and "Hangovers at work are sexy."

CNN and *The New York Times* reported that some people have taken the step to create an alias Facebook profile with an alternate name (Kristin Blue may become K. Tin Sky) to connect with friends and make it more difficult for college admissions officers, recruiters, or hiring managers to find them. However, even this step is not 100 percent secure. Even if you think what you are sharing online is private, all it takes is one person to betray your trust for that profile to become public. In addition, there are many positive applications to Facebook that you will not be able to leverage if you build your network under an alias.

Monitor Your Online Activity

In the detailed chapters about Twitter and Facebook, I provide examples of how certain online activity has been known to get people fired. Usually, the defense is that online activity shouldn't impact employers' decisions, or that sometimes things are shared in the heat of the moment or as a joke. After all, Facebook and similar networks are supposed to be private places for friends and family members, and everyone likes to let their guard down once in a while.

However, the bottom line is that employers are reviewing online profiles. More and more companies are introducing *social media guidelines* to prohibit employees from commenting about their organization online. Whether or not it is fair, or if the posted comment was in jest or in the heat of the moment, once it is posted, the damage is done. Your best bet is to vent offline!

Social Networking Success Stories

Despite the admonitions, don't let privacy issues scare you! If you spend any time engaged in social media, you will encounter many people who say that they landed their jobs as a result of connections and introductions from various sites (LinkedIn, Facebook, and

Twitter top among them). The following are success stories to consider when you think about your online strategy.

I Landed An Opportunity

Shane Mac (www.shanemac.me) asserts that his job as Marketing Manager at Gist, an online service that aims to help you build stronger relationships, was a result of his online social media engagement. He identified company members, including Gist's CEO, who were on Twitter, and got to know them via retweeting and sending them messages.

After befriending a prospective colleague who invited him to an informal company get-together, Shane had the chance to move his online networking to in person connections. His success came after three months of courting the Gist team. Shane put together a proposal of ideas to address some of the organization's challenges, which helped him land his job.

Shane considers Facebook and Twitter to be doorways, helping job seekers and others meet people they would not otherwise know. He notes that "having something to say" is imperative to successful online networking.

In fact, he created a project, AskSummit.org, where he conducts five-minute video interviews via Skype (a free online technology) with thought leaders. Arranging these interviews gives Shane a great entrée to meet and talk with people whose ideas and work he appreciates; many people are happy to spend five minutes answering questions or giving advice about a topic in their area of expertise. Shane's advice for job seekers thinking about delving into social media:

"Be fearless. Everyone started somewhere."

I Leveraged Online Tools to Land a Job
Becky Benishek calls herself a "marketer with geek skills." Formerly Manpower Inc.'s Community Manager at MyPath.com, a free online career management site, she landed the job as a result of her

online interactions. Becky was an IT contractor doing Web content management for the manpowerjobs.com website, and training countries on how to use the content management tool. She explains:

"I was also their technical writer for the documentation behind the tool. It was a great time! When the contract came to an end, I explored how I could use social media to network my way back into the workforce. I found out LinkedIn has a lot of free webinars. I started looking into the social media webinars and searching out books, and I updated my profile to let my network know what I was doing. I also made sure to keep in touch with all the people I'd met, via IM, e-mail, or other platforms. When a social media position opened up on the Global Market-ing side for MyPath, my Manpower recruiter contacted me about it. I found out during the interview that the VP of Global Thought Leadership at Manpower had been noticing my LinkedIn updates. I landed my new job as the MyPath Community Man-ager partly because I had been involved in social networking."

I Used Social Media for Outside-Of-The-Box Success

Laura Gainor's successful social media story combines an array of tools. After finding out that she and her husband would be relocat-ing to Milwaukee from Charlotte, she focused on using Twitter to network and connect with new contacts. Using Twitter helped Laura focus on the social media players in her new city, and on companies where she might like to work. Comet Branding, a social media, public relations, marketing, and branding firm caught her eye, and it turns out that they tweeted about a position she really wanted. She explains on the Comet Branding blog how she landed a job as their PR and Social Media Strategist:

"Comet Branding posted the PR and Social Media Strategist position opportunity on the same day SquarePik, an iPhone app allowing you to add a photo with each Foursquare check-in,

launched itself to the world. I utilized this social media outlet to tell my story as to how, after all of my personal and professional experiences, I thought I would be a good fit to join the Comet Branding team.

With some quick thinking on the night Comet Branding posted the job opportunity, I created their logo as a large poster and took a YouTube video to kick off my #LauraGainorToMilwaukee campaign. My husband and I happened to be leaving for Milwaukee the next day to find a place for us to live. My plan was to bring the Comet Branding logo poster with me on the plane from Charlotte to Milwaukee, where I would capture creative photos of the logo in each venue I checked in at through SquarePik and Foursquare. Throughout the process I strategically tweeted to @cometbranding to notify them of each check-in, hoping to get their attention.

As you checked out #LauraGainorToMilwaukee on Twitter, you could see the full list of my Foursquare/SquarePik check-ins with links to my Pikchur account, featuring creative photos I took with the Comet Branding logo poster at popular venues around Milwaukee. At the same time, it was also a creative way to show my husband around Milwaukee!

After returning to Charlotte that Monday, I looked to create a nontraditional presentation that showcased my social media efforts as to what I did, and how I did it. As I was creating the presentation, Al Krueger and Sara Meaney provided some great feedback after noticing my tweets from over the weekend. I was able to incorporate their immediate feedback into my presentation.

That afternoon, I launched what is now the Slideshare Presentation that got me hired at Comet Branding. Within this presentation I started out with a virtual resume of what I've done throughout my career, while also showcasing my creative and strategic talents. The presentation enabled me to tie the #LauraGainorToMilwaukee campaign together as a means to show I wanted to become a part of their team."

Takeaways

I could fill a whole book of success stories from people who know that social networking helped them land a job. The common link for successful job seekers is often being creative without seeming desperate. Those described here demonstrated that they have the skills needed (compared to just saying that they have the skills), and are willing to take a bit of a risk. The key is that the risk is a calculated one, based on what they learned about the targeted organization and its culture. Think about how *you* can turn your story into similar success.

Being Found on Google

In Chapter 1, I suggested that you should try using Google and some other search engines to determine what someone would find when they look for you online. Some people may find, to their dismay, that they share the same name as a criminal or other unsavory character. At the very least, knowing this information is the first step to combating it in the marketplace.

Many people share the name of a famous person and still manage to hold the top Google ranking for the shared name. Willie Jackson is a marketer, engineer and writer. He is proud to note that his website (http://williejackson.com/) is the first result when you Google his name, outranking Willie Jackson, the NFL player. Willie attributes his successful online indexing to:

- Owning a domain name relevant to the phrase he's looking to rank for (in this case, his name)
- Using a content publishing platform that has a history of performing well in search engines

Willie advises that all professionals own their domain name, even if they need to use a middle initial, such as www.JohnMSmith.com.

He suggests job seekers use http://flavors.me to create an attractive site that ties together all of their social networks in one easily accessible online site. He notes:

"Having an effective personal website no longer requires deep pockets or technical experience—one need only have the desire to find the right tool and the motivation to see the site created."

You can influence how your name is indexed, which is one of the most important reasons to dive into social networking. Recently, I Googled a friend's name and found that, while LinkedIn was the first result for her, the next results related to her role in her daughter's preschool Parent-Teacher Association, and an award she won in her early college years. If I were a hiring manager, I would not be impressed.

Make a note of what information is associated with your name. If there is anything you would rather not appear (for whatever reason), it is up to you to create the content that will rank higher for your name and push the less desirable information further down the page (keep reading to find out how to push unwanted search results out of the way for more recent, job-friendly results).

What if there is nothing about you online? Remember, some recruiters and hiring managers will go so far as to say, "If Google doesn't think you exist, you might as well not exist." (At least as far as your job search or professional persona is concerned.)

Don't be invisible—use the information in this book to create and manage a strong, professional online profile, to increase your chances of being hired for jobs and other professional opportunities.

How to Monitor Your Online Brand

Even if you have not created a strong brand, it does not mean that someone else has not already shared your story. If your online profile is limited and you are just starting to build it, it is important to keep close tabs on how your name is indexed.

Tools to Monitor Your Reputation

Consider the following tools to help you monitor your reputation and build your brand.

TalkWalker (http://talkwalker.com/en)

Probably the easiest way to monitor your name online, setting a TalkWalker alert involves visiting http://talkwalker.com/en and logging in to allow you to select the search terms that interest you. (In this case, you would select your name or business name.) TalkWalker allows you to select how often you would like to be notified when it indexes your search term, and asks what e-mail address should receive the notifications.

TweetBeep.com

This tool allows you to track your mentions (your name, business name, etc.) on Twitter and to receive e-mail updates when someone tweets something about you or your site, even when they use a shortened version of your URL. This is one way to capture your replies and mentions on Twitter. You can also set up alerts for topics of interest to you, including jobs or other personal or professional interests you want to track.

SocialMention.com

This tool calls itself the equivalent of Google alerts, but for social media. You can set it up to receive free e-mail messages that let you know if your name, brand, company, or any topic of interest, is mentioned online.

Tweetdeck.com, Hootsuite.com, and Twitterfall.com

These free applications let you set up ongoing searches and can be downloaded on your computer.

Clean Up Your Digital Dirt

Even if you have not posted anything online, it is likely that Google and other search engines have captured some information about you. I refer to this information as your "digital shadow" (See Chapter 1 to learn how to use the *deep web* to find information about you or others). What should you do if the information is not flattering, or if it is not what you would want someone to learn about you when Googling your name?

Create Your Own Content and Make Yourself Googleable

The most effective way to control what people learn about you online is to create your own content. Owning a blog and posting on it frequently gives you the opportunity to teach Google what you want it to know about you. Posting comments on other blogs and major media sites, and maintaining profiles on big social networks will help you influence what people see about you online.

If you are not sure that you want to go to the trouble of creating and managing your own blog, there are other options, depending on your interest. For example, you can write about just about any specialty area or interest via Examiner.com. This site has channels in most major markets and looks for local Examiners to write about everything, from restaurants and things to do to gardening and home repair (and everything in between). They like applicants to commit to several blog posts a week, but you don't have to manage or maintain your own blog. They also tend to have strong search engine optimization, so you have a chance to be indexed for words that you want people to use to find you online.

Other places to create content that search engines may index include:

- **www.amazon.com:** review books
- **www.google.com/profiles:** set up a Google Profile

- **www.squidoo.com:** a site begun by marketer Seth Godin, you may create a *lens* here and share content with readers.
- **www.ning.com:** join a community and add your insights on any number of niche topics
- **www.helium.com:** join this community and write about any number of topics
- **www.hubpages.com:** signing up gives you access to publish posts
- **www.ezinearticles.com:** submit up to 10 articles; if you meet their quality standards, you may submit an unlimited amount of posts
- **www.workitmom.com:** a niche site for mothers, where you are allowed to create a profile and post blogs

Cleaning Up Content You Did Not Create

When information that does not originate from you portrays you in a negative light, it can't hurt to ask the person responsible for the content to remove it. This is unlikely to work when the unsavory information is on a major media outlet or local newspaper's site. You have a much better chance when the offensive content is on an individual's blog. Simply write a polite message asking that the content be removed. This worked for a prospective client of mine. He had a felony on his record, and the story about his situation had been shared on various sites before the complete information came out in the press. He was able to have one site remove the information. Google still indexed it, but readers could not click through to the specifics on that site. Not surprisingly, newspaper sites informed him that they would never remove the content.

There are several companies who help identify and claim to be able to suppress negative content. You may wish to investigate the following if you are in a situation where you do not own the negative content about you online. (Please note: *this is not an endorsement of these companies, and is solely provided to help you begin your research.*)

- **DefendMyName.com:** advertises its ability to help suppress negative search engine listings about you or your company. It reportedly helps to create positive content that replaces undesirable information in early search pages. They use such strategies as circulating press releases that help push down negative results and replacing them with new information that you want people to know.
- **Reputationdefender.com:** bills itself as providing tools to monitor, protect, and improve your online reputation. This company can help have private information about you removed from some websites, but actually cleaning up "digital dirt" requires working with their staff to create tailored solutions for improving your online identity and brand image.
- **DoneReputationManagement.com:** uses an array of technologies and advanced content management systems to help you control the top 20 to 30 rankings (for your brand) on major search engines, such as Google and Yahoo.

The best way to keep a clean online reputation is to not post or do anything you would ever want to hide. When companies offer to purify your online reputation, they are typically focusing on creating new, positive links that will displace negative information from the first page or two of search results. Creating your own content via blogs, Twitter, or other sites is a good way to take charge of how you show up online.

Things to Remember

Once you identify your pitch and target the keywords you will use to share information about what you offer, it is *your* job to monitor and nurture your brand. Be the person your professional contacts would want to hire and collaborate with. Don't forget, your brand does not exist in a vacuum.

Take advantage of every tool at your disposal, including job boards, search engines, and other online resources, to help craft a desirable brand. Use descriptions and advice about leveraging the various social networks in this book to learn how to promote and extend your brand. If you do this well, you may have limitless opportunities ahead!

5 Using LinkedIn

What is LinkedIn?

LinkedIn.com is the world's largest online network dedicated specifically to professional connecting. It is a place to find and share opportunities, keep track of people you know or meet (even if they move and change jobs), and to help grow your community. LinkedIn has over 200 million members from over 200 countries and territories, and continues to expand at the rate of one new member every second.

The number of potential connections on LinkedIn is one reason it is known as a first-choice destination for job seekers looking to enhance their professional images. The LinkedIn community is made up of executives from all Fortune 500 companies. In addition, 50 percent of LinkedIn users have a bachelor's degree or higher, and there are more than 2.6 million companies represented on LinkedIn.

Tirumalai Kamala, immunologist, microbiologist, and organizer, replied to my inquiry on LinkedIn, asking people to talk about its top features. She said:

"LinkedIn allows you to establish credibility and earn trust by providing value. This is what I attempt to do by participating regularly in LinkedIn Answers, where I share the information, knowledge, opinions, and insights at my disposal. I believe the networking value of this interactive forum is incalculable. How else to get to know each other better than by analyzing how and what we ask and how and what we answer, and by engaging in dialogue and discussion?"

If you are familiar with the concept of six degrees of separation, which suggests that everyone on the planet is connected to everyone else within six steps (or friend-of-a-friend connections), you will easily understand LinkedIn's approach. The site encourages you to connect with people you know and trust; once you're "linked in," you will be connected to your friends' friends and their contacts as well.

The advantage of this approach is that your network expands every time one person in your close network adds a contact. For example, when I had 365 first-degree contacts in my immediate network, I was connected to an expanded network of more than *7,700,000 people.* My total network was growing at a rate of approximately 11,300 people every few days.

A Must-Have Professional Network

While several of the networks I describe in this book may or may not be well suited to all job seekers, LinkedIn is a must-have network for the following reasons:

- **LinkedIn ranks well for Google and other search engines.** If you have no other online presence, at least your LinkedIn profile should appear in search results about you.
- **LinkedIn gives you an easy, free, and user-friendly URL.** This is a good way for people to learn more about you and find out how to contact you. You can use your LinkedIn URL to augment other profiles (such as Twitter), or as a standalone resource for anyone who wants to learn more about you. There is an option to upgrade your profile to a paid account, but most users do not require this specialized access.
- **LinkedIn offers a way for you to stay connected.** Keep in touch with people you meet, both professionally and socially. Searching for people on LinkedIn after a networking event or social gathering, and requesting a connection, ensures you have a chance of being remembered.
- **LinkedIn lets you provide key information to contacts.** Adding your LinkedIn URL to your resume, business card, e-mail signature, and other places where you share information is a good way to provide extra details to people, as well as give them access to endorsements of your work.
- **LinkedIn provides a showcase for sharing recommendations and allows people to endorse your skills.** While some downplay the importance of endorsements on LinkedIn, the fact that the recommendation is tied to the recommender's profile does help legitimize the reference. "One-click" skills endorsing, described in-depth in this chapter, also met with critics, but will continue to be important as part of a complete LinkedIn profile.
- **LinkedIn allows professionals to share their information and expand their networks.** This is true even when they are not in job search mode. It is a great tool for passive job seekers (those who might consider a new opportunity, but are not actively looking), or job hunters who do not want anyone to know they are looking for a job.
- **LinkedIn is the go-to site for recruiters and many who want to identify potential hires.** 92 percent of recruiters use

LinkedIn to find talent, according to the Jobvite 2012 study. I have yet to meet a recruiter or who does not include LinkedIn as part of their search strategies.

- **LinkedIn helps you build an effective brand.** If you have a solid resume, you can quickly and easily build a professional profile on LinkedIn that demonstrates your expertise.
- **LinkedIn helps you protect your brand.** The nature of the site does not invite you to share inappropriate information that may damage your personal brand. I have never heard about anyone being fired from a job as a result of something posted on LinkedIn.
- **LinkedIn lets you learn and demonstrate your expertise.** It offers you a place to demonstrate your expertise and seek industry expert advice via your updates and via Groups.
- **LinkedIn provides access to an international community of professionals in 200 countries**. There are well over one million groups on LinkedIn, and more than half of LinkedIn's members are from outside of the United States.
- **LinkedIn is a good resource for new business development opportunities.** It offers a place to promote your offerings to a large potential cohort of professionals and customers.
- **LinkedIn Today.** LinkedIn allows you to cultivate useful news and information you can use to source useful links to share with your network via LinkedIn Today.

FROM THE OTHER SIDE OF THE HIRING DESK

Heather McGough, a staffing consultant who recruits within the Customer Support Organization at Microsoft, believes that having a LinkedIn profile is an absolute must for job seekers as well as professionals who are not currently job hunting. She explains:

"Recruiters use LinkedIn as a first-line source of prospective candidates. It is such a useful tool, because it allows us to find qualified people and to offer them a chance to apply for opportunities they

continued from page 98

may not have considered. If job seekers make it easy for recruiters to find them by using keywords and completing their profiles, it could improve their chances to land a new job. When creating a profile, I always recommend searching for your dream job via Indeed.com or SimplyHired.com, find the key words companies/recruiters are using in those job descriptions, and incorporate those words to jazz up your LinkedIn profile.

Some people may wonder if having a LinkedIn profile is a sign that they are looking for a job and worry that their boss or employer would view it negatively. Keep in mind, building a professional network is your responsibility and should make you desirable as an employee. LinkedIn is not a job board for active job hunters, such as Monster or CareerBuilder, where your profile obviously indicates you are in the market for a new job. If your boss is on LinkedIn, it would be difficult for him or her to say you should not be. If he or she isn't there, no worries!"

This tool allows you to select the topics that interest you. LinkedIn will collect and deliver the most relevant content to your LinkedIn profile.

Advantages of LinkedIn

In addition to the reasons already mentioned for joining LinkedIn, it also offers the following advantages for job seekers and workers:

- You can import and export contacts from LinkedIn into Excel and other supported file types. (Just go to "Contacts" from the main toolbar and scroll to the link that says "Export Connections.") It's a good idea to do this so you have a backup of your network.
- It's an easy way to touch base with your contacts regarding your professional engagements or plans. All you need to do is update your status, and LinkedIn will notify your network.

LinkedIn is also an effective research platform:

> You can use LinkedIn profiles to learn what skills others in your field or industry are marketing. Reviewing complete and well-done profiles is a great way to learn how you should be marketing yourself. Be sure to visit "Skills & Expertise" under the "More" tab to learn all kinds of data about skills you want to market.

Now that you've learned a bit more about LinkedIn, and are hopefully eager to develop your profile, here are a few other things to keep in mind:

- LinkedIn makes it very easy to search—for people, companies, and groups.
- You can easily integrate multi-media from applications such as Pinterest, Twitter, YouTube, Spotify, Scribd, and Slide Share or from your desktop. Click the blue square that you'll see when you edit your profile. Add in the URL of the information, or upload it from your computer and it will appear in your profile.
- You may request introductions to people in your extended network.
- LinkedIn allows you to communicate from within the site, which shields your e-mail address until you are prepared to share it with a new connection.
- While LinkedIn encourages you to only connect with people you know and trust, you have an opportunity to expand your network by connecting with LinkedIn Open Networkers, known as LIONS. These are people who announce their willingness to accept any opportunity to join anyone's network.
- Reconnect with people you may have lost track of. I mentioned in Chapter 3 that I located two long-lost high school friends via LinkedIn when I first signed on. It is a great place to find people you worked with years ago, and to reconnect for networking and information sharing.

- If you are diligent, you can learn all types of information about companies, including where people who work in one company tend to go next. (This information is available when you follow companies. I provide details about how to use this feature in Chapter 6.)
- An overwhelming number of recruiters use LinkedIn to source for opportunities, and it is a great place to connect with them.
- LinkedIn lets you know how many people have reviewed your profile and how often you came up in searches, which helps you gauge if your profile is attracting attention or needs to be tweaked. This is on your homepage. Assuming you allow others to see your profile when you visit their pages, you can see the most recent five people who viewed your profile with a free account. A paid account will provide additional data and analytics.

LinkedIn—Cons

There are not many disadvantages to using LinkedIn, but you should consider the following:

- It is a closed network and does not encourage you to reach out to people you do not know directly.
- For certain functionality, LinkedIn requires a fee; for example, to send InMail (a message to someone outside of your network). However, it is usually not necessary to pay for LinkedIn in order to research people and organizations, and to market your skills. Start with a free account, and consider upgrading to a job-seeker membership (described in Chapter 6) if necessary.
- As LinkedIn has incorporated more and more features, it sometimes provides utility that encourages users to meld

their personal and professional lives *too much*. Although I mentioned earlier that I have never heard of someone losing a job as a result of posting something inappropriate on LinkedIn, don't forget yourself and overshare.

Create and Optimize Your Profile In LinkedIn

When you think about what to post via LinkedIn, the most important thing to consider is that you want to make it easy for people to find you, to learn what you have to offer, and to contact you. As you will learn in the following chapters, LinkedIn provides many ways to interact with and meet new people. When you engage via LinkedIn, keep in mind that everything you do, every group you join, all the information you provide should be in pursuit of expanding your network, sharing your expertise, and providing opportunities for people you know—and those you do not know—to experience what you have to offer.

Create Your Profile

Visit www.LinkedIn.com to secure your profile. Use your real name and an e-mail address that you own, *not* one that belongs to an employer and might change as a result of a job change or layoff. You will be able to include alternate e-mail addresses once you have a profile, but sign up with a personal address as your main contact point. LinkedIn allows you to import and invite contacts from a wide array of e-mail services.

I suggest you skip all of the options to import your contacts and wait to connect to people once you have completed your profile. That way, you will be sure that everyone you contact knows who you are and how they know you. Having a fully optimized and complete profile before you try to expand your network is a good idea. (Read more about expanding your network in the next chapter.)

> ↰ **TIP**
>
> Are you multilingual? You have the option of creating a profile in a different language. LinkedIn users also have the option to add a section indicating multiple language fluencies. Simply click "Add Sections" on the Edit Profile page.

Perfect Your Pitch

Before you populate your profile, be sure you spend time perfecting your pitch and identifying the keywords (explained in Chapter 4) that people are likely to use when they search for you. Look at other LinkedIn profiles from people in your industry for ideas of strong key words and search terms.

Keywords are important to help people find you in LinkedIn. Include them in your:

1. Headline
2. Current experience
3. Past experiences
4. Summary
5. Skills

When you write your summary, be sure to include a "hook," or mini story to entice someone to want to learn more. Describe who you are and how you can help.

Answer these questions:

1. Who are you?
2. Who do you want to help?
3. How are you going to help them?

This is important advice for anyone creating and optimizing a LinkedIn profile. Just having a profile is not useful if it does not highlight what you offer. Make sure to spend some time identifying keywords appropriate for your description before you delve into creating or editing it. When you are ready, just follow the link from the toolbar to "Profile" and "Edit Profile."

ADVICE FROM THE OTHER SIDE OF THE HIRING DESK

Craig Fisher, a social business strategy consultant and LinkedIn trainer, advises job seekers to focus on their keywords:

"As a job seeker, you need keywords in your Linkedin profile that will be specific to your niche in order to help separate yours from the hundreds of less targeted profiles. Good recruiters will narrow their searches with unique keywords. Study job descriptions and other profiles to select strong choices and incorporate the keywords in multiple places in your profile—your headline, summary, in your job titles, and in the descriptions of your jobs. Having these listed multiple times in your profile will help it come up at the top of the search results when a recruiter or hiring manager searches for someone with your skill set."

Uploading Your Resume

Until LinkedIn considers your profile 100 percent complete, you will see an option to "Import Your Resume." It's important to know that LinkedIn is not actually inviting you to have a traditional resume on its platform; it allows you to use data from your resume to populate your LinkedIn profile. Even if you upload information from your resume, LinkedIn only reads content that is actually part of your profile.

LinkedIn's Help feature explains that uploading a resume is not permanent until you click on "Save Changes." Follow these simple directions:

- Click on "Profile" at the top of your home page. This will take you to the "Edit My Profile" page.
- Click "Browse" to locate the resume document on your computer.
- Click the "Upload Resume" button.
- Review and edit extracted information.
- Click "Save Changes" to complete the process or "Go Back to Edit My Profile" to cancel the import process and return to your profile.

If you are starting a new profile, it might be helpful to use your resume to fill the sections, but cutting and pasting from your resume section by section is also an easy way to populate your profile.

Profile Sections

To edit your profile, all you need to do is sign in to your profile and select "Profile" from the top menu bar. Navigate to "Edit Profile" and select "Edit" for each section you wish to update or create.

Professional Headline

This is the equivalent of your twit pitch (discussed in Chapter 4). Use your headline to clearly describe what you offer—your value proposition. There are no specific rules about what should go into this space, but I encourage you to use it to market yourself clearly and succinctly. Create a headline with a "pitch" that tells readers what you do. Include keywords to make it easier to find you.

Headlines Should Include Keywords and Your Pitch

Since your headline is the most visible information about you when your profile comes up in a LinkedIn search, it is one of the most important parts of your LinkedIn profile. Whether you are currently

HEADLINE WRITING TIPS FOR UNEMPLOYED USERS

If you are in transition, consider writing a headline that describes your professional goals. For example, if you are hoping to land an executive sales opportunity, include "Executive Sales Specialist" in your headline:

Are you wondering if it is a good idea to openly advertise the fact that you are looking for a job via LinkedIn? There are two approaches here:

1. Openly share your plans to land a new opportunity and advertise that you are in transition or seeking a new challenge.
2. Simply share your professional qualifications without calling attention to your status as a transitioning job seeker.

For example:

Option 1: Lay your cards on the table.
Project manager in transition, looking for my next role in the NYC area

or

Looking for new opportunities as a project manager with rich software-development experience

Option 2: Be the professional you are (regardless of your employment status).
Project-management professional providing exceptional value to large-scale software projects across multiple industries

or

Project manager (PMP), actively involved in multiple NYC PMI chapters—experienced in high-tech funded startups

I have spoken to many recruiters who prefer to hire passive job seekers—people who are employed. As a result, I advise you to focus on your professional skills and what you offer, without spotlighting your unemployed/jobseeker status. Anyone who spends time on your LinkedIn profile will be able to recognize you are in transition without you saying it. Hopefully, people will be so impressed by your profile your employment status will matter less than your skills and accomplishments.

However, there are a few exceptions to this advice:

continued from page 106

1. If you are a contractor, or seeking frequent, short-term opportunities, noting your availability for new challenges may be useful.
2. When you first transition to being unemployed you may want to change your headline, to alert your network of your status, by adding something such as "Seeking New Opportunities in _____." After your contacts have had the chance to see the update (about a week or two), consider changing it to a more specific, goal-oriented headline.

employed or not, incorporate specifics. Include keywords, but also include a reason for someone to want to learn more about you—a pitch. When you have a strong pitch, people who land on your profile in LinkedIn searches are more likely to click through to see your full profile. The more people who click through your profile, the more findable you become on LinkedIn.

When your write your LinkedIn profile, consider the following tips from *100 Conversations for Career Success*, which I co-authored with Laura Labovich:

1. **Identify your target audience.** To whom do you provide value (Is it universities? Fortune 500 accounting departments?) If you are unsure, ask yourself, "Whom do I want to attract with my message?"
2. **Consider the value you provide.** Be specific and narrow your focus whenever possible. This is known as your Unique Selling Proposition, or USP. Ask people you trust what they would say about what you do well. For example, are you the organizational maven? The go-to HR process expert? Marketer to small medical practices? Be sure to include your unique value (or *pitch*) in your headline.
3. **Make it memorable.** Be creative so your headline will leave an indelible mark on readers. Add humor if it fits your personality, but avoid making it cheesy or overly self-promotional.

Organizational Maven for Fortune 500 Companies: *I streamline your processes, so you can make more money*

DC-based social-media consultant (and former job seeker) Yolanda Arrington took a different spin on her profile while in transition. In her headline, she removed the jargon and touts what she can do for you:

Social Media Guru: *Need it produced, social media marketed, tweeted, Facebooked, or written? I can take care of that . . .*

Regardless of employment status, Susan Guarneri, known as the Career Assessment Goddess, insists that headlines should pack a punch like these below:

Director of Corporate Communications: *Delivering consistent on-brand corporate communications with a personal touch*

National Sales Manager: *Rainmaker and sales-team spark bringing $95 million in software sales in 10 years*

Turnaround CEO—Trade Associations: *Transformative change agent who delivers results when it matters most*

Senior Civil Engineer: *Systems maximizer who integrates projects, data, and people for quality results*

Be as creative—or conservative—as your industry requires. Remember, this is a professional network, and your headline is what everyone will see when they peruse other peoples' connections. While you may choose to advertise your job search status, do not use the entire headline to simply broadcast that you are seeking your next opportunity. Use this important space to let people know about you.

How to present yourself on LinkedIn and other social networking profiles if you are between jobs is a frequent topic of conversation in the career advice blogosphere. Harry Urschel, an executive professional technology recruiter, job hunting coach, and CEO of e-Executives, states:

"If you're currently unemployed, how that is portrayed on your LinkedIn profile can have an impact on whether you get responses or not . . . in my opinion, there is no-one-size-fits-all solution. The impression you make has a lot to do with the length of your unemployment. Your LinkedIn profile can adapt as time goes on."

Harry suggests that an effective progression on a LinkedIn profile might look like this:

- **Less than one month unemployed:** Include an end date on your last position; no other explanation or comment is necessary.
- **One to three months unemployed:** Include an update, headline, or job entry that indicates you are interested in exploring new career opportunities in your specific field or industry.
- **More than three months unemployed:** It is important to show ways you are staying actively plugged into your field or industry. Perhaps a more recent job entry from "layoff date–present" to include any applicable activity, such as:

  - active participation in (trade association name/professional association name)
  - pursuing (relevant certification/advanced degree/industry specific training)
  - leadership of (industry specific or field specific networking group)
  - writing industry-related blog, trade articles, or White Papers
  - consulting projects or assignments (only if legitimate, and include details)

continued from page 109

Harry does not believe it hurts your chances of being considered for positions if you're unemployed. There is a caveat, however. He explains:

"It is harmful to create an impression online that you are stagnant, out of touch from your career field, or simply waiting for something to come along. When you can show that you are professionally plugged in, current, showing initiative, and active in your field, you become a much more attractive candidate."

Industry

Because you must select this designation from a drop-down menu, you have a lot less flexibility with this section. Do your best to identify the most relevant industry that suits your goals or situation. If necessary, choose a broad category if a niche designation does not cover your expertise.

Photo/Avatar

LinkedIn reports your profile will earn up to seven times more click-throughs with a photo than one without a photo. You can upload a JPG, GIF, or PNG file (up to a file size limit of 4 MB). LinkedIn gives you the option to decide who will see your photo (your connections, your network, or everyone). While conventional wisdom for job seekers is to avoid using a photo on job search materials, the new standard is to include a photo online. In your settings, allow "everyone" to view your picture. This is a matter of personal preference, but I would suggest having a professional photo taken for your social media avatars (pictures).

Dress professionally for the photo. If a professional picture is not feasible, ask a friend to take some headshots. Use good lighting and practice until you have something that presents you in the best possible light—literally and figuratively. The fact is, people enjoy connecting with candidates they can picture. Displaying a photo that characterizes you as professional, approachable, and friendly is important, and will help you succeed.

Post Status Updates

This section allows you to make quick and easy notations to your LinkedIn profile, which show up on top of your main profile page. If your privacy settings allow your connections to know when you make changes to your profile, this section is an easy way to touch base with your contacts and let them know what is new with you.

Examples of good updates include, "Attending annual sports equipment show in Las Vegas," if that is relevant to your professional goals. Another example is "Speaking about travel opportunities for seniors at the annual Wayfarers Conference."

You may also include a link to a relevant article or blog post in the update section. If you use applications such as Buffer and Hootsuite, you can update your LinkedIn profile from the same platform you use to update your status in other networks. Since making a change to your LinkedIn profile is one way to push your information into your contacts' status updates, it is a good idea to make frequent updates. Consistently sharing information by alerting your network is a good way to stay on people's minds.

Websites and Twitter Integration

In Edit Contact Information, LinkedIn allows you to list three websites. Select "Other" in the dropdown menu for each site you add, and type the name into the field provided. This helps index the name of the site for searching. You may also include your Twitter URL. Remember to only add websites and a Twitter handle if reviewing them would help someone to see you as an expert in your field.

Hopefully, after reading and following the advice in this book, your social networking profiles will be unified and professional. Remember, adding online platforms where readers may learn more about you gives people the opportunity to connect easily, which is a main goal of your profile.

Public Profile

When you first sign up for LinkedIn, the site assigns you a URL that is a random set of numbers and letters, which is not particularly user-friendly (it would look odd and out of place on top of a resume or in your e-mail signature). Luckily, you can easily personalize your URL to include your name. Just click on "Edit" near the URL LinkedIn assigns. This brings you to another screen, where you can edit the link to your profile. Just type in your name (no spaces) where it says "Your current URL."

If your name is already taken, LinkedIn will let you know it is not available. If unavailable, consider choosing something with your middle initial, or a version of your name that sounds professional. This is an important step—so do not skip it. Having a personalized URL makes you look a bit more savvy than your counterpart whose public profile is a string of random numbers.

On the same screen where you updated your profile, select "Make my profile visible to everyone" to allow people to see every part of your profile. Remember, the point of social networks is to connect and share information. Hiding key details from public view is contrary to that point.

Summary

This is one of the most important sections of your profile, and one where you have a lot of leeway. The most important factor to consider is how to ensure your summary appeals to your target audience. Before writing your summary, it is a good idea to review summaries of others in your field or industry. This is another great aspect of LinkedIn—it allows you to easily research how people in your field market themselves. If you are in a very conservative field, a tongue-in-cheek summary that intends to make readers laugh will probably not win you any points. However, if you are in a creative business, being a bit casual and fun can demonstrate that you have what it takes to get the job done.

While searching, you will likely find summaries written in the third person. For example, "John Smith is a driven, enthusiastic, and creative communications expert." A lot of professionals use this format because they believe it sounds more formal. I advise clients to write the summary in the first person. You may also incorporate pronouns such as *I*, *me*, or *my*, and describe yourself from a personal perspective. For example, "I author a well-regarded career advice blog, advise and coach clients in the U.S. and abroad regarding career transitions, and teach job seekers and entrepreneurs how to use social media."

Walter Akana, career and life strategist at Threshold Consulting and co-developer (along with Carol Ross) of the Online Remarkable Profile, believes a LinkedIn summary should tell a compelling story about the person. This before-and-after summary from Traci Maddox is one example:

Sample Before and After LinkedIn Summaries

Traci Maddox

Before headline:
President and Founder at Sage Peak Associates, Inc.

Before summary:
Author & Speaker, Certified Professional Co-Active Coach, and seasoned program manager with extensive experience in implementing change in both large and small organizations, as well as strategic planning, coaching, and team leadership. Skilled in various change management methodologies, including Kotter and ADKAR. Primary strength is a holistic approach; providing top quality products and services to clients while furthering organizational goals and keeping within cost, schedule, and performance requirements. Recently published The Essential Employee, *a book about five key employee behaviors in the workplace.*

Traci Maddox

After headline:

Executive Coach, Author, and Organization Development Consultant

After summary:

I am an adventurer. Whether I'm bicycling across North America or finding a new way to help an organization be more effective, I want to create an experience that brings people alive! If you want to have fun while learning and growing, I'm the right person for you.

I started my career as a computer scientist back in the day when personal computers were new and exciting! While I loved using my technical background to work with a team and create new technology products, I quickly found that my passion was the team—not the technology.

Throughout my federal career, I loved the big picture and strategy components of what I did and gravitated toward those kinds of jobs. First, that led me to program management—big, complex systems with people as the backbone. Once I was a program manager, I led large and small teams, and found I loved motivating people and leading them to their best performance. This, I realized, was my true passion and would be my legacy.

So I pursued my passion and went back to school for Organization Development, using my work for practical applications of my new training. I moved into the Corporate Business Office and created structures for organizational success—linked, of course by the people who are critical to the success of any change.

I started my own business in 2002 and found my true calling: helping people and organizations reach their peak! Along the way, I achieved my certification in Co-Active coaching and use that training and all my accumulated experience to coach executives and facilitate groups.

My newest adventure is that of author and speaker. My first book is based on research, but is written as a novel. It's about the five key behaviors you must have to be considered essential in the workplace. The Essential Employee *is my vehicle to help all entry-level employees—even those I can't connect with personally—reach their peak.*

What's the next adventure? I'm excited to find out!

Additional Examples of Summaries

Teresa Basich—http://www.linkedin.com/in/teresabasich

I'm a marketing and communications pro with a penchant for words and the digital space. My work experience lies mostly in managing creative projects, writing and editing copy for marketing pieces and business-to-business magazines, and designing marketing collateral for a variety of industries including commercial real estate, the automotive aftermarket, and mass transportation, among others.

My professional passions include social/new media marketing, integrated marketing communications, employer branding, internal communications, public relations, and ad and copy writing.

Robyn Cobb—http://www.linkedin.com/in/robyncobb

Highly focused, passionate marketing and business leader with extensive experience championing sales and profit growth. Proven ability to envision creative marketing strategies and programs to deliver immediate results. Experience in revitalizing organization performance via cutting-edge analysis, strategic planning, and business development programs. Recognized as an energetic leader, strong motivator, noteworthy communicator, and exceptional innovator with superior business acumen.

Sections

If you have specific certifications, languages, projects, patents, publications, or specific skills that someone might search for if they wanted to hire someone like you, be sure to fill in those sections in your LinkedIn profile to make it easier for people to find you.

LinkedIn is adding new options for your profile all the time. Also consider including test scores, courses, and certifications. If you volunteer for a cause you'd like to share, add the Volunteering & Causes section, too.

Add Rich Media

You can include links to online work products via your LinkedIn profile. What kind of information might you consider adding? Some examples: PowerPoint presentations you created and uploaded to Slideshare, blog posts or guest posts, and YouTube videos. All you need is a URL for the information you want to share, or share via uploads from your desktop. Add it by editing your profile and selecting the blue box icon that sits near the little "pen" and the up-and-down arrow when you edit a section of your profile. Experiment with different content and decide what looks best; this is a great way to build out your LinkedIn profile and to showcase your best work.

Experience

This is an important section, and one which most closely resembles your resume. In fact, you can likely copy and paste sections of your resume in the Experience section, assuming you have a strong resume that includes keywords and is optimized for your profession.

Use very targeted phrases and keywords, and include skills and accomplishments (including numbers, as long as they are not proprietary). It is up to you how far back you choose to go with your experience. There is no rule that says you are required to list all of your jobs if you have a 20-year career. However, listing them provides more opportunities for people to find and connect with you, which is one of the advantages of LinkedIn.

Recommendations

Having recommendations helps you come up in search results and improves your opportunities to connect with people who are hiring via LinkedIn. Some may require viewable recommendations to consider you for opportunities, so reach out to LinkedIn connections who can reasonably and strongly recommend you once you have a finished profile. Make an effort to offer to endorse others, even before they request something from you. Just follow links from your profile on the main toolbar to "Recommendations" to manage and request endorsements. Read more about LinkedIn recommendations in Chapter 7.

Skills

If you haven't already created a Skills section, you will be able to add it via clicking on the link to add skills on the right side of your screen when you are in Edit mode. You must choose five skills for a complete profile. While you can add up to 50 skills, I'd advise you to limit your choices to the most specific and targeted choices you think people will want to know about you. (Choose the words people will use to search for someone like you—your keywords.)

LinkedIn allows and encourages people to endorse your skills via a one-click option indicating they agree you know about the skills you've added, for example, "accounting" or "social media." You can endorse people by visiting their profiles and either accepting the suggestions LinkedIn may provide to endorse people or by scrolling to their Skills section (usually toward the bottom of their profile). Just click on the "plus" sign next to each skill you wish to endorse, and that's it! Your photo will appear next to the skill, and your contact will get a little boost on their profile.

Many people believe endorsing skills is too easy and frivolous. I've even seen members of the career coaching community say they did not plan to participate in skills endorsing. That is a mistake. Be aware that LinkedIn will incorporate data from Skills and Endorsements to fuel its own search algorithm. In other words, the more endorsed you are for your key skills, the better it is for you. So, endorse others, and you will likely see endorsements in return. In this case, reciprocal endorsements do not seem to pose any problems at this time.

Have a Complete LinkedIn Profile

It is important to have a complete LinkedIn profile. LinkedIn notes that you are 40 percent more likely to be found in search results if your profile is 100 percent complete, compared to a 90 percent complete rate. How do you reach a fully complete profile? These are LinkedIn's requirements:

- Include your photo. You can use the privacy settings to determine who will be able to view your picture, but I suggest making it publicly available.
- List all of your jobs and descriptions of your roles.
- Have five or more skills listed in "Skills."
- Write a summary.
- Fill out the education section.
- Fill out industry and postal code.
- Have 50 or more connections.

If you finish these steps, you should achieve all-star status.

How Much Time Should You Spend On LinkedIn?

You may be wondering how much time you should spend on LinkedIn to get the most out of it. This is always a difficult question to answer, as it really depends on the person and his or her goals and needs. I asked Jason Alba, founder of the job search organizer JibberJobber.com and creator of the *LinkedIn for Job Seekers* DVD, for his opinion. He replied:

"I tell people they can have a two-minute strategy or a two-hour strategy, depending on what they need to do. At a minimum, spend time to get your LinkedIn profile just right. Then, spend a

minimum of a couple of minutes a week going in and accepting invitation requests.

If you have more time, you may try the two-hour per week strategy, which might include updating your status, participating in Group discussions, and using the advanced search feature to find people to expand your network. There are a lot of proactive steps to take, but at a bare minimum, having a complete profile is key.

If a job seeker told me he was spending hours a day on LinkedIn I would think that is okay, as long as he or she has a serious focus and is involved in activities with a high return on the time investment. Unlike other social networks, people aren't going to LinkedIn for fun stuff; it's important to go in with a purpose. Identify your goals, do the job, and then get out so you have time to use other networks and focus on other important aspects of your job search. This is a tool, not a place to hide."

Back Up Your Profile

Be sure to backup your LinkedIn Profile:

- Go to View profile.
- Select the Edit profile dropdown in the main section of your header.
- Click "Export to PDF."

You can also back up your first-degree contacts using these instructions from LinkedIn's site:

- To export your connections list from the Connections (http://www.linkedin.com/contacts) page:

  1. Move your cursor over *Network* at the top of your homepage and select *Contacts*.

2. Click the *Export connections* link in the bottom right corner of the page.

3. Leave the *Export to* field as it appears and enter the security text if prompted.

4. Click *Export.*

5. Save the file in a location where you can easily find it, like your computer's desktop.

   Note: If you're using Internet Explorer and see a yellow pop-up blocker across the top of the page, click the yellow bar and then select *Download File.*

Things to Remember

Be sure to perfect your "pitch" before you create your LinkedIn profile. Choose your keywords and think about what story you want to tell about yourself to help people learn more about you. Make it relevant to the reader and incorporate details they need to know.

Incorporate as much useful information about yourself as possible. Don't forget to post a photo, update your status frequently, and spend as much time as necessary engaged on LinkedIn to be worthwhile to grow your network and demonstrate your expertise.

Now, keep reading to learn how to expand your network and for tips and tricks to make the most of your time on LinkedIn.

CHAPTER

Making the Most of LinkedIn

After Your LinkedIn Profile is Optimized

One of the most important and overlooked aspects of social networking is the fact that it encourages you to be generous, and to benefit from the generosity of others in return. While LinkedIn is designed to connect you with friends of friends, it provides channels that allow you to meet new people (via Groups, Jobs, etc.), so it is likely that you may find yourself in a position to provide advice and information for strangers, and they for you. If you are a true *connector*, meaning that you thrive on connecting people and being a networking hub, you will embrace the opportunities to interact and extend your network beyond your close circle of friends.

> ⇨ **TIP**
>
> Meeting people online is all about being generous with your time, resources, and information.

The most successful social networkers do not solely focus on themselves and what they want to gain from using LinkedIn and other networking tools. Instead, they think about how they can be of service to others and what they can do to help their communities. If you optimize your LinkedIn profile and begin searching for people to help you without first reaching out to the community and focusing on what you have to offer, you may find your efforts fall flat.

People enjoy meeting and working with others who behave generously. Think about what you offer and share it online; you may find yourself repaid nicely. I constantly hear stories about people who received just the information or help they needed from strangers.

PEOPLE WHO HAVE BENEFITED FROM A STRANGER'S KINDNESS

"I met a colleague through a LinkedIn group I manage. He shared my website on job search with another one of his LinkedIn groups. A fellow member of that LinkedIn group reached out to me to offer a very gracious comment. In thanking him, I shared the site (www.candidateschair.com), which I explained was a bit of a 'doctor heal thyself' project, as I had just kicked off a search for a CFO role. He e-mailed me back that they needed a CFO—two weeks later we were off and running."

–MARK RICHARDS,
Financials OnDemand

"I got a sales manager job by using the Request for Introduction to a third-level connection after I had applied in the normal way. I still don't know the name of the third party, but he passed on my request with enough passion (and trust of my contact) to get me the interview and thus the job."

–BRYAN C. WEBB, Former President/CEO,
Norton Scientific Inc.

continued from page 122

> *"I showed someone how to use the search function to find partners in India and two weeks later, she introduced me to someone who became a paying client. There have been many, similar situations for me and others I know. LinkedIn is the biggest and best professional networking platform on the planet."*
>
> —TIM BOND, Online professional networking strategist, business development

Developing Your Network

The size and strength of your network will impact how useful this tool is for you. The more people there are in your first-degree network (the ones directly connected to you), the more people who may notice when you update your status, or make a change to your profile. Additionally, your name will appear in more search results if you are connected to an extensive network of people.

Another reason to grow your network is because LinkedIn easily allows you to connect with people who are already your second-degree contacts. Using a free account, it gets more complicated to connect if you are not a close contact with your target "connectee." Additionally, if you do not know anyone in common with another Linkedin user, you will not be able to view that person's profile if you have an unpaid account.

Managing Your Network

As you use LinkedIn, you will receive invitations from people you may not know asking to connect with you. If you prefer to keep your network restricted to those you actually know personally, you may wish to ignore these invitations.

If you plan to focus on growing your network to be as large as possible, accept all invitations. You may even want to consider identifying yourself as a LinkedIn Open Networker (LION), which would make you part of a hub of connectors. When I originally joined LinkedIn, I was very particular about connecting with people, and ignored all requests from people I did not know. After speaking to many LinkedIn users, I decided to expand my view of who could be a good connection, and I now generally accept any invitation that is personalized and lets me know why the person wants to join my network. For example:

- "I follow you on Twitter, enjoy your advice, and would love to connect here."
- "I read your blog and would love to connect on LinkedIn."
- "I am in the middle of a long job search and am expanding my network. I would appreciate connecting with you."

CONSIDER BECOMING A LINKEDIN OPEN NETWORKER (LION)

Dave Maskin, owner of WireNames.com, a leading trade show booth traffic builder, says the following:

"By becoming an open networker, or LION, I have done more to expand my business on this site than any other single thing. The concept of networking with folks other than those you already know helps expand your horizons. It allows networking between total strangers who might otherwise not even know each other. This, to me, is real business expansion.

For folks like me, who are hired by total strangers all the time, connecting with people I've never worked with before makes very good and logical sense for my business needs. In the business world there is no such thing as a one-size-fits-all plan, but I have found it profitable to be a LION."

Guy Shute, IT Team Leader at Mantech International Systems Recruitment states:

"I became a LION two years ago and went from about 20 first-level connections to about 1,500. This has given me far greater reach

continued from page 124

and ability to either connect with others or track down experts when I want to contact a thought leader on a certain issue.

"When I started using LinkedIn, I did research about networking, super connectors, and social networking, and read about successes such as Steve Burda, who is an open networker and also called the Mother Teresa of Networking."

"I became a LION with the idea that 'those who give will receive.' I have come across very nice people who are happy to help and focus not just on connecting, but on building trust and relationships. I have read (and agree) that social networking is not like a sprint, it's like marathon. Take time to build trust and relationships. It's important not to solicit new contacts prematurely."

—DINESH RAMKRISHRA, India's Top Recommended
Business Development Manager

Don't forget that accepting all invitations also has some drawbacks. While you will have a larger network and access to more people via LinkedIn, you will not personally know most of your connections. If someone asks for an introduction, you will not necessarily be able to confidently pass along the link as you would if you had a personal relationship with the person.

WHY NOT TO BE A LION

The larger my connection base has grown, the more I realize how crucial it is to be a discriminating networker with a highly focused and, hence, more personally valuable list—one that I'd want to think twice about sharing indiscriminately. Now that I'm at 700-plus connections, that truth has become obvious to me. It's pointless collecting links like postage stamps. My LinkedIn homepage, now clogged with updates from virtual strangers, reminds me of that with every visit."

—JUDY B. MARGOLIS, business writer, editor, blogger,
strategic marketing communications expert

Other suggestions to help you expand your network:

- Share your LinkedIn URL in your e-mail signature, on all of your correspondence, your resume, your business card, and via any social and in-person networking that you do.
- When you meet someone (at a networking event or any situation), mention you are expanding your connections on LinkedIn, and ask if they are a member and if they would accept an invitation. Then, be sure to follow up. Don't forget that personal friends and contacts make good LinkedIn connections. Your neighbors, people who are on your sports teams, your kids' friends' parents; all are potential connections.
- If you do decide to expand your network broadly, feel free to ask connections on other social networks (such as Twitter or Google+) to invite you to their LinkedIn network. Several prominent social media stars send out messages via Twitter occasionally, reminding people to feel free to connect via LinkedIn.
- Be sure to open your LinkedIn profile to everyone via the privacy settings. (Find Settings under your picture on the top toolbar. Check your "Privacy Controls.")

Finding New Contacts and Requesting Connections

You will need to decide on your own strategy and comfort level when it comes to including people you do not know well in your network. LinkedIn allows everyone 3,000 lifetime invitations. (This is why LIONs often prefer to ask you to extend an offer to connect. It is possible they have no remaining invitations.) This is more than enough for most LinkedIn users.

It is easy to request a connection via LinkedIn. When you are on a person's profile page and you are connected by at least a second degree, directly under their picture, you will see an option that says Connect.

Simply click on it, select how you know the person (you may need to include his or her e-mail) and personalize a message. Write a short, targeted message to the desired contact. LinkedIn provides a default message: "I'd like to add you to my professional network on LinkedIn." Sending this note does *not* do much to help you convince someone to be a connection. Instead, use your note to make it clear how you know the person (even if it means reminding them of where you met) and why you want to have them join your network. Your goal should be to invite only people you actually do know or those with whom you share a reasonable connection.

I listed a few introduction message examples in the "Developing Your Network" section early in this chapter. Make it clear why it makes sense to connect. For example:

- "I noticed that you contribute to XYZ group and post about insurance regulations, which is a topic I am making an effort to understand for my professional development. I hope you will agree to join my network on LinkedIn."
- "We are both members of the Health Informatics Technology group here on LinkedIn, and I really appreciate your contributions and news items. I hope you will agree to join my network."
- "I see you attended the University of Wisconsin-Madison and studied psychology. As a current student there, I am hoping to connect with alumni in my field of interest to expand my network in advance of graduation. I hope you will 'link in' with me. Go Badgers!"
- "We met last night at the Chamber of Commerce dinner. (I was the one wearing the red scarf.) It was great sharing our mutual affection for losing baseball teams! I hope you will agree to connect here so we can stay in touch."
- "Thank you for answering my question posted in the nonprofit accountant group, about best practices for using LinkedIn. I'd love to connect with you for potential networking opportunities in the future. I appreciate your consideration!"

> **⇔ TIP**
>
> LinkedIn provides many opportunities to find people to con-
> nect with you. Use all of these, along with appropriate and
> personalized messages to grow your network.

Ways to Find People to Add to Your Network

- Search "People"
- Groups—many people find new connections in common interest groups.
- View your friends' connections—you never know when a friend of a friend will be a good connection for you.
- Click "Add Connections" on the toolbar under Contacts. Review the suggestions, including colleagues, classmates, and people you may know.
- "People You May Know" tool—LinkedIn will suggest people you may know. You may be surprised by how many you actually *do* know!
- Navigate to Network on the toolbar and click Contacts. Click "Add Contacts."

Import Your E-mail List

Once your profile is ready to show off and you know how to request a connection, you can use LinkedIn's import tools to find people you may know to invite to connect. For complete instructions, click on the "HELP" button on LinkedIn's toolbar and search "import contacts." You will find instructions to help you import contacts for a variety of e-mail services. LinkedIn offers you the option to invite your contacts to connect via LinkedIn once you import your list.

If you notice friends or contacts who don't seem to be on LinkedIn, consider inviting them to join. You will be doing them a favor and help-ing yourself at the same time. When I first joined LinkedIn, I invited a very well-connected friend to join. (She used to send out e-mails to hundreds of her friends at once.) Before I knew it, my network expanded exponentially as she became an active member and connector.

Link to Some LIONs

As discussed in the previous chapter, LinkedIn suggests you connect with people you know and trust. However, it is not a bad idea to search for some LIONs who share common professional interests with you and ask them to connect. Remember, the benefit of linking to people who have a lot of connections is that their extended network becomes part of your network, which increases the chances that your actual name (not just an anonymous profile) will appear in searches. Anyone who self-designates as a LION agrees to connect with anyone who asks for a link.

To find LIONs, navigate to the top toolbar and do a search for "People." Type in {LION, keywords relevant to you}. For example, if you are in the insurance industry, your search would be {LION, insurance}. If you want to be more specific, consider adding a location—either in your city or a city where you might like to work or live.

LinkedIn will show you people who have your keywords highlighted in their profiles, which will include those who are currently in your targeted field (in this example, insurance), as well as those who used to work in that area. Remember, most LIONs probably do not know most members of their network very well, so keep this in mind when you begin to try to ask for introductions via LinkedIn.

Another search to consider is simply, {LION, your city or target city}. Even though LIONs probably have contacts all over the world, by narrowing your search to a few targeted open networkers, you will increase your chances of connecting with a great contact. The main advantage to linking with a LION is that you will expand your network exponentially; your name will appear in many more searches, more people have easy access to your contributions to LinkedIn, and your updates will go to more people.

If you really want to target your search, use the "Advanced" link (directly to the right of the search bar). For keywords, select "LION," choose a location via the drop-down menu, and choose an industry or industries of interest. When I searched in a 50-mile range of my zip code for LIONs in the accounting industry, I found nine results.

Try some searches, and narrow down the search to find an open networker who fits your specifications.

Research New Potential Connections

If you have already exhausted the suggested ways to find connections, look through membership directories of organizations you have joined to find the names of others you may connect with on LinkedIn. Do searches in LinkedIn (using the "People" search tool on the toolbar) to find as many of those people as possible within the network. As I mentioned, be sure to pay attention to LinkedIn's suggestions of "People You May Know" when you sign into your profile. It still amazes me how many colleagues and friends are not already first-degree connections to me. While some of LinkedIn's suggestions are random (for example, suggesting I know people just because we share a last name), recently, I have been following up with at least one of the suggestions each time I sign on to connect with someone I should have in my network. You never know who may be the person to connect you to the perfect information or opportunity.

LinkedIn Alumni

Found via www.linkedin.com/alumni, this is a useful LinkedIn tool to research information and grow your connections.

LinkedIn's blog notes, "Gathered from the profiles of more than 200 million members, LinkedIn's Alumni tool helps you explore alumni career paths from more than 22,000 colleges and universities worldwide—and build relationships that can help you along the way." They suggest you check out your own school, or use the "change schools" button to learn about other schools. What can you find out? Where graduates live, the organizations they work for, and the types of jobs they pursue. You can also change the dates to track careers of specific graduating classes.

Plus, LinkedIn notes, "You can now explore alumni careers based on what they studied, their top skills, and how you are connected on LinkedIn. All the graphs are interactive, just click on the bars to drill down to the specific careers most interesting to you."

Learning About Companies

One of the most useful tools LinkedIn offers is the opportunity to follow companies and learn who is joining and leaving organizations of interest to you. From LinkedIn's main toolbar, select the "Interests" tab and choose "Companies."

Type a company you want to research in the search field. LinkedIn will show you an overview of the company, those currently in your network who work for the organization, and typical career paths for employees. For example, Ameritech employees have a tendency to go to work for Cisco or Motorola. Some companies also show where people come from before they work there. If you click the tab to "Follow Company," you have access to additional information, including when LinkedIn members join or leave the company you follow. This may be a great way to learn about potential openings or to find new people to network with you. If you view the current employees who are in your network and select "See More," you will see a page with additional connections as well as a sidebar on the left that allows you to filter your search. Take advantage of all of these tools to find connections of interest and to learn about organizations.

Advanced Searching

Something easy to overlook on LinkedIn, even though it is right out in the open, is the "Advanced" search tool. (I mentioned this in the section about finding a LION.) Located in the main toolbar at the very top of your screen, on the right of the search field and the magnifying glass, click the word "Advanced" to find in-depth search options.

Take advantage of these specific searches to find and target exactly the information you need. Susan Adams of Forbes.com authored a series of articles about using LinkedIn. She interviewed career expert and LinkedIn spokeswoman, Krista Canfield, who suggested a useful tip for all professionals: Fill in your job title in the search field and click "Advanced" search. Once in the Advanced search fields, click on the "Location" field and search for people with the same job title as you. Adams notes that Canfield suggests making connections with as many of those people as possible.

Looking for Specific Jobs

Don't forget that LinkedIn also has its own job board. Follow the top menu bar's "Jobs" link. The most efficient search to run is a search of keywords to find opportunities of interest to you. Just follow "Advanced Search" to reach a detailed menu. Once you find opportunities of interest, LinkedIn will give you the option to save the job or to apply.

Looking for jobs on LinkedIn is unique in that LinkedIn connects a position to the person who posted it, and LinkedIn tells you how you are connected to that person (via which of your connections), as well as who might connect you to the organization or company. It also suggests links to similar jobs and allows you to apply for the posted job. LinkedIn makes it easy to request a referral if you do have contacts that lead you to the person who posted the job.

LinkedIn's Job Search offers all users:

- Advanced search options to target open positions by country and zip code, industry and function.
- Options to view most recent jobs by showing new results from saved searches
- Access to LinkedIn's list of "Jobs you may be interested in," which helps you find possible jobs of interest based on what's in your LinkedIn profile.
- An opportunity to overview your favorite job postings by clicking on the "Save Job" link on jobs you really like and want to track on your LinkedIn Jobs page.

Job Seeker Premium subscribers also see:

- A feature to help you find jobs that meet your salary requirements.
- Embedded tips to help you find a job faster.

Lindsey Pollak (www.lindseypollak.com) is a nationally recognized expert on next-generation career and workplace issues. She is the author of *Getting from College to Career (HarperCollins, 2012)* and an Ambassador for LinkedIn. These are her suggestions to use LinkedIn to actually apply for jobs:

- Include keywords in your summary statement. The "Summary" portion of your profile provides a chance to share the highlights of your bio in your own words. It's also a place to include key words and phrases that a recruiter or hiring manager might type into a search engine to find a person like you. The best place to find relevant keywords is in the job listings that appeal to you and the LinkedIn profiles of people who currently hold the kinds of positions you want. Check out LinkedIn's Company Pages feature to search through the profiles of employees at your dream employers.
- Make sure that your contact settings include "Career Opportunities" as one of the reasons you are open to being contacted. Many recruiters limit their searches to people who have opted for that communication. (Find this setting in the "Edit Profile," "email preferences," "types of messages you're willing to receive.")
- Follow-up is crucial, and you have a better chance of receiving a response when you follow up on LinkedIn. Sending your communications through the professional network of LinkedIn can not only help you stand out from other candidates, but it also helps you continually build your case. Every time you send someone a message or InMail on LinkedIn, they can easily click over to your profile and check out your credentials.

- Consider Job Seeker Premium. Once you have a strong LinkedIn profile, you want to make sure it gets to the top of recruiters' inboxes when you apply for jobs. LinkedIn offers an upgrade feature called Job Seeker Premium that, among other benefits, places your profile at the top of the list of applicants to any job you apply for on LinkedIn. Premium subscribers are twice as likely to be contacted by recruiters and 80 percent more likely to be found in search. Check it out at http://www.linkedin.com/jobseeker.

And here is Lindsey's advice for job seekers on writing connection requests:

- Write a brief, customized, polite note to explain why you want to connect.
- Thoroughly read the person's LinkedIn profile and mention something that stood out to you or something you have in common.
- Do not directly ask for a job in a connecting request. I recommend using the request to build rapport and establish contact, and then once the person accepts, you can ask for advice or for the person to keep you in mind if he or she hears of any job opportunities that might be a good fit for you.
- One great strategy is to offer to help each person you'd like to connect with. You might say something like, "Please let me know if there is anything I can do to support you."
- Remember that HOW you build your network is just as important as why you build it. Always be authentic, polite and positive. People will remember that when they hear about job openings.

Privacy

Who's Viewed My Profile (and Whose Profiles am I Viewing?)

With all of this searching possible, it is easy to overlook the issue of privacy and tracking. Once you begin to use LinkedIn frequently, you may notice that your homepage includes a section called "Who's Viewed My Profile?" (To see this, follow the Home button on the main menu bar; scroll down and view the right side of your screen.) You can tell how often you showed up in search results. Depending on the viewer's privacy settings, it may be very clear exactly who has visited your page. Other times, you will only learn his or her industry, field, and location. When you view profiles, LinkedIn will track you, as well. If you do not want anyone to track your digital LinkedIn footprint, you will need to adjust your privacy settings.

From above the search bar, click on the small photo of you on the top right side and choose "Privacy & Settings." Select "Profile."

> **⇨ TIP**
>
> Keep an eye on how often your profile comes up in search by tracking the "Who's Viewed My Profile" section on your LinkedIn homepage. Consider tweaking your profile by incorporating extra keywords and experimenting with different descriptions if people are not finding your profile as often as you might like.

You may choose how you will appear (or if you will appear) on people's results. LinkedIn allows you to show your name, just your industry and location, or be totally anonymous. You decide if you want people to know whose profiles you visited on LinkedIn and select the choice that works for you. One thing to consider—if you have an interview for a job, it may not be a bad idea for the interviewer to know that you have researched his or her profile. Consider various ramifications of your selections and think through different scenarios before you make a choice.

LinkedIn's Privacy Settings

Review the various options LinkedIn gives you under "Settings" for privacy.

> **⇨ TIP**
>
> In order to appear in search results, you must allow a public profile (under "Profile," "Public Profile") to be visible and set to display full profile information.

You can make decisions about who can see what, including your member feed, if your connections are allowed to view your other connections, and if LinkedIn notified people when you update your status.

> **⇨ TIP**
>
> Before you make these choices, be sure you know the ramifications of your decision. Remember, the point of LinkedIn is **not** to lock down a private vault of information. The idea is to share your information and to make it accessible. The exception might be if you are currently employed and in the midst of a major overhaul to your profile that you do NOT want your boss (a connection on LinkedIn) to notice, you may wish to temporarily change your "Profile" and "Status" updates so you can make changes to your profile without alerting your network. Once you have finished making updates, be sure to re-visit the "Profile" and "Status" setting so it will alert your network of updates going forward, as these updates offer terrific ways to touch base with network members.

Additional Tips and Tricks to Maximize Your LinkedIn Use

Don't forget, LinkedIn includes sections to list certifications, languages, patents, publications, projects, test scores, courses, and honors and awards. Follow the link when you edit your profile to add these sections.

Rearrange Your Profile

You may change the order of your profile sections (Background Experience, Honor and Awards, Skills and Expertise, Publications, etc.) Rearranging these sections allows you to decide what people will see first when they view your profile. For example, if you want to highlight an impressive recommendation, you have the option to do that. These are LinkedIn's instructions for reorganizing your profile's sections:

1. Click on "Profile" in the top navigation area of your home page. This will take you to the "Edit My Profile" page.
2. Hover your mouse over the up and down arrow icon, directly to the right of the section you want to move. A hand appears and you can drag and drop the section.
3. Click and hold down your left mouse button and drag the section to the area you want it to appear. (Sections cannot go above the blue box on the Profile.)
4. Release your left mouse button to drop the section into place. Your changes will automatically be saved. After you drop the section, no further action is required.

Mobile Applications

If you like to access LinkedIn on the go, be sure to click "Mobile" from the bottom toolbar to learn about applications to use with your smart phone or tablet.

Keep Up-to-Date

LinkedIn is making changes all the time. Learn about updates by frequenting the site and making a habit of clicking through the various options and applications. It is a good idea to keep an eye on LinkedIn's blog (http://blog.linkedin.com/). You may access it via the bottom toolbar on LinkedIn. Developers and contributors write frequent posts and provide information, advice, and tips to help you optimize your LinkedIn experience.

Things to Remember

Using your LinkedIn profile well is not difficult if you know the steps to take to put yourself in the fray. Once you optimize your profile (as described in Chapter 5), leverage all of the tools this network provides, and you may benefit from a stranger's generosity.

Develop your network via:

- Being on the lookout for prospective contacts and knowing how to ask for a connection.
- Linking to a LION—or by becoming one!
- Knowing how to research connections and how to get in touch with targets who don't make it easy to reach them.
- Using the "Jobs" feature and taking steps to leverage it for your needs.
- Setting appropriate privacy settings to make sure that people are able to see the information you want them to see.

Chapter 7 explains how to build on this information to really build your brand (your reputation) using LinkedIn.

Using LinkedIn to Build Your Brand

Once you have built a network of people, created a strong, keyword-focused profile that makes it clear what problems you solve, and leveraged the LinkedIn tips and tricks described in the previous chapters, it is time to focus on how LinkedIn can help propel your career forward.

Whether or not you agree with the concept of considering yourself a *brand* (as described in Chapter 4), it is important to remember that demonstrating your expertise via the social web provides opportunities and advantages you may not have considered. In this chapter, I'll share success stories and focus on how LinkedIn can help you share information about yourself and connect to the people who may be able to give your career a boost.

Make It Easy to Find and Contact You

You can use LinkedIn to share information that allows people to contact you without needing to jump through a lot of hoops. And while it is possible to use LinkedIn to communicate with people all over the world without even sharing your e-mail address, I suggest that you consider sharing contact information on your profile. Go to "Profile," "Edit Profile," and scroll down to "Additional Information," edit "Personal Details." You have the option to list contact information, and even your birthday and marital status. Depending on your business, you may want to consider sharing some direct contact information, but I don't suggest sharing your birth date or marital status. An e-mail address should suffice.

Go back to the top and select "Settings" from your photo. Carefully scroll through each choice of the settings menu. Under "Groups, Companies & Applications," you can decide how to display your groups, and turn on or off notifications. Be sure to leave notifications on, or you will miss possibly important information.

Choose email preferences and select the type of messages you are willing to receive from LinkedIn. I suggest you select "Introductions and InMail." List the best way to reach you via an email address under "advice" to people who are contacting you.

> **↪ TIP**

> LinkedIn will e-mail all invitations, opportunities, and inquiries to the address you indicate. Be sure you check that inbox relatively frequently, or you may miss unexpected opportunities.

I have a client who, after putting together his resume, optimizing his LinkedIn profile, and going through some interviews, decided that he needed a sabbatical to spend some time fixing up his house and taking some classes. He put his job search on hold. Months later, out of the blue, he received an e-mail from a recruiter asking if he would be interested in a job. She found him via his well-written, fully optimized LinkedIn profile that included his e-mail contact information. When he told me about it, he said, "Miriam, I thought it was an April Fool's joke! I couldn't believe that a job would just land in my lap." My client took that job, and now advises others to focus on LinkedIn and to have references and job search materials ready to use at a moment's notice. If he had used an e-mail address that he did not normally check, the recruiter's inquiry would have gone unanswered and he would have missed a great opportunity.

Ways to Connect: Invitations, InMail, and Requests for Introductions

LinkedIn makes it possible to contact people who do not show their e-mail address via three tools: invitations (explained in-depth in Chapter 6), InMail, and requests for introductions.

At this writing, LinkedIn is offering job seekers several discounted membership plans that include some benefits to job seekers, including InMail messages. Follow the "Jobs" link from the LinkedIn toolbar and click on "Job Seeker Premium" to learn more about these options. LinkedIn says that "Premium subscribers are two times as likely to be contacted by recruiters," so trying out a plan for a month may be a good idea. Just be sure to use your time well so you may realize a return on your investment. If you are not a job seeker, you may click the "Upgrade your account" link found at the bottom of your homepage.

METHODS TO CONNECT USING LINKEDIN

Ellen Sautter and Diane Crompton are career coaches and social networking enthusiasts, and authors of *Find a Job Through Social Networking* (JIST, 2010). In it, they outline the various methods LinkedIn provides to contact people:

Invitations: Inviting others to join your network or accepting their invitation. When a contact accepts an invitation, you will be in each others' first-level contacts. This is free. LinkedIn allots 3,000 invitations to each member, and invitations others send to you do not count against that total. There is no cost to issue or accept invitations.

continued from page 141

Introductions: Requesting that contacts introduce you to one of their first- or second-level contacts sets off a chain of communication from you, to your contact, to the target contact, or to another intermediary contact, and then to the target contact. These are also free, and, with the free LinkedIn account, you have five of these to use at any time. LinkedIn credits you back when the introductions are forwarded or you withdraw them.

InMails: Sending an e-mail-like communication directly to someone not in your first-level network through the LinkedIn communication channel. Upgraded memberships include a varying number of InMails, or you may purchase these for $10 each.

To purchase individual InMails, follow the link to "Settings" by clicking on the small photo of you in the top right. At the top of the "Settings" page, there is an option to purchase individual InMails.

LinkedIn explains how to send an InMail once you have them credited to your account:

1. Search for the member you wish to contact in the "Search" feature at the top of your home page. A page of results matching that name will appear.
2. Hover your mouse over the name of the member. This section will turn blue and reveal links on the right side of the result area.
3. Click on "Send InMail." This will take you to the InMail "Compose your message" page. By default, the "Include my contact information" box is checked.
4. Enter the contact information you want to share.
5. Select a Category from the drop down to identify why you are sending them an InMail. Information posted on the right indicates under which circumstances they would be open for contact.
6. Enter a Subject.

7. Select a Salutation.
8. Create your message. The note under this box shows how many InMail credits you have.
9. Click "Send."

CLEVER WAYS TO INCREASE NETWORKING CONTACTS

Optimizing LinkedIn sometimes requires leveraging more than just the obvious approaches. Debra Feldman (JobWhiz—http://jobwhiz.com/) is an executive talent agent who combines the skills of a corporate sleuth with the savvy of a matchmaker to develop and implement targeted networking connections. Debra suggests the following to make the most of LinkedIn to connect with people you might not otherwise be able to access. Try these approaches when you cannot easily connect via e-mail and when you want to build relationships with targeted contacts before you approach them:

1. Once you identify someone you want to meet, research to find out which groups they joined and ask to become a member of that group. This will not only allow you to participate in group conversations and demonstrate your knowledge and expertise to the entire membership, but you may be able to reach your target via an e-mail because you are members of the same group.
2. Join a group whose members are likely to have connections that you want to establish. Once you get connected, ask these new contacts to make an introduction on your behalf.
3. Ask a question in a group that is likely to solicit answers from your target contact or from those who may be connected to that individual. Similarly, you may answer questions in groups to expose you to those with similar interests and concerns; this will attract desirable new connections, especially individuals affiliated with your target employers.

Debra explains,

"These tactics—commenting, questioning, and posting to discussions—are effective to attract new connections that match your new contact specifications. While you may not be able to make a direct

continued from page 143

connection with Sue at XYZ company, you may be able to reach Bill at XYZ company who can recommend you to his colleague, Sue. Or you may be able to connect with Savannah at UVW who knows people at XYZ. Don't rely on LinkedIn only for direct connections. Use LinkedIn as a powerful and far-reaching networking tool for an ever-expanding pool of contacts."

Raise Your Profile

Recommendations

We all love to have people say something nice about us. LinkedIn allows you to compliment colleagues and contacts. From LinkedIn's top menu bar, follow "Profile" and select "Recommendations." This is where you can request recommendations from business partners, colleagues, clients, or supervisors who may reasonably endorse you. You may also offer unsolicited endorsements of colleagues, subordinates, contractors, and others whose work you want to recommend.

Giving Recommendations

Before you write a testimonial, focus on the person's key skills. What would be most useful for you to highlight about their abilities? Think about their accomplishments and provide specific examples to support your points. Keep it short (you are not writing a biography). *Give before you get* is a good rule of thumb, so make an effort to think about whom you may wish to endorse.

Why Should You Care About Recommendations?

Recommendations are an important part of LinkedIn for several reasons:

1. LinkedIn has noted that "users with recommendations are three times as likely to get inquiries through LinkedIn searches."

2. When people review your profile, seeing some recommendations indicates you are well-respected.

3. Having people positively describe your work ethic, abilities, and skills may help you get hired, makes it easier to find clients or colleagues, and enhances your reputation/brand.

You decide which recommendations you want to show on your profile. Don't be shy about requesting recommendations; you may even manage recommendations and request revised testimonials if appropriate. (Just go to "Profile" from the toolbar, "Recommendations," and follow the prompts to ask for updates.) Think about good times to ask for recommendations, even if you are *not* looking for a job. For example, if at annual review time you receive a positive evaluation, you may wish to ask your supervisor to share some comments on LinkedIn. (Note that some companies prohibit their employees from giving public recommendations. You will want to consult your organization's guidelines.) If you are doing contract work, take the opportunity at the end of the project to request a recommendation from the client. Having these referrals posted online may help you provide content for your resume. (Many professional resume writers now include endorsements on resumes).

Since LinkedIn recommendations are tied directly to a user's profile, it is clear that they originated from the person. Some suggest that these recommendations are useless because many are given in kind—"you endorse me and I will say something nice about you." So, it is a good idea to make sure that not all of your recommendations are reciprocal. The bottom line for LinkedIn recommendations: they can only help you. Don't overlook this useful tool.

Endorsing Skills

As noted previously, in addition to formal recommendations, LinkedIn also encourages you to secure endorsements of your skills. This type of endorsement is much simpler than recommendations, as it only requires a one-click response. It is an easy way for people to acknowledge your skills and abilities. People choose skills you've added in the skills section to endorse, or they can even add additional skills. (You have a choice to show these endorsements on your profile or not.) Remember: take this seriously. LinkedIn will use these one-click endorsements to help rank your profile in search.

Extend Your Brand By Joining Groups

One of LinkedIn's most useful features is that it offers a platform for people with common interests to join groups where they can share news, jobs, and information about their fields. In Chapter 5, I noted that there are groups for all types of professional interests. From the LinkedIn toolbar, simply select "Interests" and "Groups," then review the Groups Directory, which allows you to search key words to find a group that is well suited to your needs. Don't join the first group you see; take some time to review the choices. While LinkedIn's limit of 50 groups is pretty generous, you want to identify and join groups that seem to have active memberships and are well suited to your professional needs. Note that some groups are carefully moderated and will require the group owner's approval before you can join.

After you have found several groups based on professional interests to join, be sure to review the list for:

- School alumni groups
- Fraternity and sorority groups (if applicable)
- Groups associated with current or former employers. There are even alumni groups for companies that no longer exist. This can be a great way to keep in touch with former colleagues.
- Membership and association organizations.
- Locally based groups, including chamber of commerce and geographically specific business associations.
- Personal interest groups. Never overlook the fact that connecting on a personal level is a great networking strategy. If you skydive, look for skydiving groups. (As of this writing, there are 18 such organizations.) Maybe you prefer a sport that is more grounded. There are 134 groups associated with

biking. Theater is more your interest? You may be surprised to learn there are 643 groups in response to that keyword. Clearly, no matter your interests, professional or hobbies, you can easily find and join a group (or several groups) to help meet and connect with like-minded people.

Find the Best Groups

You want to be sure to make the most of your time using groups, so select the best groups for you. Evaluate any group you may want to join by clicking into the group and scrolling down your screen until you see a box that says, "Check Out Insightful Statistics on this Group." Click it and you will be able to view demographic information, the group's growth and activity data, and you can see the seniority level of the group's members. Knowing this information will help you decide what groups have active members most likely to help you.

Group Settings

Once you decide to join a group, LinkedIn asks you how you would like to receive information from the group. You can decide if you want to display the group's badge on your profile, what e-mail address (if you use several in LinkedIn) you wish to use to use to receive information from the group, if you want the group's announcements and digest (which I recommend if you plan to be an active member), and whether or not group members are allowed to send you messages.

⇨ TIP

Keep in mind the purpose of joining the group when you make decisions about these settings. Why join the group if you do not want updates and notifications? If you are in active job hunt mode, receiving updates daily may be a good idea; if you are a more passive networker, you may choose to let more time go by before hearing from the group.

You Joined a Group. What's Next?

Joining groups is a first step to expanding your network, sharing your expertise, and enhancing your ability to become known as an expert in your field. However, just joining and adding the group's badge to your profile alone is probably not going to get you very far. LinkedIn's group pages are very engaging. Take advantage of your memberships by adding news items, sharing job postings (when applicable), and replying to discussions. If there are group members who might be good contacts, request a connection or ask for a phone call or meeting once you establish yourself as an active group member. Like any social network, you can only get out of LinkedIn what you put into it. Make the time to engage.

Getting Help Via Groups

Groups can be very powerful, especially when comprised of people whose goal is to help someone. JobAngels is a group that began on Twitter (it's no surprise that this success story has its roots in multiple social media channels). Mark Stelzner, founder and principal of Inflexion Advisors, a respected and active thought leader in the HR community, launched JobAngels with a single tweet. He asked:

> *"Was thinking last night that if each of us helped just 1 person find a job, we could start making a dent in unemployment. You game?"*

LINKEDIN GROUP SUCCESS STORY

If you doubt that connecting with a stranger via a group can make a difference in your career, read this story that Mark shared about one job seeker who only needed to connect with one *right person*:

"What the heck is a LinkedIn?" The question drew heavy laughter from the audience of 3,000 unemployed skilled laborers just outside of Pittsburgh. I spent the next 15 minutes explaining the power of a tool

continued from page 148

that more than 90 percent of this audience had never heard of before that day.

The gentleman who had posed the question—let's call him Charlie—approached me after the session and gave me a hearty handshake and a pat on the back. He's a burly, middle-aged electrician who had been unemployed for nearly seven months. "Thanks for not treating us like morons," Charlie said with a big grin. "So many people talk down to us and most of us just want to leave these meetings a little smarter than when we arrived. We need help, not a pat on the head."

Charlie's story isn't unique. The housing market had dried up, which meant that new construction came to a screeching halt—and since Charlie worked for a number of developers his fate was in the hands of forces he could no longer control. The hammer fell and he and his crew of ten suddenly found themselves out of work and out of luck. "I think back on that time with a heavy heart," said Charlie. "My family could get their head around the fact that this wasn't my fault, but it didn't cover the shame and fear in their eyes." Bills piled up and the family tightened their belts. Everyone went without, and time seemed to stand still.

Shortly after I met Charlie, he sat down with a local career counselor who helped him set up an account on LinkedIn. Charlie had remembered my JobAngels group and asked that the volunteer counselor help him get connected. He put out a simple request for help. "It was a Hail Mary but what did I have to lose? I just couldn't get a break. That is, until I met Evelyn."

Evelyn is a public school official who happened to join the JobAngels LinkedIn group after she read about it in the newspaper. "I wanted to help people, but didn't know how. I'm not very good on the computer, but that didn't stop me." Her warm laughter filled my ears when we spoke. "I think fate brought me and Charlie together."

Evelyn saw Charlie's request for help and wrote him a note suggesting that they talk. She told Charlie that her school district was in the midst of a rebuilding project that was fully funded but they were having some trouble with the electrical systems. Would Charlie mind talking with the general contractor to see if he could help? "Would I ever!" said Charlie. "This was the first bit of good news I'd had in seven months. I jumped at the chance." As you might suspect, all went as planned and six days later, Charlie and his crew arrived on site for work.

continued from page 149

Both Charlie and Evelyn get misty-eyed when they think about the odds of finding one another at that particular moment. "Charlie doesn't think of it this way but he helped ensure that our kids were able to get back to school on time," shared Evelyn. "He's a kind and generous man who is such a hard worker. We're blessed to have found him." And Charlie?

"I think about all the little decisions I made that helped me find Evelyn. Going to the auditorium to hear you speak. Scheduling time with the career counselor. Signing up for LinkedIn. Joining your group. Posting a message. It just goes to show that you're never going to succeed if you sit on the sidelines and expect the world to save you. You need to take control and put yourself out there. It's scary, but man, is it worth it."

In the time since that tweet launched JobAngels in January 2009, this grassroots movement grew to an active community of more than 90,000 members strong with platforms on Twitter (@jobangels), LinkedIn, and Facebook. As a result, over 1,700 people they have tracked have found gainful employment through association with the movement. JobAngels merged with Hiring for Hope. Learn more by visiting www.hiringforhope.com.

JobAngels and Hiring for Hope members have sent millions of messages of encouragement, job postings, networking, and feedback.

Ask Questions in Groups

One way to get some help is to ask questions in groups. Here are some suggestions to help you effectively use questions:

College Students: If you are a college student, LinkedIn provides access to a diverse community of people in every industry to ask a question that might help steer your career plans. For example:

- How did you decide on your major in college, and does it impact what you do in your career today?

- I am thinking of studying journalism at Northwestern University, but am concerned about the job market after I graduate. If you work in this field, what would you advise?
- As a writer and photography blogger about to graduate with a double major in film and English literature, I am interested in meeting and/or speaking with other artists who have successfully leveraged their skills either in their profession or via a hobby. Please share some advice and let me know if you would be willing to arrange a brief phone call or meeting.

Experienced Professionals: A more experienced professional might ask questions to draw information or expertise, to extend his or her network, or to seek collaborators for a project:

- I am expanding my event planning business and hope to hire one or two interns to help manage my social network. Please let me know if you know of anyone—location does not matter.
- Please suggest experts who may be available to speak about "green" office spaces in the Dallas area. I am co-chairing a large conference and hope to find someone who could effectively keynote our program for over 1,000 participants.
- What's on your ultimate VPS wish list? Features? Packages? Software? Configuration?

Career Changer: A career changer may ask questions to conduct general research and gather opinions:

- I'm making the move from a career in banking and looking at going back to school for accounting. If you have experience or a background similar to mine, please share your suggestions. I would enjoy the opportunity to touch base.
- What advice do you have for someone transitioning from being a stay-at-home parent with background in mechanical engineering to having a career as a business consultant?

- How may I best leverage my background cataloging government documents? Please let me know if you have suggestions for professions that would benefit from my skills, including: detail oriented, organized, research focused, computer literate, quick learner, and fast worker.

START YOUR OWN GROUP

You may wish to create a group if you don't find exactly what you are looking for, but be aware that running a successful group is a bigger commitment than being a member. In Chapter 2, I shared information about Tim Puyleart, who initiated and manages a group for environmental, health, and safety professionals in Minnesota. He described some of the benefits of administering a group. Here are a few additional thoughts about the pros and cons of managing a LinkedIn group.

TARGETED GROUPS ARE EASIER TO LAUNCH

Chris Perry, a brand and marketing generator, entrepreneur, career search and personal branding expert, and the founder of Career Rocketeer.com says,

"Starting and managing a LinkedIn group is a great way to boost your brand, build a network, and identify opportunities. Your members come in contact with you at multiple touch points, including your announcements, discussions, and external sites/ networks, and can't help but view you as a leader in the area or industry associated with your group. As the owner/manager, career stakeholders, including both member and non-member recruiters, employers, hiring managers, and potential partners will view you as an industry leader."

Chris suggests the following to leverage your role and enhance your personal brand as a LinkedIn Group leader:

continued from page 152

- Share unique and insightful news and resources on a consistent, but not overly frequent basis.
- Limit self-serving updates or promotions to 20 percent or less of your outgoing outreach and interaction.

Chris cautions,

"Unless you already have a large network prepared to join your newly created group, these groups take time, effort, and planning to build and manage and must be launched and nurtured strategically. As a result, growing a group to any substantial size is an impressive accomplishment to share in your interview or with potential networking contacts."

Chris has started two LinkedIn groups: Career Rocketeer and MBA Highway.

Chris notes that growing a targeted group is easier than building a general membership. He says,

"I started MBA Highway as a targeted networking group for MBAs and MBA employers and recruiters to fill an unfilled group niche. As a result, this group grew quickly, especially as I invited MBA programs to share the group with their students at the same time as those programs were discovering the value of online networking to enhance their students' job search. This group has grown to more than 34,000 members thus far, and is still going strong."

If you don't have the time or desire to start your own group, Chris suggests getting active in someone else's and asking them how you can become involved and potentially help them as a manager. He explains,

"This will inevitably help you build your brand within the community without the trials and errors of launching your own group. When doing this though, be cognizant of the group owner's guidelines, needs, and comfort zone."

THE GOOD AND THE BAD OF CREATING A SUPPORT GROUP

Tim Tyrell-Smith is a marketing consultant and author, and the founder of *Tim's Strategy: Ideas for Job Search Career and Life*, a fast-growing blog and website, http://www.timsstrategy.com. He started writing his blog in September 2008 and realized that he wanted to create a place online where job seekers and career experts could help each other. He chose LinkedIn because all of his business friends were already there and could help seed a strong group. The group he started is called *Tim's Strategy—Ideas for Job Search, Career and Life.*

Tim does his best to personally connect with the 3,400-plus members in the group, and he noted that there are both struggles and joys when managing the group:

A few struggles:

- Maintaining a group on LinkedIn takes a lot of time, no matter the size. Tim remembers writing late into the night many times to personally welcome every new member, respond to people who had questions, and cheer them on when they had good news.
- Running a group for job seekers means that your audience is transient by definition. They become active at some point in their search and eventually become less active as they find a new role. Some of the most active members that gave the group its early character inevitably move on. It is important to constantly encourage activity, which is hard to do!
- Creating strict rules about acceptable content and self-promotion was critical to keep the group genuine, especially for the first few hundred members. Unfortunately, there is a good amount of spam on LinkedIn. Tim explains, "Creating and enforcing rules isn't always fun, but people appreciate it for the most part."

A few joys:

- Tim enjoys watching the group grow steadily and meeting all the new people; especially those he can help personally. He notes, "It is really what makes running a group so rewarding— that perhaps your initiative helped someone or someone's family get back on their feet."

continued from page 154

- Tim says, "Participating directly is great, but watching members help members is also great to see. You can't always be there for every conversation, and so I love to see a few leaders stepping in to provide a significant piece of advice for someone else."
- Tim's favorite ongoing discussion is about members sharing their small wins. "Reading about those small wins that became a big win helps others see how they might start to break out of their situation and feel good about the group's role in sharing a positive message."

Tim notes that groups ebb and flow.

"There are great runs of new membership and great interaction for weeks. And then just the opposite will occur. And you wonder if you've done something wrong. But in the end, as a group leader of a job search and networking group, it is all worth it when word comes back that someone has arrived at a new job."

Keep Your Profile Updated

Once you have gone to all the trouble to optimize your profile, expand your network, build your brand, and increase your visibility by joining groups and engaging with new contacts on LinkedIn, don't forget to keep your profile current and to post updates frequently. In fact, even if nothing changes in your work history, it is a good idea to consider tweaking your headline occasionally, and to continue to collect recommendations and to expand your network. Taking these steps will push your updates into your connections' regular e-mail from LinkedIn (assuming they elect to receive occasional updates). You have certainly heard that "out of sight is out of mind." In LinkedIn's case, if you don't make updates, you are invisible to all but those who purposely seek out your profile and the searches you might come up in. Pinging (touching base with) your contacts by creating frequent updates that LinkedIn will share with your immediate network is a good way to stay on their minds. It is not difficult, does not take much time, and is worth the effort.

Success Stories

What is more important than seeing results? No one likes to spend time on something unless there is a reasonable return on the investment. If you're on a diet, avoiding all your favorite junk food, you want to watch the numbers on the scale drop. If you're working out, spending all kinds of time sweating at the gym, you want to see some muscle definition. It's motivating to read or hear stories of how other people have succeeded. While I don't believe that jumping online and engaging in social media to propel your career goals forward is as hard as losing weight or shaping up, I do know it is a process. You are not likely to see results immediately. (Although, it has been known to happen.)

⇨ TIP

> When you grow your network, remember, any one person could make the difference in your career path. Hopefully, that will motivate you to continue to expand your circle of influence and participate in social networking.

I hope the following stories help further motivate you to take charge of your LinkedIn profile and to mobilize a plan that will optimize this tool to work for you.

JOB SEEKER BENEFITS FROM LEVERAGING LINKEDIN

Sital Ruparelia, career search expert, talent management consultant, speaker, writer, and a member of Microsoft's talent acquisition team, shared this success story:

I coached a senior director, in his early 50s, with a consulting background. He wanted help figuring out what he wanted to do for his

continued from page 156

next and final role before retiring and to learn how to find that role when most firms were laying people off.

He asked, "Sital, what shall I do over Christmas break?"

My reply was:

1. **Be visible.** Attend every Christmas party, gathering, event you get invited to. Meet and re-engage with friends, family, and contacts.
2. **Join LinkedIn.** Set up a basic profile and start re-connecting with ex-colleagues and clients.

The first point he was fine with. The LinkedIn suggestion met resistance.

I gave him a brief demonstration and showed the benefits, but he was not keen at all. After much arm twisting, he reluctantly agreed that he "may look at it" if he got a chance.

Fast forward to the middle of January when we next met.

He was all suited and booted with a smile on his face. Apparently, he had a second interview that afternoon for a role with the firm that he actually wanted to work for (the same firm that all the recruiters were telling him was not hiring).

"So, where did that opportunity come from?" I asked.

"Well, you know that LinkedIn thing you suggested? Well, I had a play on it one afternoon and signed up. I started to connect with people like you suggested. One of them was an ex-colleague from KPMG. We'd lost contact and hadn't spoken in five years. He mailed me via LinkedIn and asked, "So, what are you up to?" I explained I was between roles. We agreed to meet up in the new year to catch up. But then, just into January, he mailed me again via LinkedIn to ask for my resume. Apparently he met someone over Christmas who was hiring for someone with my exact background. They moved quickly and completed the first interview over the phone and then invited me in for the second interview today."

To cut a long story short, he was offered the role about two months later. They basically adapted the role to suit his needs and requirements (based on the work we had done). Why were they willing to negotiate and change the role to suit him?

continued from page 157

1. He was clear about what he wanted and what he didn't want.
2. Little competition: They were at very early stages of the recruitment cycle and had no one with his experience and skills in the frame.
3. Cost saving: The referral helped them save in the region of £50k ($75k) in recruitment fees compared to using a recruitment firm.
4. He had fairly specialized skills and client relationships that were not easy to find.
5. A credible ex-colleague recommended him.

Every time I come across a client reluctant to use LinkedIn, I share this story. It works every time!

LINKEDIN CONNECTS USERS TO BUSINESS OPPORTUNITIES

Lisa Rangel, PHR, is the Managing Director of Chameleon Resumes (www.chameleonresumes.com) and a former recruitment leader. She explains how she used LinkedIn to fuel her own business plans:

I was at a crossroads whether to look for a new position or launch Chameleon Resumes. To bridge both paths, I updated my LinkedIn status and title to "Seeking New Business Development Opportunity." A former college classmate (whom I had not spoken to in years) approached me via LinkedIn after seeing my status change. It turned out he is a leader of a learning and development firm and needed targeted sales development work done on a contract basis. I happily obliged, and this work helped me get my resume writing/job search consultancy business off the ground. Additionally, I handled employee outplacement and student career services for them. It was a win-win all around, and it started by simply changing a status on LinkedIn, telling my connections what I was looking for, and letting myself be found.

COMBINING TWITTER AND LINKEDIN CAN RESULT IN NEW PROSPECTS

Kevin Shannon, an integrated marketing communications director focused on the intersection of transportation and technology, explains how LinkedIn (combined with Twitter) helped him:

> I was let go from a job in September as a marketing director with a growing focus on integrating social media. While I am close on a few things, I have used the transition time to do some project work and connect with others on LinkedIn and Twitter. After leaving, I started a new and separate Twitter account to listen, learn, and engage with others with a specific industry focus. My Twitter account is @ConnectedCar.
>
> On my Twitter profile page, I had not posted a link or profile. One day, I changed my profile to include a link to my LinkedIn account. Within a few hours, I had requests to connect through LinkedIn from some new Twitter followers. One of the connections also wanted to schedule a phone call to talk about my background and interests. As a result of that conversation, I wrote two articles for him and continue to stay in touch, with more articles coming.
>
> As a result of posting the article links on Twitter and LinkedIn, I was connected to a few more people, including one with similar interests. We had a few conversations, and he has been helpful in providing suggestions of companies in my area who might need some help. In addition, he has also offered the possibility of working on some projects with him.
>
> Beyond that, I have had four or five additional phone calls with people I follow on Twitter to ask their advice and suggestions for industries and companies I have targeted. One new connection even worked at the same organization as me but at different times, all discovered with some LinkedIn research.
>
> My lessons:
>
> - Have a plan. Have a focus with your message, your industries, groups, and targets.
> - Learn as you go. I have learned that while some have privacy concerns, sharing, being open and engaging with others does create a relationship. I try to give back, share insightful trends and news, and not be sales-y in my approach.

continued from page159

- *People surprise you. Some of your close friends who you thought would be helpful, are not—they don't return phone calls and they have no idea how to help. It has been those who I have not known who have surprised me the most with their introductions, suggestions, and advice.*
- *Many things online often create an offline connection and conversation allowing things to become more personal.*
- *Both Twitter and LinkedIn have offered the opportunity to demonstrate expertise and create relationships and connections during my transition. I have some part-time contract work because of it, and some of the connections have offered me the opportunity to add to my portfolio, which helps me stand out.*

Things to Remember

Follow the steps outlined in this chapter to use LinkedIn to build and expand your brand. Luckily, this network is relatively easy to mobilize; all it takes is a little extra effort to give you the chance to create your own success story:

- Make it easy for people to find and contact you.
- Use the tips and tricks suggested in this chapter to reach the people you want to meet. A little know-how, some ingenuity, and follow-through may get you exactly what you need.
- Connect with everyone you can reasonably add to your network and continue to expand it.
- Give and request recommendations; sometimes it is a good idea to focus on giving before receiving.
- Join groups and use them to the fullest by participating in forums and discussions. Consider starting a group; use the advice from the group leaders highlighted here to conceive of and launch a successful group.
- Keep your profile up to date and tweak it by adding status

updates or changes, even if you are not making major career changes.

- Be inspired by the success stories in this chapter (and in the rest of the book). You can create your own success story. It is up to you!

8 Twitter— Why You Should Tweet

The name *Twitter* does not necessarily inspire confidence for skeptics. With a cartoon bird for a logo, Twitter, unlike LinkedIn, was not conceived as a professional network for job seekers or business owners. In fact, the simple question it originally asked people to answer was "What are you doing?"

This resulted in people sharing information that was frivolous at best and narcissistic at worst. Many viewed Twitter as the place where people told their networks what they were having for lunch or dinner, or how long they waited at the grocery store.

When I first started using Twitter, I thought it was a big waste of time. I didn't appreciate reading peoples' dinner menus and I didn't care how delayed their flights were. Then, I found a group of colleagues who tweeted, and everything changed. Twitter became a place where I met new people, shared and received advice and information, solidified relationships with people I otherwise would never have met, and conducted business.

Now I am a bit of a Twitter evangelist; I believe Twitter is one of the best social network's for job seekers and professionals. In this chapter, I will share information and stories that I hope will inspire you to enlist Twitter as one of your primary networking tools.

Today, Twitter bills itself as a place to discover what's happening right now, anywhere in the world. If you watch TV, you'll certainly see mentions of it on any major broadcast. With the right strategy and approach, you can not only find out what's happening anywhere in the world, but (more importantly) what is happening in your industry—and position yourself as an expert in your field.

What is Twitter?

Twitter is an online microblogging platform that allows participants to send brief, 140-character messages to a group of people who choose to "follow" them. (As a frame of reference, the previous sentence included 141 characters. Twitter messages, known as *tweets,* are brief!) Your Twitter name (or handle) begins with an @ symbol. For example, mine is @Keppie_Careers. To find my tweets, go to http://twitter.com/keppie_careers. You don't need to have a Twitter account to view the messages people send on Twitter, but you will need an account to respond or interact.

Your tweets display on your profile page, on the home page of each person who follows you, and in the Twitter public timeline (tweets are saved and indexed by the Library of Congress). Using Twitter is the equivalent of participating in an open chat room or texting many people at once.

You can send your messages using the website directly, through a number of applications that help you manage your time on Twitter, and from any number of mobile applications (see the *Resources* section for suggestions).

There is no doubt that you will find people on Twitter sharing trivial information that will not interest you, but many people consider Twitter a platform to demonstrate their expertise and find out what is going on in the world. Some have referred to Twitter as "an entrée to real-time relationship building," "better than e-mail and phone calls combined," and the "best way to share and discover what's happening *right now*."

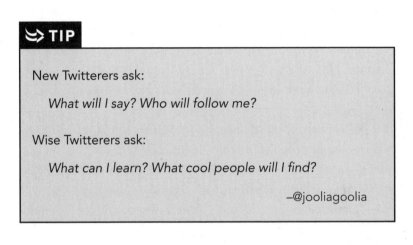

TIP

New Twitterers ask:

What will I say? Who will follow me?

Wise Twitterers ask:

What can I learn? What cool people will I find?

—@jooliagoolia

Use Twitter to Help Position Yourself as an Expert

Twitter is a great way to share ideas, insights, and information, and to demonstrate expertise to a broad audience. It provides a venue to share resources in quick, pithy bursts of wisdom, which is perfect if you don't have the time or energy to create a blog. Many tweets include a URL, which leads to a post or article that will be of interest to *followers* (people who elect to receive the tweets). Some tweets simply state a fact or make a comment. Many people share quotes that relate to their niche.

The following are examples of typical tweets from @FastTrackTools, owned by Ken Revenaugh which provides information and resources in the fields of sales, branding, and leadership. (Note that *RT* designates a *retweet*—meaning that the person is endorsing and forwarding information that has already been tweeted by someone.)

- *Free #PowerPoint template to communicate your personal brand: http://bit.ly/bDAXSw*
- *3 Ways to "Achieve Your Goals: Flow and Attraction" http://is.gd/gt0jA*
- *What Motivates Us To Do Great Work? http://t.co/OvovRxs*
- *Star performers teach for differentiation, tailor for resonance and assert control. How sales playbooks can help: http://bit.ly/9vULJq*
- *RT @Hoovers: 16+ ways to avoid sales mediocrity http://ow.ly/33e3F*
- *RT @TanveerNaseer: Today's post: 3 Steps To Help Get Your Leadership Groove On http://bit.ly/aHMlQZ*
- *To be a learner, you have to be ready to share your experiences and listen to the experiences of others.*
- *"Show me your friends and I'll show you your future." ~John Wooden, former UCLA coach*

Sending tweets such as these, in addition to interacting via Twitter with other people in the sales and leadership field on a daily basis, helped position @FastTrackTools as a go-to leader in the field. As a result, Ken attracted business and consulting opportunities, in part due to a Twitter stream rich in advice and information. This can happen in any field, and anyone can use Twitter to showcase their expertise.

HOW TO "COME RECOMMENDED" BY POSITIONING YOURSELF AS AN EXPERT ON TWITTER

Heather R. Huhman (HeatherHuhman.com) is a career expert and founder and president of Come Recommended, LLC, a content marketing and digital PR consultancy. You can follow her on Twitter at @heatherhuhman. She explains:

"Twitter provides a fairly easy and inexpensive way to establish yourself as an expert in your field. Being viewed as an expert helps

continued from page 166

you become more visible to potential clients and establish a trust with your audience."

Here are her suggestions to consider when positioning yourself:

- **Choose your focus.** It can be confusing to your followers if you try to be an expert in multiple subjects. Review your competition. Is there someone with high visibility who has already established him or herself as an expert in your niche? How are you going to differentiate yourself and show that you have value?
- **Build credibility.** Help your audience by sending out relevant and useful content. You'll be able to establish a bond with followers who appreciate the information; they will eventually trust you as an expert. Be patient—this takes time and won't happen overnight.
- **Be retweetable.** When you're pushing out content that is useful, valuable, and interesting to your followers, they'll want to share it with others. This immediately increases your visibility to all of their followers, too.
- **Don't put all the emphasis on pushing your content.** While you may want to direct readers to your website (if you have one) or services, or share information about your job search needs, you don't want to put all your effort into pushing your own content or talking about yourself. On the same note, don't become a cheesy salesperson. Twitter users can be turned off by just one or two tweets that seem too "spammy." And of course, it doesn't hurt to retweet others' content once in a while!
- **Have original thoughts and opinions.** Experts have opinions on recent news and emerging trends. If you're going to position yourself as an expert, don't be afraid to be wrong or disagree with other experts in your subject area.

Some people choose to create two Twitter personas—one personal and one professional. If you do this, you will want to be very careful not to accidentally send a personal tweet to the professional account (or to send the same tweets to both accounts simultaneously) if the point is to keep them separate. I do not advise having different accounts, since it provides a false sense of security for people who believe their personal account will not impact their professional life. I recommend creating a Twitter account that will appeal to your target professional audience; determine what people will need from you before you create your Twitter stream.

How you build credibility and an audience on Twitter depends, to some extent, on your target market. David Benjamin, a consultant on digital communication strategies, explained that he realized growing his network required him to provide value in different areas. He notes:

"It meant helping answer questions or retweeting messages to my network, to help amplify questions I could not answer. In some cases, I learned that making someone laugh or smile when they were having a hard day was just what the doctor ordered."

HOW TO USE TWITTER TO POSITION YOURSELF AS A SUBJECT MATTER EXPERT

These are David's suggestions for Twitter success:

- Use one of the various listening tools to capture every time someone mentions your name, company, brand, industry, competitors, etc. For example: www.twilert.com, Google alerts, and a keyword search on Twitter Search. These tools can track a word or phrase (such as your name, Twitter name, business, etc.), and alert you when it appears online or via Twitter. It helps you know when someone is talking about you or your business.
- Focus on helping everyone in your network prosper, which increases the likelihood others will want to help you in return.
- Learn to be a connector. It's great to be viewed as a valuable member of your community.
- Respond to the majority of your personal mentions—unless your brand/name is mentioned so often that you need a team to tackle this task.

continued from page 168

- NEVER get involved in an online fight. There are no winners, no matter what the outcome.
- Take personal conversations off the mainstream. Anything more than a couple back and forth tweets to one person most likely belongs in a direct (private) message.
- Adjust activity if your desired outcome is not occurring, after you have enough data to evaluate it.

⇩ TIP

When professionals share information and advice, make it available to the masses, and actively engage in the Twitter community, they deepen their digital footprint—that is, they make themselves searchable via Google and other search engines, and have the opportunity to extend their reach beyond the walls of their office.

Extend Your Network Beyond Your Immediate Circle

Hopefully, you are already convinced that having a strong professional network is important for career and business building. Twitter is a wonderful resource to help grow the number of people who know and care about you, even if only virtually. As an active social networker, I have been amazed at the open and giving nature of interactions I've witnessed and experienced. Many people (and it seems a significant majority of online networkers) enjoy helping their contacts. Meeting people you would not otherwise encounter can open doors to opportunities you may have never considered.

Twitter helps provide exposure and credibility. This is useful for job seekers and business owners interested in raising their profiles in their niche. Hannah Morgan (http://careersherpa.net), a career and social media strategist, explains that Twitter's lack of barriers to entry, focus on personal interactivity, and opportunities to follow the best and brightest in any field makes it a worthy network.

Hannah explains:

As a new business owner, I knew my niche, my target audience, and the value I provided. The challenge was in getting the message out to my audience. I had three goals to achieve: establish credibility, build my brand, and develop relationships. Along the way, I learned the following lessons:

- *Maintaining a blog helped me build credibility, but blog writing is not for everyone. Starting a dialog was important, but difficult, since I had few blog subscribers. I sourced other blogs that discussed similar topics and issues, so that I could comment on established and recognized expert sites. Comments led to e-mail conversations, which led to phone conversations with prominent bloggers.*
- *Twitter became a great equalizer. With no barriers to entry, all I needed was an account and unique thoughts that added value to join the conversation.*
- *I retweeted links from people whose work I admired, and submitted comments on other blog posts, which resulted in growing important relationships for my business. People followed back and even added me to Twitter lists, suggesting their followers learn more about me.*
- *Twitter morphed into a tool to not only build and grow my brand, but it also became a place for relationship building. Each request for information has the potential to result in a stream of offers of assistance and new opportunities. Each interaction is the beginning of a new relationship. Twitter relationships can be nurtured effortlessly, through a direct message or a retweet offering genuine thanks or praise. Each exchange moves the connection closer and establishes trust.*
- *Partly as a result of my relationship-building efforts through Twitter, Miriam Salpeter and Jacqui Barrett-Poindexter invited me to contribute to the Career Collective, a group of social media savvy resume writers and career coaches. Associating with this group helped me continue to advance my career,*

continued from page 170

and provided additional opportunities to build relationships and business.

Twitter, more than any other social media tool, enabled me to establish a recognizable presence and brand online. I highly recommend that everyone—even jobseekers and business owners who do not have an interest in blogging—experiment with Twitter. If you focus on building relationships instead of self-promotion, you may be surprised at just how quickly you can launch your career or business objectives.

Unique Aspects of Twitter

Twitter provides networking opportunities that LinkedIn and Facebook do not. The following are some compelling reasons to include Twitter as part of your social networking strategy:

- Twitter offers an unfiltered opportunity to connect. You don't need introductions to contact another Twitter user. You may find and share information, resources, and friendships. It's the online equivalent of a backyard barbeque.
- It is acceptable (and expected) to follow and connect with people on Twitter because your friends or connections do. (Unlike Facebook, where "friending" all of your friends' friends is not always socially acceptable.)
- For many industries, there is no better place to find out what is going on in your field *now*, in real time. You may be able to learn what captures the attentions of industry leaders, what the latest trends are in a field, and who to follow to learn more.
- Twitter is the place to be if you want to stay ahead of the curve. It's also a great resource if you have a technical question about your computer, need to know how to do something, or even where to eat or what to do in a city you'll be visiting. Just ask, and the responses are sure to come pouring in.

- Twitter offers the opportunity to see who is following whom and provides a tremendous chance to connect and learn from people you might not otherwise know.
- Leaders in your field may share advice, links to important news, resources from conferences, and other information. Communication that occurs in the public realm opens up opportunities to learn new things daily.

Who is On Twitter?

You may already know that celebrities and media personalities are on Twitter. However, you may not have heard that many CEOs, entrepreneurs, top-level executives, hiring managers, recruiters, reporters, writers, prospective mentors, and other people just like you use Twitter—to connect, share information, and enhance their reputations as experts in their fields. You may be surprised to find that stars in your field may follow *you* if you reach out to them! Twitter is a democratic gathering place to share ideas, and helps create a level communication playing field.

Twitter affords unprecedented access to other professionals. When you follow industry leaders, you'll know who spends time with them, what conferences they attend (and what they think of the speakers), what they're reading, and what problems they want to solve. This is great information to leverage when job hunting. When you follow the right group of people, Twitter helps you keep your finger on your industry's pulse. If your industry is not well represented, you have a chance to be a leader in your field via this network.

Becoming a part of a strong Twitter community may save you time and help cull down the informational overload we all face on a daily basis. Let your *tweeps* (Twitter friends) tell you what's worth reading.

IF YOUR INDUSTRY DOES NOT PARTICIPATE ONLINE, YOU CAN LEAD THE WAY

Brett Vanderwater MBA, CIA, CMA, CTP, is a strategic financial leader who believes that social media is useful for all careerists, even those in fields without significant representation. He tweets @BrettVanderH2O. Brett answered some key questions about the topic:

Many people believe that social media is only useful for certain industries. As a finance/business professional, what made you turn to blogging and Twitter, and how have they helped you advance your career?

My first introduction to social media was LinkedIn. I stumbled onto the fact that companies were performing a Google search prior to my interviews, based on the fact they knew I was a runner and member of several professional organizations. I did land a job at Kellogg Company, in a controller role at their Atlanta, Georgia facility.

After obtaining my job, I continued to study the communication power of social networking. I optimized my LinkedIn to include recommendations, news postings, discussions, and groups.

I also expanded my efforts to include blogging, which allowed for further creativity and helped me spread the word about my expertise in finance. The finance profession can be an introverted group, and admittedly, I did take a deep breath prior to sending out the first blog post. Of course, I assumed 10,000,000,000 people would instantly read it! After realizing very few read it, I started advertising the blog on LinkedIn via groups and added Twitter to further leverage and market my blog.

I found Twitter to be a simple, yet confusing tool. This is when I sought professional advice on how to represent a professional image and further leverage networking opportunities. I contacted Keppie Careers.

While I am still adding to my social network, a key career value is the circle/network that it has created. The world I once played in was limited to the city where I lived. Now, the landscape is broad, and I have met professionals from all over the world. I have had the opportunity to speak at several Atlanta area professional forums, to further leverage my growing brand. These events were directly related to my use of LinkedIn, Twitter, and blogging.

continued from page 173

Since there is not a critical mass of people in your field on these networks, how have you increased your following and how has that helped you?

The finance field is not very active on social networks, so I broadened my definition of a finance person. I now refer to myself as a Strategic Financial Leader, and network with all levels of professionals in an organization. As a result, my LinkedIn contacts increased from 380 connections to 550. My Twitter followers expanded from 175 followers to more than 8,100.

What I learned was to utilize a skill I have been using in my business career—leadership. When a profession is not at the same place that you want to be, you have two choices: 1) Conform to the profession's expectations; and 2) Redefine it. I chose option 2.

Would you recommend that others in industries like yours (where there are not already a lot of people involved online) try using social networks?

I recommend that people in the finance industry use the power of social networks and embrace the changing communication landscape, to enhance knowledge sharing and actualize the globalization that we talk about in the conference room.

I believe the finance industry will embrace social networks and fully leverage its power. The driving factor is that adopting these tools will save money and speed communications, thereby resulting in cost savings and exponential gains to corporations in the future.

Turn Tweets into Press Opportunities

If you follow the right people on Twitter, you never know when keeping up with their tweets might result in an unexpected opportunity. For example, I follow a reporter for the NBC affiliate television news channel in Atlanta. One day, he tweeted that he was looking for experts to comment on a story about job searching. I tweeted him back, and before I knew it, he was bringing a camera to film a segment to go on the air.

Kerry Noone, former Senior Marketing Manager for SodexoCareers, saw a tweet from Tory Johnson (@toryjohnson) from Women for Hire (and a *Good Morning America* Workplace Contributor) asking if anyone had ever gotten a job through Twitter. She responded immediately that Sodexo had two examples of Twitter hires, and that she would be happy to share the details. Tory replied that she was interested in the example, but needed the information right away because she was working on a segment for *Good Morning America* with George Stephanopoulos the next morning. Kerry connected her with Trish Freshwater, who was a recent hire through Twitter. The conversation resulted in an article and a segment on *Good Morning America*.

Turn Tweets into New Business Relationships

One story that I enjoy telling stems from two (seemingly) totally frivolous tweets, which resulted in a terrific business partnership. Early in my Twitter tenure, I was reviewing my messages and saw a tweet from a colleague I followed, but did not know well. He tweeted something to the effect of, "I am watching *The Biggest Loser* while eating a hamburger and fries. Is that wrong?"

Obviously, he was just being facetious, but I wanted to respond. Since I was very focused on only tweeting career advice messages, I hesitated before sending the following reply: "I think it is okay, as long as you don't follow it up with a big piece of chocolate cake." The next thing I knew, he messaged me back that he and his company were interested in expanding its resume writing services, and asked if I would be interested in this opportunity. From two silly tweets, a business partnership was born!

Ashley Bennett was a student at Pennsylvania State University. She explains how she benefitted from her participation on Twitter:

"Heather Huhman was one of the first people I started following on Twitter when I became actively involved in social media. I loved that she always posted internship opportunities on her Twitter account, and seemed genuinely interested in helping Gen-Y students succeed in their professional endeavors.

Heather posted an opportunity to work where she worked, and I immediately replied. After e-mail communication, one phone interview, and one in-person interview, I got the job. Heather allowed me to run a nationwide campaign; I released two nationwide press releases, gained experience with media pitching, and was published in the company's magazine.

Heather became not only a PR mentor to me, but also a friend and trusted colleague. I learned and produced more in that internship than I have ever done in any academic classroom or other internship to date! I always tell people about how I got my first internship through Twitter and no one believes me. I think this experience illustrates the impact that social media is having on the professional world today."

Use Tweets to Find Job Hunt Support

Alisun Hernandez (@SunnyinSyracuse) had been working in the world of education for six years, teaching social skills, coordinating youth programs, and conducting mediations with inner city students. She describes how Twitter played a role in her career plans at that time:

"Initially, I thought I would be avoiding Twitter at all costs. My opinion started to change after a friend (@JPedde), who also felt

the same as I did about Twitter, entered the job market and was surprised at its value. Curiosity got the better of me and I joined Twitter at a social media conference I attended.

Several people described Twitter as a conversation; just join in when you have something to add. As someone who visited chat rooms in college, this made perfect sense. As a result of the conference, I immediately gained a few followers—and that was enough to start noticing how they were engaging and who they were engaging with. I started adding to the conversation and following people who had really thoughtful things to say or links to provide. Before long, I had built a network of great people that I have learned from, conversed with, and even met in person.

When I knew I would need to start job searching, Twitter was the first place I started. I needed help with my resume, information on cover letters, and interview tips. I noticed a friend was participating in a Tweet Chat with the hashtag #jobhuntchat. I joined one night and found a plethora of advice.

Then I went to my personal network, where some of the people I was engaging with were tweeting about job tips. I read all of the information they posted. Finally, I sent a tweet out to my network that it was time for me to start looking for a new job. I immediately got offers of help and resources from those I conversed with regularly.

Forming a relationship first is crucial. Someone who immediately hops on and begs for help before letting people get a feel for who they are can be detrimental. Once you feel comfortable conversing, my advice would be to find communities who are offering job search help. Follow Twitter accounts posting jobs in the areas/fields/locales you want to be working in. Above all else, remember to be yourself!"

More Twitter Success Stories

Connie Reece (@conniereece) is a writer, speaker, and social media/networking consultant who joined Twitter when it was still a small, niche network of tech geeks and early adopters. She shares one of her many Twitter encounter stories:

"One of the first friends I made was Jim Long, . . . @newmediajim. As a news junkie, I figured that Jim, whose profile stated he was a veteran cameraman for NBC News, looked like someone interesting to follow. That hunch was certainly correct. Jim would tweet from the White House lawn, the nightly news set, or the Meet the Press set.

He demo'ed Twitter for Tim Russert and countless anchors and correspondents, as well as producers, engineers, and light and sound techs. Jim was unflappable. He seemed to be able to tweet on his smartphone with one hand and run the camera with the other.

'Going live with Brian Williams in sixty seconds,' he would tweet . . . and many of us would flip on the TV to see what Jim was seeing through his camera lens.

After a while, Jim's followers noticed a pattern: when his Twitter account would go silent for 24 hours or more, it meant he was preparing to take off in Air Force One (or one of the press planes accompanying it), and he could not tweet his whereabouts for security reasons. After a hiatus of a day or two, Jim would resurface, tweeting from Iraq or Afghanistan, or wherever the president happened to be. To this day, he still takes his Twitter followers along on his travels, giving us the feeling of being insiders to history.

Jim and I tweeted back and forth a lot. In June 2007, while President Bush was visiting his ranch in Texas, Jim invited me to drive up from Austin. I spent a dusty, miserably hot day at a middle school in the tiny town of Crawford, which served as headquarters for the White House press corps when the president was in town. But what an unforgettable experience it was getting to meet the people who bring the news into our living rooms, and especially getting to visit with an online friend who became an offline friend as well."

Building Community and Expanding Your Network Via Twitter

Leah Barr calls herself "proof that Twitter can be a life-saver for someone who's just moved to a new city and knows virtually no one." A casual tweeter before relocating to Indianapolis, she connected online to a community that led to in-person meetings and conferences. She explains:

"On @amy_stark's recommendation, I joined smallerindiana.com, a site that helps connect locals via Twitter. The number and diversity of my friends skyrocketed! Instead of meeting fellow recent grads or people still in school, I met professionals, including Generation X/Y cuspers like myself, as well as executives and entrepreneurs who have been in business for decades.

@robbyslaughter helped me revamp my resume when I was despairing in a dead-end job. Friends like @exrev, @bgkahuna, @edeckers, and @bethg40 banter daily, giving me reasons to laugh. We meet in-person for food and drinks to extend our Twitter friendships. I landed an opportunity to contribute as a writer @indygeeknet via @alxconn. I even met my mechanic, @mycardoc, via Twitter.

My Indianapolis Twitter community cheers each other in the good times, and consoles and helps in the bad. For example, when @msswank gave us the stunning news that she was just laid off, for the sixth time in her career, it was amazing to be a part of the cocoon of love and encouragement that surrounded her within mere minutes. She instantly had about 20 people offering kind words, and sending her name and qualifications among their own connections, to lend a helping hand."

Meeting New Local Friends

Susan Pogorzelski is a freelance creative writer and author of *Gold in the Days of Summer*, a novella, finds truth in fiction and explores the world through words. She explains:

> "I first joined Twitter to keep in touch with bloggers from around the country with whom I'd formed a community, based on our shared interests and life experiences. It was a way to further connect with new friends, share our experiences of discovering the world and ourselves, and help each other navigate adulthood in areas such as careers, relationships, and life in general.
>
> While Twitter made the world seem that much smaller, I didn't realize how close to home it would actually reach. Within a few months, those relationships expanded to include people from my local community that I may never have otherwise met—with in-person meetups enabling us to take those online discussions offline and form true friendships. Twitter is a remarkable platform that enables you to go beyond networking—to form lasting connections and strong friendships stretching from those faraway corners of the world to your own neighborhood."

Tweeting as a Skill

Some believe that being able to use Twitter well actually helps qualify people for jobs that require strong communication skills—and what job does not require this? Many people, even writers, comment that using Twitter really forces them to get to the point quickly. When writing a tweet, there is not much space, so you need to be brutal in editing. It helps you focus and gain clarity about what is important in what you are trying to share, and to think about how to communicate in a way that is interesting and makes sense. Using Twitter may help you clarify your value proposition. Remember—less is more!

> ⤳ **TIP**
>
> In today's fast, give-it-to-me-now, digital age, being able to communicate in 140 characters or less is a skill worth practicing. If you can learn to tweet with impact, without resorting to a lot of *txt spk*, you are even better off!

You Can Always Meet In Real Life (IRL)

Remember, just because you meet someone on Twitter does not mean that you can't network in person! If someone seems like a good contact, and they're accessible, invite him or her to meet for coffee or lunch. If not, set up a time to speak on the phone and see how you can help one another. Never forget to make personal connections.

Be on the lookout for Tweetups in your area. These can be fantastic networking opportunities, and a great chance to put a face with the names of some of the people you're engaging with on Twitter. Try to find and follow your local community by searching the geolocation/Twitter resources I provide later in this book.

Things to Remember

Twitter has many benefits; this powerful tool allows you to:

- Position yourself as an expert in your field (if you are one).
- Extend your network and grow relationships to the next level.
- Engage in a community with low barriers to entry, learn what your mentors and colleagues are thinking about, and discover what is important to leaders in your field.
- Find and follow everyone—from CEOs to people just like you—and engage in powerful one-on-one dialogues that may lead to in-person meetings.

- Be a leader in your field, even if there are not many of your colleagues participating online.
- Take advantage of a wealth of opportunities, such as press encounters, new business relationships, jobs openings, internships, mentors, and support for job hunt activities.
- Meet and befriend local and international people.
- Practice and hone all-important writing skills.

The next two chapters provide additional testimonials about Twitter's benefits, as well as detailed advice about how to get started efficiently and effectively. I hope you will take this information to heart, and learn how Twitter can help you get where you need to go.

CHAPTER 9

Getting Started with Twitter

In this chapter, I will walk you through getting started using Twitter—signing up, selecting your settings, and explaining what to tweet, how to tweet, and who sees your tweets.

Your Twitter Name and Handle

You will never know if Twitter can help you unless you sign up! Go to http://twitter.com/ to get started. While the sign-up form is short, it asks you to make an important decision—choosing your Twitter name (or *handle*). Don't make a quick decision about this. While it is possible to change your Twitter name, it is best to make a careful choice from the start.

My first suggestion is to think about creating a name that is easy to type using smart phones and other on-screen keypads. You have several options to consider:

- **Use your name as your Twitter handle.** For example, I would be @MiriamSalpeter. This seems an obvious choice, but there are several issues to take into account:
  - ➤ If you have a very long name, including it in a tweet will use up much of your allotted 140 characters. This can also be difficult when people are retweeting (forwarding) your messages, and may make using Twitter seem more cumbersome.
  - ➤ If you have a common name, someone may already be using it.
  - ➤ If you are not already well known in your field, using your name alone will require people to conduct a little due diligence, to decide if they want to follow you. I typically reciprocate follows when their Twitter handles clearly indicate that they may tweet about career or business related topics. For example, if @HRjohn or @CareerSpecialist follows me, I will probably follow back without investigating their Twitter streams (I can always unfollow later if necessary). If @John follows, I will not automatically follow back.
- **Use a combination of your name and expertise.** For example, @Miri_OrgChange, @ITBeth, or @AccountantJeff. If you are using Twitter to build a professional reputation, it is a good idea to consider including your profession in your name. The caveat is that you don't want a long name. Twitter only allows you 15 characters.
- **For business, use your business or blog name.** For example, I tweet from @Keppie_Careers, which is the name of my business and blog. Susan Pogorzelski, who writes a blog called Twenty (or) Something, tweets via @20orsomething.
- **Use your title.** Are you a camp director? Consider tweeting @CampDIR.
- **Consider a tagline.** My friend and colleague, executive resume writer Jacqui Barrett-Poindexter, tweets @ValueIntoWords, an abbreviated version of her tagline, "Your value into words."

Once you sign up with your username, password, and e-mail address, Twitter invites you to go through several steps to find people to follow, including the following: selecting from a list of people who tweet about various topics, connecting with Gmail, Yahoo, AOL, and LinkedIn contacts, and searching for people or companies of interest. I suggest that you skip all of these steps and move directly to confirming your account via the e-mail message Twitter will send you. This step will provide you with complete access to your Twitter account.

If you are interested, you may also activate your account via your mobile device. But know that you do *not* need to plan to use Twitter on the go to get the most from it.

Create Your Profile

From the bicycle cog icon, select "Edit Profile." Follow these important steps to complete your profile:

Photo/Avatar/Header

Upload a photo (it can be a JPG, GIF, or PNG, up to 700k). It's a good idea to use a clear picture that shows your face and makes you look friendly and welcoming. Also consider choosing an avatar (photo) that you also use for profile pictures on other networks. This makes it easier for people who don't know you well to remember and recognize you. You may also add a "Header," which is the background for your avatar.

Name, Location, and Website URL

Enter your real name and location. City and state are fine, even if you choose the closest metro area. There are applications that help people find contacts who live nearby; by indicating a city, you will help people who are searching via geographical locations. This does not let people know where you are when you tweet.

Add a URL for a website if you have one. If you do not have a site or a blog, use your LinkedIn URL. Providing easy access to more information will help anyone who wants to learn more about you find exactly what they need.

Bio or Twit Pitch

Your twitter bio (or *twit pitch*) is a 160-character or less summary of what you have to offer. It must include keywords that will make it easy for people who search for your expertise to find you. Focus on promoting your value proposition across Twitter with a strong statement.

Project the same message through your Twitter bio as you do on LinkedIn and other social networking profiles. Consistency is important, especially when you are looking for a job—use every word to your advantage.

Here is an example of a twit pitch (from @KarenBice) that wasn't targeted enough to help propel her job hunt:

Executive assistant job hunter, Marine mom, history geek. Tweet on various subjects which rock my world, especially the job market.

As a job seeker, that bio did not pack the punch it needed. Using her space to share personal information did not leave enough room for targeted keywords. Here was her transformed bio:

Executive assistant, "right-hand" for VP/C-suite execs seeks job using organizational/project management/communication skills. Adaptable. Love challenges.

Clearly, the revised bio includes many more power-packed words and uses her space more efficiently. When she is not job hunting, Karen may wish to change it back to include more about her personality.

It is fine to include something about your hobbies or personal interests in your Twitter bio, but when you are job seeking, be aware that focusing on hobbies or family interests over skills and accomplishments may detract from your goal—demonstrating what you have to offer professionally. The following are examples of strong bios, some of which include personal information:

- @LarryEngel: *10+ years experience in Advertising & Marketing, Certified Google AdWords Professional, SEM Search Engine Marketing, and LinkedIn / Facebook PPC Advertising.*
- @MikeRamer: *Careers / Employment * International Trainer * Executive Recruiter * Social Media Enthusiast * Love Travel, Wine, Cars, Skiing * Very Fun Dad!*
- @jobhuntorg: *Job-Hunt.org connects you to resources that will help you find your next job: employer recruiting pages, associations, networking, careers, advice, and more.*
- @TrishMcFarlane: *HR Director/ HR Blogger, HR & Social Media speaker, HRevolution co-creator, Mom of Twins.*
- @steviepuckett: *webmaster, content creator, career coach; military spouse, eduflexing mom; if I don't have something positive to say, I don't tweet . . . that's just how I roll. ;)*
- @JennyDeVaughn: *Pay-It-Forward Social Media and Digital Enthusiast, Relationship Builder, HR Brand Ambassador, Entrepreneur, Recruiter, Mobile Geek + a Dale Jr. NASCAR Fan!*

Design

You have the option to personalize the background image people see when they visit your Twitter page. There are several options:

- You can select a new default theme that others may also be using, but can personalize it beyond the default offerings. Once you are in the "Design" view, select one of the tiles shown to change your background. You can also change the design colors in this view.
- You may also try customizing a background using the *Themeleon* link, on the right side of the "Design" page, which gives you many options to customize your page (you will need to login to your Twitter account to save the background).

- You can create your own background using any number of applications (and a little creativity).
- You can hire someone (or a service) to create a personalized background.

Since many people view Twitter from various applications and rarely ever visit an actual Twitter page, and because Twitter's interface takes up a lot of screen space, I am not convinced that it is important to worry about your Twitter background. I'd suggest spending a minimal amount of time customizing it.

> **⮡ TIP**
>
> It is important to create a completely filled-in account (populated by tweets) and a bio with a photo that explains what you have to offer *before* you begin to follow people. If you do not take these steps first, people you follow receive a notification that you are following them, but would have no way of knowing anything about you—and no reason to follow you. I receive a lot of notifications of followers with no bio and an "egghead" (Twitter's default avatar) for a picture. I never follow them back.

Twitter Location and Privacy

From Twitter's top toolbar, click the gear icon, and "Edit Profile," then select "Account." This is where you can enable Twitter to track where you are when you tweet. This is different from the location you will list in your Profile, which is where you currently live and/ or work. When you tweet from a device that is GPS-enabled, Twitter may track and share your location with others. This can be useful if you want to find people who are at the same event, or want to know what is going on in a particular place. However, it does present some privacy and security questions for people who are not convinced that it is a good idea for others to be able to track their whereabouts. Choose what seems most comfortable for you (I do not enable this setting).

Twitter also allows you to protect your tweets. If you check this box (found under "Account"), only people whom you approve will be able to view and follow your tweets. This setting may work well for a family trying to use Twitter to keep in touch with each other, but it is not conducive to building your brand and demonstrating your expertise online. I do not recommend that you select this option if you are planning to optimize Twitter to improve your career prospects.

Notices

From Twitter's top toolbar, select the bicycle cog image and then "Edit Profile." Email notifications is where you can decide if you want to receive e-mail alerts about your Twitter followers and decide when you receive direct (private) messages. This is probably not necessary if you make an effort to review your messages using Twitter or another application on a regular basis.

How to Tweet Effectively

It is very important to know who sees your messages. Some people who have been using Twitter for years still do not know this information!

Always include a Twitter name in your message if you want a particular person to read it. If you use someone's Twitter handle (@Keppie_Careers, for example) in your message, it will appear in their *mentions*, even if the person is not following you. You may view your @mentions by clicking on that tab on your Twitter homepage. This is the great advantage of Twitter—you can reach people, even if they do not know you.

If you begin a message with @ATwitterName (an *at message*), that message goes to the direct Twitter streams of that person, and everyone who is following both of you. It also goes into the public stream. For example:

@beneubanks Those babies look like dolls—literally! So adorable!

I wrote that tweet directly to @beneubanks as a reply, and while I do not mind if other people see this public message, since it is intended for him, it works well as an @ message.

If I want a tweet to appear in the public stream, and also want a broad audience to see it, I would not start the message with an @. For example:

@careersherpa offers great tips for commenting on blog posts: http://bit.ly/9nuZ2N

While this message is in the public realm, only people who follow me *and* @careersherpa will see it in their Twitter streams. This is not a useful message if I am hoping to introduce a new audience to @careersherpa.

One option for this tweet is to set it up with a period at the beginning:

.@careersherpa offers great tips for commenting on blog posts: http://bit.ly/9nuZ2N

This signals Twitter that this message is for everyone, without using many extra characters. Anyone who follows my Twitter stream will have this message in their Twitter messages. @careersherpa also receives a copy of this message in her mentions, so she will know I was recommending her.

A different option is for me to send a message such as:

Great tips for commenting on blog posts from @careersherpa: http://bit.ly/9nuZ2N

Similarly, this message goes to everyone who follows me, and @careersherpa receives a copy of this message in her mentions.

Private Messages

If you want to contact someone in private via Twitter, you may send a private, or "Direct Message." The caveat is that you may only send private messages to people who are following you. When you visit a person's Twitter page, if he or she is following you, there will be an option on the dropdown menu that looks like a shadow face to tweet to or send a direct message to someone who is already following you. Following that link will allow you to send a private message. If there is no "Direct Message" button, it means the person is not following you. You will find messages people send you via the gear icon on Twitter. Choose "Direct messages."

What Not to Tweet

Remember, unless you lock down your Twitter profile (which I do not recommend), everything you share is part of the public stream and is categorized by the Library of Congress—and indexed on Google. Therefore, try to follow some logical rules about what you share on Twitter. Here are some tweets that I saw today that would be on my "not to tweet" list:

- *Having lunch with my gorgeous wife on a gorgeous day in #NYC—too bad I have to go back to work. Bleh.*
- *I hate when ppl come in the office at work and interrupt my sleep!*
- *I hate work . . .*
- *I hate waking up for work. ;(*
- *Ugh I hate today is payday and I gotta close at work. I kinda feel like callin in sick I already got my check lol!!!*
- *I'm gonna be late to work but I hate that place now lol*

Don't Miss Any Tweets

Using the Twitter client itself (https://twitter.com), you can easily view messages that include your Twitter name (if there are any) by clicking on "@Connect," located on the top tool bar of your Twitter profile, when you are on your homepage. This is important, because the only other way to see who has mentioned you via Twitter is to read through every single tweet. When I first started using Twitter, this is exactly what I did—I didn't want to miss replying to someone mentioning my name, so I fervently trolled the entire stream, looking for my name. You don't have to do that!

You can also view your private messages by clicking on the gear on the Twitter toolbar and follow the link that says "Direct messages." Be sure to review these, as you never know who may be trying to get in touch with you.

What to Tweet

Knowing what to tweet is easy, once you identify your goal. If your goal is to build a reputation as an expert in your field, you will need to tweet information that indicates you know what is important and comment on developments and news to indicate you are up to date on the latest trends in your industry. Tweet links to news, share information, describe events, and share advice about all of these topics via your Twitter stream.

Making Sure People See Your Tweets

When you are tweeting, and few people are following you, it is a good idea to include other peoples' Twitter handles in your tweets, as this makes it likely those people will actually view your tweets. Also, consider including hashtags (using the # sign and a word or phrase that will be searchable) when you tweet, as some people do search for terms (for example, #jobs, #jobsearch, etc.), and may come upon your tweet in the public stream.

> **⇨ TIP**
>
> Visit http://hashtags.org to find helpful information pertaining to tags, users, and hashtag trends.

It is important to structure your tweets to have the greatest impact. Consider the following:

As noted, many tweets include links to additional information. Sharing these links suggests that you know what is going on in your field. Some experts tweet short advice or quotes and do not include links to further information. These pithy tweets provide useful recommendations and demonstrate knowledge and expertise about a topic.

For example, Gayle Howard, award-winning master resume writer, author, and personal branding strategist, frequently posts advice and information without links from her account @GayleHoward. For example:

- *#Jobseekers. The onus is on you to question the contact person/recruiter and discover more about the role to determine if you are qualified.*
- *#Jobseekers. Ask the employer at interview: What major challenges are currently facing the management team?*
- *#Jobseekers Transitioning from the private sector to the public sector can be confusing. Take a close look at position responsibilities.*

Gayle explains the following:

Twitter, for me, provides the mechanism to do two things: advance the legitimacy of the resume writing sector, which for most people is either unknown or misunderstood; and second, to provide free, rapid-fire assistance to people who want instant advice. Most of my tweets do not contain links to articles as I'm

*not using Twitter as a sales channel to drive people to my web-
site. Instead, my tweets aim to inform, sometimes challenge, and
elicit comments and observations from others that expose jobseekers to a flash meeting of experts. The conversations hopefully
will test pre-conceived notions and allow jobseekers to pursue
strategies that will differentiate them from others in this highly
competitive world.*

You may also wish to ask questions or engage your community
in discussions. Feel free to reply to messages on Twitter that other
people send. Just include @ and their Twitter name (for example,
@Keppie_Careers if you wanted to reach me) in the message to
reply or respond.

Also consider retweeting something that someone whom you
admire sent. Depending on what application you use, there are
many ways to do this. The best way is to be sure your tweet actually
includes the other person's @name in it, and that it begins with
"RT." You may wish to comment on the information, but sometimes, you may just forward the tweet. Retweeting is a great way to
get someone's attention if you hope they might notice you in the
Twitter stream.

For example, I retweeted the following tweet without a comment.
@HeatherHuhman forwarded a link written by @AskAManager.
She included a hashtag—the # sign with a word after it, which indi-
cates a topic that is searchable via Twittter:

*RT @heatherhuhman: What Hiring Managers Want by
@AskAManager—http://bit.ly/cEMOyL #JobAdvice*

I also retweeted this post, originally sent by @JTOdonnell, and
added the comment "Don't do this if you are job hunting!":

*Don't do this if you are job hunting! RT @jtodonnell: What's
Wrong with My LinkedIn Request to Employers? http://bit.ly/
aXu0RQ [JT & Dale]*

HOW TO SHORTEN URLS

Since you only have 140 characters for each tweet, you will want to shorten lengthy URLs so the links do not take up your entire tweet. An application such as Tweetdeck (http://www.tweetdeck.com/), owned by Twitter, is a free download, and automatically shortens links. So does Hootsuite.com. Some other choices include:

- http://Bit.Ly—which allows you to track clickthroughs on your links. Be aware that links do expire, so do not use a Bit.ly link that you expect to make permanent (for example, on your blog or website).
- http://tinyurl.com—TinyURL links do not expire.
- http://ow.ly—used with Hootsuite (a Twitter application), these links will also expire.

Keyboard Shortcuts

While we're on the subject of shortening, be sure to look at Twitter's "gear" dropdown menu for "Keyboard Shortcuts." It lists all kinds of useful ways to easily navigate Twitter.

TWEETING WITH IMPACT

Tweeting with impact requires some finesse. You don't want to send out a string of messages full of abbreviations and text speak that are not easily scannable. If you are reaching other tweeters who follow many people, you need to tweet so that you attract their attention. Jacqui Barrett-Poindexter is a Certified Master Resume Writer who composes career-positioning documents for executives and professionals. (http://careertrend.net)

I have many friends who tweet, but I am always impressed by how Jacqui manages to compose tweets that capture the necessary information or endorsement without reducing the tweet to a string of abbreviations. Jacqui's Twitter handle, @ValueIntoWords, suits her well, as she demonstrates how to unearth and translate value into words—even in the short form.

continued from page 195

HOW TO TWEET FOR IMPACT

Here are Jacqui's suggestions to help you tweet with impact:

- The key for a high-impact tweet is focus. If you are a job seeker interested in attracting hiring managers, company influencers, industry recruiters, human resource professionals, and others who may have a reach into the organizations where you want to work, tweet using proper context, good grammar, and minimal abbreviations to help you extend your influence.
- It may be tempting to tweet stream-of-conscious, spur-of-the-moment thoughts, but these result in hollow posts with less impact and undesirable grammar, spelling, and punctuation habits, including text-speak (txt spk).
- Powerful tweets lead readers to more substantive material that extends and expands a short Twitter message. Here is an example of my own such Tweeting:

> In Resume Writing: LESS is 'not' always more: provide meaningful, MEATY story content framed in a digestible, 'newsy' style.

This pithy tweet was the impetus for a beefier blog post message flush with contextual detail.

Now, imagine that tweet in "txt spk":

> In resme wrtg, less=not mre; prvde meaningfl, meaty stry contnt. frmed in digstble, nwsy style.

This may seem like an exaggerated example, but I know tweeters who truncate all of their messages to pack in more words. Although I value words, I know that forcing words into tweets detracts from your message (at best) and makes it difficult to read your tweets (at worst).

I encourage job seekers, and all tweeters, to consider the value of your message and the substance of your words. Make sure that what you are saying resonates with your core belief system and with the opportunities you wish to attract.

For example, I follow a social work career transition tweeter (and blogger), @DorleeM, whose tweet stream centers on career advice and psychology. Though her industry focus is social work, her tweets equally promote career transition strategies as she personally navigates the job

continued from page 196

search maze. She feeds her target audience meaningful content, and often uses Twitter to lead into her own social work career-transition blog. For example:

- *Racial/Ethnic Disparities to be Reduced in #Healthcare Reform @nationalcouncil http://bit.ly/96AALE #socialjustice #diversity*

- *A Course Load for the Game of #Life (NYT) http://nyti.ms/djzGyL learn some economics, statistics . . . #highered #education*

- *How To Build #Reputation w/#Blog: Create Value @MikeRamer @sueyoungmedia @colinismyname http://bit.ly/buZDzJ < gr8 post #marketing*

She adds hashtags to help people who don't follow her find her tweets, and also avoids abbreviating (unless absolutely necessary) to make her point. She states:

"Apply this type of targeted, quality tweeting to retweeting. Read other people's tweets, and the blog posts and articles to which the retweeted messages link, and interject your value-add insights. In other words, instead of simply clicking the retweet button, pull content or create a short summary of the targeted blog post to use as a lead-in to your retweet. Show that you read and understand the tweeted content and share that value with your readers.

For example, when retweeting a message from the author of this book, in which she linked to a *New York Times* article that quoted her, rather than simply sending on her tweet, I pulled a snippet from the article, and wrote:

Expand your "Sphere of Influence" says @Keppie_Careers in NYT article on Social Networking http://nyti.ms/9Pn9D7.

Effective, impactful Tweeting centers on thoughtful, focused, synergistic ideas that flow, versus staccato, hurried word rivulets. If you trust your instincts, take a few moments to stew in your thoughts before developing your clever, pragmatic, impassioned, precise, and/or compelling ruminations through the Twitter stream; I think you'll be kindly rewarded. The business and career relationships and partnerships that will ensue, the advocates that you will cultivate, and the learning experiences in which you will indulge are just some of the perks of Twitter engagement."

Finding People to Follow

Once you have completed your profile and posted tweets for several days, it is time to follow people. Revisit the @Connect link on Twitter's top toolbar. Browse the choices to connect with people you may know or want to know.

Once you follow people, it is a good idea to review whom they follow. Simply go to their Twitter profile and click on "Following," on the left side of the screen. They will then be listed in the stream, along with his or her Twitter bio. It is perfectly acceptable to find people to follow by seeing who other people follow. Another good way to find people who may tweet interesting information is to review Twitter lists.

Find peoples' lists by visiting their Twitter profile and following the links under "Lists," below their profile/bio. You can easily follow individual people on the list, or agree to follow the whole list. Review lists via Twitter profiles or use available tools, such as the following, to find people to follow:

- **http://wefollow.com/:** search for terms, topics, or people of interest and follow them
- **http://search.twitter.com/:** Twitter's advanced search tool
- **http://www.twellow.com/:** Twellow, the Twitter Yellow Pages
- **http://justtweetit.com/:** a directory to help you find other Twitter users
- **http://twibes.com/:** lists to review
- **http://www.followerwonk.com/:** allows you to search bios on Twitter

> **⤳ TIP**
>
> When you start following people, build your list slowly. If you follow too many people before people have a chance to follow back, you will get to a point that Twitter freezes your ability to follow other people until your "Following" number is a greater percentage of those you follow. Try to keep your "Following" and "Followers" in proportion, to avoid Twitter assuming you may be running a spam account.

Tweeting Etiquette

While I am not an advocate of hard-and-fast rules for using any social network, there is no doubt that each has its own set of suggested etiquette. Dawn Bugni, (www.write-solution.com), a Master Resume Writer who has been published in several books, is a former recruiter with more than 25 years of corporate management experience. She is a tell-it-like-it-is Twitter enthusiast, and offers the following advice to new and budding Twitter users:

> *"Not sure how to behave on Twitter? Evidently, you are not alone. Googling 'Twitter etiquette' brings back 9,960,000 results. Twitter is yours. However, in making it yours, consider your audience and your message. Think about the impact you have on your follower's stream. More importantly, consider the message you're sending about yourself, especially if you're in a job search or building a professional image. Common sense and courtesy go a long way in developing your public face.*
>
> *To help cultivate what is not always so common, here are some basics to consider as you explore:*

- *Be interesting. Interact. Retweet (RT) and mention others, but tweeting only links and other people's thoughts is not engaging.*
- *Many tweets in rapid succession take over the stream. Write a blog post and tweet the link if you have a lot to say. If they're random thoughts, space out your musings.*
- *If you use Twitter to update other social media platforms, do it selectively, so your posts and quantity are appropriate to those venues.*
- *If you tweet a link, make sure it's publically accessible. Don't make followers go through Facebook, sign up for an e-letter, or join a site to read an article.*
- *Take time to say thank you—it has an added benefit, it helps your followers connect with each other.*
- *Space out #FollowFriday, thank you, and other lists. No one wants to read list after list of names.*
- *Move long personal conversations out of the public stream, unless they're beneficial to your followers.*
- *A little self promotion is okay, but don't make it the primary focus of every tweet. Interest in what you do comes with interaction.*
- *If you acknowledge new followers using automated direct messages (not recommended), don't make the first contact something like "Check out my blog, download my e-book, or use my services."*
- *Keep it positive. You can disagree with someone without saying they're wrong. State your position, independent of the offending tweet. Twitter is about sharing; not drama and being right.*
- *Invite someone to participate in projects or events behind the scenes. Public stream invitations potentially put that follower on the spot—not good when asking a favor. With permission, promote participation publically.*
- *Refrain from bad language in online conversations. Don't make someone's first (or last) impression of you a poor one.*
- *Unless you're tweeting for a business, avoid joint or couples accounts. People want to know you as a whole, not as half of a couple; this is especially important if you're a job seeker.*

You'll find hundreds of other guidelines out there. Adapt what works for you, but always give more than you take. The most important thing to remember: Tweet others as you would like to be tweeted."

Following Etiquette

One question that seems to puzzle many new Twitter users is "Do I follow everyone who follows me?" I do not personally adapt that philosophy to my Twitter use, but I do try to make a point to try to follow anyone who retweets my messages or asks me a question in the public stream. That way, those people may contact me on Twitter privately if they so choose.

I also make a point to follow those who follow me if their Twitter name and/or most recent tweet (the one that shows up when I review them in my list of new follows) seems relevant to career topics.

Erin Kennedy (http://exclusive-executive-resumes.com) is a certified professional and executive resume writer/career consultant, and the president of Professional Resume Services, Inc. She tweets @ErinKennedyCPRW. Erin has a different take on the subject, and I think it is valuable to share her ideas, to illustrate that there is no one right way to use Twitter:

> *"After spending lots of evenings on Twitter studying other people's feeds, watching responses, and seeing what people were retweeting and talking about, I finally started to understand it. People have different ideas about this, but I follow just about everyone that is not offensive.*
>
> *Whether you are building your network for business reasons, promoting your product, or just looking to make new contacts, the bottom line is that you want people to find you. If you limit people you follow to just those you know or people in your industry, you will severely limit your visibility. I am amazed by followers who DM me or retweet my posts that are on Twitter for completely different reasons and yet, they found my article or tweet useful.*

You may get to the point where you want to unfollow people who don't follow you back. Whatever your reasons are for unfollowing, there are a few different ways you can do it. One is to manually unfollow. This is a good choice if you only have a handful of followers you don't want around anymore.

However, if you want to go through and get rid of 50 or more followers, it can be time consuming, and you will want to use a program. I use www.justunfollow.com. All you have to do is add your user name and it will bring up your entire list of non-followers and followers. You can easily make your choice of who to unfollow.

Keep in mind that some people/companies will probably never follow you. These are most likely the bigger names, who will only follow a handful of people but have followers in the thousands, hundreds of thousands, or more. If you like what they have to say, then keep them in your list.

The bottom line is to not be afraid to follow people out of your comfort zone. You never know who you might strike up a conversation with!"

Things to Remember

This chapter gives you all of the information you need to get started on Twitter, from signing on with a handle/name, forming your bio, tweeting, and understanding who sees what tweets.

Review tips about what to tweet (and how to do it well), explore proper Twitter etiquette, and find people to follow. This will help make your Twitter experience useful.

Unless you have stopped and taken some time to actually follow the steps I suggested, using Twitter may still seem difficult. I encourage you to pause and take some time to get yourself set up with an account. Once you are signed on, it will be easier for you to envision how you will be able to optimize your Twitter experience, which I describe in the following chapters.

10 Getting the Most from Twitter

Twitter continues to improve its interface and functionality. Several companies market free applications to use from a desktop, so you have choices regarding how to use Twitter— as a power Twitter user, I read and send tweets via an application known as Hootsuite.

This chapter covers some of the available applications that you may want to try. Everyone has their own preferences, and new players continue to join (and leave) this fast-changing market. To keep track of what is happening in the technical world, visit Mashable (http://mashable.com/).

TweetDeck

TweetDeck is owned by Twitter. Available for desktop, as a web interface, and for mobile devices, TweetDeck (http://www.tweetdeck.com) allows you to customize your Twitter experience and view your messages via columns, which you choose. You can set up groups to follow, save a search for a keyword, name, or company so you can return to it easily, and have TweetDeck capture the mentions. It is easy to join conversations via automatic URL shortening, to retweet, and to schedule tweets to send out later.

When you download TweetDeck, you will be able to easily set up columns to store tweets from specific people, follow hashtags (#), and track conversations that interest you. This makes it easier to keep track of what is happening on Twitter without feeling the need to watch your stream 100 percent of the time.

Tweetdeck also allows users to filter and search within columns, and to mark tweets as read. If you have more than one Twitter account, you can manage it from the same desktop and integrate Facebook, or multiple Twitter accounts simultaneously. (Visit www.Tweetdeck.com to download the desktop or web version.)

Hootsuite

With a web application that does not require a download, as well as having desktop versions available, this tool (Hootsuite.com) allows you to track and follow updates from multiple accounts, and also integrates with Facebook, LinkedIn, Google+, FourSquare, and others. With paid and unpaid options through the site, you can run searches, maintain user lists, manage your responses to your networks, and be notified and respond through the Desktop Notifications feature. Hootsuite also offers mobile applications for iPhone, iPod touch, Android, and Blackberry. Visit the site to learn about its recent updates.

How Much Time Should I Spend On Twitter?

A lot of jobseekers worry that they are spending too much (or not enough) time on Twitter to make it worthwhile. One true thing about Twitter—there is enough information and resources there to keep you busy for a very long time. If you are someone who is easily distracted, and who does not typically manage your online time efficiently, Twitter may present a challenge.

I recommend setting up some tools to help you get the most of Twitter:

- Use a Twitter application (as such as Tweetdeck or Hootsuite), and set up columns and lists of people to follow, whose tweets you wish to track closely.
- Conduct searches on terms with hashtags that interest you, save them, and review them all at one set time during the day. For example, #insurancejob if you are looking for an insurance job.
- Use scheduling tools to automatically post tweets during the day, which will reach different audiences of people on Twitter during different hours of the day.
- While I try not to automate too many updates, my favorite tools include:
  - **Bufferapp**—this application has an extension for Firefox that allows you to easily post links and updates directly from the page you want to share. You can simultaneously post to Twitter, Facebook, LinkedIn, and other networks you include in your account.
  - **Tweetdeck and Hootsuite**—both of these tools have scheduling mechanisms that make it easy to post updates

at a specific time or to automatically populate updates at pre-designated times.

- Identify goals (for example: two direct interactions, four things to retweet, gain five new followers today), and do what you need to do to accomplish those goals for the day.

Taking steps to streamline your Twitter time will help make it seem more manageable. However, be sure you spend as much time as seems useful to you. Setting a timer and spending 15 minutes at a time throughout the day may work well; however, just as I would not advise you to attend an in-person networking event and leave after 15 minutes, I do not advise you to limit your Twitter time to a specific amount.

How to Get More Followers

This is a popular question from people who are just starting out on Twitter. After all, how can you increase your influence and raise your reputation using Twitter without followers? While there are rogue programs that promise followers in exchange for following or tweeting something, I suggest you avoid any quick-fix schemes. Even if you may be able to raise your follower count using these programs, you will not have the type of followers you need to move your career forward. The followers are not likely to be members of your field, and what good is it to have a long list of followers who are not interested in your tweets?

It is possible, using Tweetdeck, Hootiesuite, or other Twitter applications, to set up lists of people to follow closely. In other words, some Twitter users may technically follow many people, but may not actually view all of those tweets. Categorizing people this way allows users to follow numerous Twitter accounts without actually viewing the tweets of most of the people they follow. As a result, just having a lot of followers will not, in itself, be very useful for you.

Provide Quality Content from the Outset

The best way to attract followers is to provide useful, quality content. Your goal should be to demonstrate your expertise to your colleagues, so make an effort to keep up with the news in your field and to share that information. In previous chapters, I suggested several tools to help you keep your finger on the pulse of your industry, including setting Google alerts for keywords in your field as well as visiting Alltop.com (http://alltop.com), to review blogs centered around your subject matter.

If you create a Twitter account and manage a Twitter stream of interesting, useful tweets before you find people in your field and industry to follow, it is much easier to attract an audience than if you find and follow people before you have something to offer them. In the same way that you wouldn't expect people you don't know to take the time to attend a party at your home, you cannot expect people on Twitter to decide to follow you before they know what you offer. While some people do automatically follow back, plan to build your following by being someone with something interesting to say.

Connect

If increasing your number of Twitter followers is a goal, after you focus on providing quality content, make an effort to help your target audience notice you. The best way to do this is to join conversations, to retweet things (with your comments added) from people you admire, and to visit and comment on their blogs (if they blog). Following these steps will help ensure that people you want to know, and follow, will notice you.

Create Lists

While it does not mean people will follow you, creating and curating lists in Twitter is one way to reach out to users you admire. In Twitter's top toolbar, click on the gear icon and select "Lists." Select the "Create lists" button. Create a name for your list; for example, "Architecture Experts," "Business Leaders," or "HR Pros."

Name your public list in a way that makes it clear what people are tweeting about and compliments members. Then follow Twitter's steps to add people to the list, either with the search tool or by typing a Twitter name (for example @Keppie_Careers) into the field.

While this method is not as direct as sending messages to people you admire on Twitter, getting involved in conversations, and retweeting, it is always flattering to be on a list, and it is another way to try to grow your Twitter community.

Save a Search

In addition to using lists, you may want to conduct searches to save and refer back to later. Twitter allows you to do this easily. Just type keywords into the search field relevant to your interests, like "HR" or "emotional intelligence." Then, save the search by clicking the gear icon and "Save Search." Just click the search toolbar to review a saved search whenever you want. This is a great way to track and keep up with ideas, conferences, and information that is useful for you. It also helps you find great information to pass along to your Twitter followers.

#FollowFriday

A Twitter tradition that seems to persist, despite the fact that many claim to dislike it, is #FollowFriday or #FF. This is when many Twitter users take the opportunity to share lists of people they believe their followers should be following. #FollowFriday lists may include a list of Twitter names with another hashtag, used to indicate why you might want to follow these people, or it may actually be personal endorsements of individuals.

No matter what you think of this tradition, it is a nice gesture to mention and recommend someone to your community (even if your community is very small). If you are interested in attracting a particular follower, you may want to consider a personal #FollowFriday recommendation. For example:

- #FollowFriday @valueintowords because she offers top-tier career and resume advice and regularly shares ideas for #jobseekers.
- #FollowFriday @lruettimann because she tells it like it is for #jobseekers while offering great advice and stories to keep you laughing.
- #FollowFriday @smartbrief for interesting tidbits and news you need to know.

These tweets will go into the target's mentions. If these contacts were not already following you, these types of tweets may result in reciprocal follows.

Learn About (Or Run) Twitter Chats

Twitter chats are a good way to connect with others who tweet in your niche. Rich DeMatteo, co-founder of Bad Rhino, Inc, a social media marketing firm, also runs CornOnTheJob.com, a job search, recruiting, and HR blog. Find him on Twitter @CornOnTheJob, where he co-moderates #JobHuntChat, a Twitter chat for job seekers that is over three years old. Rich offers the following advice for anyone considering starting a Twitter chat, and explains how chats benefit Twitter users:

> *"I won't lie. Running a Twitter chat isn't easy; it is a large commitment. It requires tons of planning, scheduling, and collaboration with co-moderators, and chats require you to reinvent your product on a weekly, bi-weekly, or monthly basis. So why do it?*
>
> *Running a Twitter Chat allows you to push your brand in whatever direction you'd like. What do you want people to know about you? What expertise do you hope to portray? Are you a social media savvy golf enthusiast? Great, start #GolfChat on Tuesday nights and talk about Tiger Woods, 9 irons, and golf carts. Make it yours, champ, it's your chat. See where I'm going?*

I run a blog called Corn on the Job. It's a place for job seekers to come hang out, learn about the job search, and be part of a community. I started #JobHuntChat, the very first job search focused chat on Twitter, to support and enhance my brand and reputation.

Every Monday night at 10 ET, Jessica Miller-Merrill (@Blogging4Jobs) and I co-moderate #JobHuntChat. We both work in the HR/Recruiting industry, so our involvement in #JobHuntChat boosts our brand significantly. We've built up our community, and we've witnessed many participants benefit from their participation. For example:

'Finding #JobHuntChat catapulted me into the world of online networking. As a college senior, I'd barely built up a network, and had zero connections in the industries I was interested in. #Jobhuntchat—along with its amazing moderators and participants—taught me that it was imperative for me to put myself out there, both in person and online. Connections I've made with people online and at networking events have led to great relationships and multiple job offers!"

—LINDSAY GOLDNER, @linzlovesyou

"Through #JobHuntChat, I was able to utilize the power of the chat and actually obtain an internship! Three months later, it's going strong and I have been able to build up my own network and influence. This has given me the opportunity to work with non-profits and recruiters, in the hopes of finding a long-term job in social media and marketing. I was also named the new co-moderator of a generational chat, #genychat."

—BLAKE MCCAMMON, @rblake

"The beauty of #JobHuntChat is its simplicity: question, interact, learn, network . . . You get back what you put in."

—STEVE LEVY, @levyrecruits

If you want to start a chat, these are my suggestions:

- *Pick a subject you love and know a lot about. Remember, it's your brand and you'll be seen as an expert on the topic.*
- *Read David Spinks' (@davidspinks) guide:* How To Start and Run a Successful Twitter Chat. *It was my bible when creating #JobHuntChat (link provided in the Appendix).*
- *Find one or more co-moderators. You'll lean on each other more than you think.*
- *Don't get frustrated if the number of participants is lower than you expected. You'll have high points and low points.*
- *Have fun with it and get creative. With so many people on Twitter, similar chats will always come up. Each individual chat should be innovative, to keep the community engaged.*

How to Connect With Targeted Tweeters

The most important thing you will do on Twitter is connect with and meet new people. For someone new to social media interactions, it can be awkward to finesse these introductions. When you are new to the medium, it is hard to know when it is appropriate to reach out to introduce yourself.

J. T. O'Donnell is a nationally syndicated author, career expert, and founder of the popular career advice blog, CAREEREALISM.com. She explains how to use Twitter's powerful resources to reach people you might not be able to connect with otherwise—and why it might actually be easier to touch base with your targeted mentors via Twitter:

"Because interactions are limited to only 140 characters, Twitter enables people to engage on a simplified level—an attractive option for busy professionals. If you want to meet someone in your industry that you feel might be difficult to reach, Twitter

may be your answer! Here are four steps for successfully connect-ing with professionals on Twitter:

1. *Find the top players in your industry and start following their Twitter feeds. Create a list in Twitter to monitor the tweets of this group. By checking their tweets daily, you'll learn a lot more about what the thought-leaders of your industry are thinking!*

2. *Re-tweet the best tweets from the list. This will bring your feed to the attention of these industry players, because they will see that you mention them. Re-tweeting is a sign of respect and it is greatly appreciated. Over time, your Twitter feed will be memorable to them, since you will have likely re-tweeted their ideas several times.*

3. *After a week or two of following and re-tweeting industry experts, they may choose to follow you back; when this hap-pens, you will be able to send the individual a private tweet via the Direct Messaging option. If they don't follow you, it's okay to ask a question via an @ message (use a Twitter name in the message)—just be sure it's a good question! For example, if someone tweeted about a new product/service/ idea in your industry, ask their thoughts about it. Offer your opinion as well. Begin a simple dialog. That is the beauty of Twitter. Someone is more likely to respond since it only takes 140 characters to do so!*

4. *After a few dialogs, you can ask to take the conversation off-line. For example, you could see if the individual would be willing to connect with you on LinkedIn. Once connected, you can send more lengthy e-mails and even request an informational conversation.*

Remember: Not everyone will opt to connect with you. But if you follow these steps, you will increase the chances that they will. The key is to be articulate and patient. Establishing a rapport with top profes-sionals means making an effort to gain their respect."

Using Twitter to Hire People

More and more companies are turning to Twitter to source candidates. In Chapter 1, I mentioned several services that share job postings through Twitter feeds. Searching #job on Twitter will always yield many results, so it is clearly a venue for sharing hiring opportunities. The Jobvite 2012 survey says 54% of recruiters use Twitter to source hires, and 42% of job seekers who used social media to find jobs said Twitter helped them.

Samuel Dergel, formerly of CFO2Grow (www.cfo2grow.com), responded to my tweet asking for people who use Twitter to hire in fields not traditionally associated with Twitter. He responded to the following questions:

What type of people are you seeking?

"We look for financial executives and professionals for our clients. Our clients give us the mandate to fill their important financial roles—CFOs and their teams."

How do you leverage Twitter to find people?

"At CFO2Grow, we believe in relationship recruiting. This means that building relationships with candidates allows us to be the preferred recruiter for people in our niche.

Twitter, for us, is a part of our Web and social media strategy, for staying on the minds of forward-thinking finance professionals. Twitter is a key part of our relationship building process. We have made placements through Twitter by:

- *Being referred candidates*
- *Candidates following us on Twitter who said, 'Hey, I could be good for that role'*
- *Getting clients and mandates from followers and referrals from Twitter*

We expect Twitter to become an even larger resource for us as its popularity continues to grow within our niche."

How can candidates connect and find you?

"We aim for our audience to be:

- *CFOs*
- *People who want to become CFOs*
- *People that hire CFOs*

Many of our tweets are aimed at these audiences by using the hashtag #CFO as much as possible. Our goal for our Twitter stream is to be relevant to our audience."

What do you look for?

"We look for the following:

- *Referrals from our network*
- *Finance people with something relevant to say."*

What helps people stand out on Twitter?

'In our niche, if people are tweeting and willing to put their opinions out there, we see them as progressive. Finance people will usually not be as outgoing as marketing people—so if they are Tweeting, believe they have value in what they have to say, and are not afraid of being visible, they will stand out. Our clients are looking for these rare financial executives.'"

Useful Data From Twitter

Check out "Twitter Ads" under the gear icon. Sign in and then choose "Analytics" from the top toolbar. You can view some interesting data about your tweets, such as how many people are seeing and retweeting them as well as details about your followers.

Twitter Gets the Word Out

Daniell Morrisey is a career writer and coach. He notes that he uses Twitter as one of his recruitment tools—both for general callouts and specific roles. He says, "I have found it really useful for quickly getting a message out to market. The beauty of Twitter is that people send the message on, so you quickly can target a wide community in your field. I've found many talented individuals through this and other social networking."

How Twitter Helps Find Jobs

Members of mainstream media often contact me to ask for my expertise about how using social media can help job seekers. When I review the quotes I share with them, there is often a common theme: Twitter (and other social media) does not automatically win people jobs. It is important to manage your expectations. Twitter is not a magic job wand. I tell my clients that Twitter is not about finding a job; rather, it is about demonstrating expertise, and creating and managing the relationships that may lead to job opportunities.

It takes time and effort to build the online relationships and spheres of influence that could help carry you to your next job offer. The more people who learn about you and know what you have to offer, the more likely you are to be successful.

It is your job to hone your skills, via internships (even for more senior professionals), volunteer work, and by managing your career to include opportunities to improve your skills. While I believe that being able to use Twitter and social media effectively demonstrates an important skill set, the most important thing you can do to improve your chances of getting a job is to be good at what you do.

Things to Remember

There is a lot to say about Twitter. There is a lot of information, and many ins and outs to this network. I hope the stories, testimonials, and advice provided from my Twitter friends are good enough reasons to consider making Twitter a part of your toolkit. Almost every expert opinion in this book is from someone I would likely not have known if I had not used Twitter! I hope these stories and experiences will resonate with you.

Keep in mind that if you choose to tweet, Twitter is also about you, and what type of image you want to project. There are no firm rules, only guidelines. Don't let anyone tell you how often to tweet, how much time to spend tweeting, or what percentage of your tweets should be personal or professional. Use the information in this book, what you see other people doing on Twitter, and your own professional instincts to guide your networking.

You will get out of Twitter what you put into it. Don't hesitate to tweet me @Keppie_Careers if you have a question I did not answer in this book.

Making the Most of Facebook

ne lesson I hope that everyone takes away from this book:

"Don't underestimate the capacity of any social networking tool to impact your job search and career plans."

JOB SEEKERS CAN USE FACEBOOK

It seems contradictory to suggest that Facebook, a clearly personal network better known for helping people lose their jobs than find work, can actually be useful to job seekers. In a recent conversation with an organization that was planning to hire me to speak to their students, I mentioned including material about social networks in my talk. My contact immediately assumed that the information would be about what not to do on Facebook if you are looking for a job.

There is so much press about people being fired due to Facebook that it is easy to see how many people could overlook opportunities inherent in leveraging this social network. After all, this is a network aimed primarily

continued from page 217

at having fun, sharing vacation pictures and photos of your kids or parties, waxing eloquent about random, frivolous topics, describing musical interests, and playing video games. Facebook does not seem like a network you would consider as a go-to job-search aid. However, you may want to rethink this.

Why Should You Care About Facebook?

Facebook is the largest social network, with more than 1 billion active users as of this writing. Its members, if they were a country, would be the third largest, behind only China and India. Members can post photos, links to outside sites, and share news and status updates with those they have elected to allow join their communities.

Why Use a Social Network for Professional Purposes?

Research shows that up to 80 percent of firms locate their hires via personal referrals from employees. A report from CareerXRoads, a consulting practice that studies recruiting technology solutions, shows that nearly half of all companies hire one of every five refer-errals. *As Time* magazine notes, "The difference today is that a lot more of those recommendations start with connections made through online networks." Based on this data, it is easy to make a case for using social networks to expand your connections. Throughout the book, I share stories from people who have benefitted from the kindness and generosity of complete strangers. Facebook plays a unique role in the networking puzzle because you have a tendency to connect there with people who actually know you (or people who "knew you when").

Keith Ferrazzi wrote a book about networking and the power of connecting, called *Who's Got Your Back?* (Broadway Books, 2009). In it, he describes the concept of having *lifelines*, or people who are there to help you. These people are invested in you and your success—they're the ones who have your back.

While he suggests having a few lifelines, the concept easily translates to a larger network. The people with whom you share a history or a childhood (those you may find on Facebook) are likely willing to go to bat for you when you need it. If you can create a profile on Facebook that connects you to a group of people who think of you fondly and wish you well, it is definitely worth the time and effort.

Joining Facebook provides access to potentially millions of contacts and opportunities, to share information with people from all over the world. On the other hand, the types of activity these sites invite, including sharing highly personal and sometimes publicly inappropriate information, has been known to get people in trouble professionally. Jobvite's research says 66% of recruiters use Facebook to recruit.

The survey shows:

- 80% of recruiters reacted positively to evidence of memberships in professional organizations, while two-thirds like to see volunteering or donating to a nonprofit.
- Content that recruiters especially frown on includes references to using illegal drugs (78% negative) and posts of a sexual nature (67% negative).
- Profanity in posts and tweets garnered a 61% negative reaction, and almost half (47%) reacted negatively to posts about alcohol consumption.
- Worse than drinking, grammar or spelling mistakes on social profiles saw a 54% negative reaction.
- However, recruiters and hiring managers tend to be neutral in their reactions to political opinions (62% neutral) and religious posts (53% neutral).

If you follow some very basic guidelines when creating your profile, and maintain a professional page, I recommend considering becoming one of the more than 1 billion (and counting) active Facebook users.

Your Professional Profile

It's easy to create a free profile. Just visit www.facebook.com and sign up with an e-mail address and password. You must include your date of birth to verify your age, but you will be able to hide this information once you have a profile. Once you verify your e-mail address by clicking the link that Facebook will send you, it directs you to go through some steps to find friends via your e-mail contacts. It is up to you whether or not you want to do that right away, but, as with Twitter, I would suggest waiting until you complete your profile.

Fill out the "Info" page with complete details about your educational and work history. You will want this information to remain public for everyone to see. As you are filling in your profile, decide which other details you want to share. For example, you may not wish to share political and religious views.

Do not feel compelled to fill in all of your music, movie, and personal interests. If you do include this information, try to think of it from the perspective of someone who might want to hire you. If you are applying for a daycare or teaching position, it may be detrimental for a potential employer to learn you favor very violent or otherwise potentially offensive music. Even though you can adjust privacy settings, do not consider anything in your profile private, as any of your friends may share information from your profile with someone you would rather not know it.

⇢ TIP

As a rule of thumb, consider everything you post on Facebook to be public information, for everyone to see, read, and share.

Privacy

Facebook makes regular changes to their privacy settings. Review your settings regularly, to be sure things are set to your satisfaction. To set and monitor what people can find out about you, click on the "gear" icon and "Privacy Settings." This will take you to a page where you can identify who will be able to access the information you share. You can adjust your settings any time.

You can choose who sees your posts:

- Public friends
- Friends of friends
- Friends except acquaintances
- Friends only
- Only me
- Custom
- Other

The "Customize" feature allows for additional choices. This gives you the chance to identify individuals in your list of friends who will not be able to see your update. For example, you could post something about a surprise party and exclude the guest of honor. These detailed selections may be useful, but always keep in mind that you should never post anything that would result in negative ramifications. For example, in theory, you could complain about your boss, but exclude everyone who works with you from seeing the post. But it still is not a good idea to use a social network to complain about work. As a rule: *If you need to go to extreme efforts to cull your list of friends before sharing an update, take that as a sign that you should not post it.*

Click through all of the various settings on the left side of your screen, such as "General," "Notifications," "Security," and "Mobile."

Read the choices carefully and be sure to choose the privacy and security selections that make the most sense for you.

Be aware, no matter what settings you use, certain information is visible to everyone:

- Your name and profile picture, which will also appear if you write on someone's wall
- Your gender
- If you select to be a member of a network (for example, University of Arizona)
- Your hometown and interests
- You can view your profile as someone else will see it if you'd like to double check your settings and evaluate what people who do not know you can or cannot see.
  - Click the Privacy Shortcut Button (it's on the top Facebook toolbar, to the right of the home button and looks like a lock).
  - Click "Who Can See My Stuff?"
  - Click "View As." You will be able to see how the public or a particular person sees your Facebook profile and content.

Edit Your Profile

Upload a picture. You can select one from you computer (up to 4MB in size). If you have a recent professional picture, use it and be consistent with photos on other sites, such as LinkedIn. If you do not have a professional picture, take a nice, basic photo of you alone. Ideally, it would be helpful to be able to see your face, and you should consider a friendly looking picture. Many people include pictures of their friends or children in their profile pictures, but when you are using Facebook to help you professionally, it is best to use a current picture of just you. You should also upload a photo to headline your Facebook timeline. This picture appears at the top of your Facebook page and is quite large.

Fill in the various sections as necessary, with a specific focus on Work and Education. Make sure the information (degrees, dates, etc.) that you share on Facebook matches what you share on your resume and other online profiles. Complete the "About You" and include professional information.

> **⇨ TIP**
>
> Synchronize your various social networking profiles. You want to tell the same story in each place. It's okay to show more of your personal, fun side on Facebook, but be sure you are still painting a picture of a professional that will appeal to anyone who might want to hire you.
>
> Be sure you receive Facebook notifications at an e-mail address you regularly read.

Find Friends

Once your profile is filled out completely, you'll want to add friends. You can search for friends in a variety of ways.

One way is by typing their names or email addresses in the search bar at the top of any Facebook page. Facebook notes, "If you don't see the person you're looking for, you can filter your search results." They instruct:

1. Type in the name of a friend in the search bar
2. Click the "See more results . . ." link at the bottom of the dropdown
3. Click "People" from the Search Filters menu on the right
4. Use the filter dropdown menu to filter your search results by location, education, or workplace, or add another filter option (for example, searching for your hometown will show you all of the people who have that town listed on their account as well)

You can also type "find friends" in the top search bar on Facebook and review the selections. Once you have a list of friends, Facebook will suggest contacts based on your mutual contacts.

Facebook allows you to easily invite your personal contacts from your email account or Skype, for example, from the "find friends" landing page. Facebook says you'll have the option to send a friend request to any of your friends that already have a Facebook account; however, I usually avoid taking advantage of this option due to concerns that the system may decide to email people I do not really want in my network.

Of course, you can also invite friends individually by looking up their names in the top toolbar and requesting to be friends. Facebook's search, known as a "social graph," makes it very easy to identify people to add as friends. For example, you can type a query such as, "People who went to my high school and graduated in 2009" (assuming you listed your high school and they did, too) and Facebook will provide those results. You can ask Facebook any specific search question by typing it in the top search bar. Another example, "People who work at IBM and live in Atlanta." Of course, Facebook will only be able to provide results from public information in their bios, but the search options are endless!

When you decide to ask for someone to be your friend on Facebook, you have an opportunity to write a brief note. As with LinkedIn, explain why you'd like to connect if it would not be obvious to the recipient.

⇨ TIP

Don't forget that people will be able to see information from your contacts, so choose your friends with care. Consider the adage "guilt by association" to be true. If your friends' profiles are full of profanity and drunken photos, you may wish to distance yourself.

Updating Your Status

Once you have a profile, you'll want to say something smart! If you connect to a number of friends, you will probably notice that status updates run the gamut. Some people will tell you what they are making for dinner, comment that it is really hot outside, or that their car broke down. Others share a link to an interesting story or news item and make a comment about it.

It is pretty easy to get the hang of posting. Next to the button that says POST, you should see a drop-down option to help you choose the privacy status of your post. What you see will depend on how you set up your privacy settings, but be sure to make a point to check it before each status update.

How to Leverage Facebook Status Updates for Professional Reasons

If you want to really leverage Facebook for professional reasons, set a Google alert for keywords important to your field or industry. For example, if you are an educator, set a Google alert for {education, reform}. When you receive e-mails with links to stories pertaining to education reform, read them, share the links, and comment on your page. This is a great way to demonstrate your expertise and present a strong, professional presence on Facebook. (You may also want to share this type of information on Twitter, which you can do if you synch your accounts.)

You have a few options on Facebook to keep your personal and professional updates separate. One is to create a Facebook page, as noted above. Typically, businesses or brands use pages to promote themselves, but you can choose to identify yourself as a "public figure" and have a page. Note that you will not have the same flexibility as you do in your personal profile when using your page.

Another option is to allow people to "follow you" on Facebook. These people are not technically your Facebook friends, but they subscribe to your public updates by clicking a follow button on your timeline page. Facebook explains, "When you allow people to follow you, anyone can follow you to get your public updates in their news feed, even if you're not friends on Facebook. You can have an unlimited amount of people following you, and you can follow as many as 5,000 people. You can have 5,000 friends on your personal account." If you'd like to offer people the option to receive your public updates, follow these steps:

1. Click the gear icon in the top-right of your screen
2. Select "Account Settings"
3. Click "Followers" on the left side
4. Check the box next to "Allow Followers"

Facebook notes that you can only allow people to follow you if you are 18 or older.

⮑ TIP

Another option to make sure people will notice your updates is to use hashtags on Facebook. Hashtags, which are indicated by a # sign (for example, #Job for a job posting), are searchable on Facebook. However, if you post a hashtag in an update for friends only, it will not be searchable beyond your friends list. This is why it may be helpful to create public updates and include hashtags in them. See Chapter 9 for more information about hashtags.

Etiquette for a Professional Profile

Whenever you plan to use social networks for professional purposes, it is important to follow some guidelines. Here are some to consider when developing a professional/social online presence:

- Even though you can see all of your friends' friends, don't reach out to them unless there is a specific reason for doing so. It is okay to ask mutual connections if they would broker an introduction. Making these connections is a lot less formal than via LinkedIn, for example, but certainly possible.
- Remember to personalize your invitations.

HOW TO CREATE AND MAINTAIN A PROFESSIONAL PROFILE IN FACEBOOK

Chris Perry is a brand and marketing generator, entrepreneur, career search and personal branding expert, and founder of Career-Rocketeer.com. These are his suggestions for creating and maintaining a professional Facebook presence:

- **Plug your personal brand.** Prominently highlight your personal brand and supporting pitch or statement on your Facebook profile to help communicate and reinforce your brand to current friends and attract new friends and prospective employers.
- **Professionalize your profile.** Keep your profile updated with your current activities and contact info. Include multiple website addresses such as your LinkedIn profile, Twitter and Google+ accounts, blog, and other online brand-building efforts in your bio, so that your network can easily access them.
- **Help your network help you.** Let your network of friends and family know that you are seeking new opportunities via your status updates or by posting messages. Not only do they know you best and can attest to your strengths and skills, but your friends and family should be interested in helping you.
- **Claim your domain.** Make it easy for others to find your profile, and for you to refer professionals to your profile, by claiming your own domain name on Facebook, if available (e.g., http://www.facebook.com/johnsmith). To claim your name, log in to your Facebook account, and then visit http://www.facebook.com/username.
- **Be a resource.** Don't just use your status updates for personal statements or comments. Share professional resources (articles, websites, book reviews, etc.), to show you not only have expertise, but that you generously share your skills and knowledge.
- **Engage others.** Go beyond one-way communication with status updates. Be sure to initiate and maintain consistent dialogue with your Facebook friends and network. This will encourage others to interact more often with you, as well as to share your updates or resources with others, inevitably increasing your visibility and opportunities to network.

continued from page 227

- **Separate your work life from your social life.** If you don't want recruiters to see your personal profile, limit external visibility to your profile and consider starting a public Facebook page. You can do this by logging into your Facebook account, visiting http://www.facebook.com/pages/, and clicking the "Create a Page" button. A public Facebook page (you can choose "Public Figure" as your category) can be similar to a personal profile, but allows you to introduce yourself to employers and recruiters before a phone or in-person interview ever takes place. Photos of you in professional attire and even videos in which you are talking about your experience or career objectives can help convince others of your qualifications.

- Avoid taking a lot of Facebook quizzes, such as "What superhero are you?," and don't plan to join groups that might cause a hiring manager to reconsider your professionalism or suitability (for example, "I hate people, but love dogs"). Even if you have privacy settings, that is no guarantee of real privacy.
- If you link your various networks (for example, Facebook and Twitter), be careful about your updates. You do not want to overextend your welcome on your Facebook friends' feeds if every Twitter update you make is posted to your wall. If someone hides you (by rolling the curser over your update and selecting "Hide"), you won't have an opportunity to touch base with that person via passive updates. Don't ruin the opportunity to reach out to casual friends and contacts.
- Don't use the "Events" option to try to sell things, or to invite out-of-town friends to events they are unlikely to attend. This seems very spammy.
- Limit inviting friends to "Like" or join causes to those that are really important to you.
- Share photos that demonstrate a professional demeanor. Pictures of you in a bikini, with a lampshade over your head, or at events that you wouldn't want your boss to know you attended, are best left off.

ENHANCE YOUR CAREER VIA FACEBOOK

Alexis Grant is the owner of Socialexis, where she coaches small businesses and organizations about how to use social media. She suggests the following tips for successfully leveraging Facebook for job hunting and career enhancing purposes:

- While Facebook is for fun, every one of your friends could be the connection or provide the lead you need to get a job. Don't overlook the value of your friends, even if you know them personally and not professionally.
- One benefit of Facebook, compared to some other social networking sites like Twitter, is that you probably know all of your friends personally. They like you, and probably have a stake in helping you get a job. They want to help you—so let them.
- While you may not be comfortable e-mailing friends you have been out of touch with over the years to ask them to help with your job hunt, it is easier to communicate with them through Facebook for career advice and assistance.

- Be aware of your status updates and how they may make you appear. For example, if you review your updates and 75 percent of them involve complaining, take note. Don't feel compelled to tell your network how tired you are on a regular basis. Do an audit of your own profile, and make sure your updates portray you positively and professionally.

Find Groups to Join

In the top search field, type "Groups." It will provide results of open groups you can join. However, you can also refine your search by using the search fields on the right of your screen. For example, add a name to your search, such as "paralegal," to find groups related to that profession. You'll see some groups are "closed," but others are open and available to join. In Chapter 7, I suggested including personal interests and hobbies in the groups you considered joining through LinkedIn. You may remember there was a large skydiving group. A search for skydiving in Facebook yields many specialized groups. That certainly boosts your networking options.

On the other hand, Facebook has many groups that might provide networking options, but would not be very flattering on your profile. For example, *I Hate Mondays* would not be a good choice. Remember, keep your profile clean and focused on telling a professional story.

Liking Companies

Jenny DeVaughn, a senior director, employment branding and social media expert at Randstad Sourceright, notes the following:

Career pages may give candidates insights into the company's culture and events like career fairs. You may also find that a former colleague or co-worker is employed with that organization for an employee referral.

When you like a company on Facebook, the administrator of the page is able to view that you have liked it and can click to see the public information available on your profile. When you post information to the company page, it is also publicly shared for others to read. Also, when you mention a company name in your status, it is displayed as a related post to the community page of that organization.

Facebook is actively monitored by recruiters and hiring managers alike. Even though it should not be used as a tool for background checks or candidate screening, job seekers and professionals should be aware of the pitfalls that exist from sharing information, photos, or videos on Facebook. Everyone should use caution and good judgment before clicking the 'Like' button on the web or within Facebook, since you are publicly approving of that brand and the content it displays."

FROM THE OTHER SIDE OF THE HIRING DESK—A RECRUITER'S PERSPECTIVE

David Cherry is Senior Recruitment Business Partner, for McAfee, Inc., and co-creator of McAfee Careers' Facebook page. I posed the following questions to David about what job seekers should expect from the Facebook experience, and what the company hopes to gain by having a Facebook presence.

What tips and suggestions do you have to help job seekers take advantage of the opportunity to connect on Facebook?

"Be interactive, don't just visit a page and leave; if you like it, become a fan. Leave comments, ask questions—actually engage with the company. Use the discussion forums to recommend suggestions about what you would like to see on the pages. The most common thing I try to encourage is feedback, as the page will never evolve without user feedback."

What are you looking for from applicants?

"Facebook is part of our social media strategy, along with Twitter, YouTube, Digg, etc. . . . we try to not just list a constant stream of open positions, but to also offer tips, career advice, interview techniques, and explain what applicants can expect during the interview process. We want to offer insight into what it is like to work at McAfee, a chance for potential employees to interact with people who work at McAfee, and the opportunity to learn about the culture of the company.

As a user visiting our page, there isn't a set guideline about what we expect; the user should drive it and we can then respond according their needs. Key advice: Don't be afraid to ask questions. It may be a corporate username, but we're real people at the other end, answering questions and writing the comments."

Is there something that a Facebook contact can do that would help him or her advance in the application process?

"They could mention in their application that they came to us through Facebook. We monitor the page around the globe, and with several members of the Global Talent Acquisition Team,

continued from page 231

uploading content and responding to questions. Everyone that we invite for an interview is given the same opportunity. All I would say is that those who have visited the page will gain more information on the company, and may be more prepared for their interviews than those who do not."

What should job seekers avoid? What, if anything, would prevent you from hiring someone based on Facebook profiles?

"Don't openly criticize the company where they want to work! Realize that depending on the question you ask, you may not get an immediate response; sometimes we have to find the right information internally before responding. Like Twitter, comment and ask questions, but not every 10 minutes. Give the team time to digest questions and respond.

I don't believe there is a situation where we wouldn't hire someone from looking at a Facebook profile, and we wouldn't use a Facebook profile as part of a selection process or as a decision-making tool."

Do you have any good stories to share?

"We have had some success with Facebook, and currently have several people going through interviews who contacted us through Facebook, which is great news!

We have had some great conversations and feedback on the content we're posting, which is nice to see, especially when it's not all about recruitment. The other day, we had someone ask our advice about a training company he was planning to pay for McAfee training; we can advise about a lot of different topics."

Why is your company on Facebook? What is your goal in adding that to your recruiting arsenal?

"The end goal and strategy is to encourage and drive traffic to our careers page (www.mcafee.com/careers/default.html), so we receive more applications. Alongside this (and something I believe is just as powerful), it's important to give people information about our culture, promote our brand as a great company to work for, and to give job seekers the opportunity to speak to someone in a more casual environment."

What Not to Do On Facebook

It is common to hear stories about people who have lost their jobs as a result of something posted online. Typically, the offending social networker uses Facebook to complain or share a gripe, which gets passed along to an employer.

Fired For Complaining About Customers

The Charlotte Observer reported the story of a waitress at a North Carolina pizzeria, who was fired after posting a derogatory message disparaging a couple who stayed in the restaurant for three hours, which required her to stay an hour beyond her normal quitting time, and only tipped $5. While the *Observer* reports that she did not name the customers, she clearly named the restaurant, which led to her bosses firing her for presenting the restaurant in a negative way.

Fired For Conflicting Religious Beliefs

The *Gazette Online* reported that a teacher in a Catholic school in Fort Dodge, Iowa, was fired after she responded to a Facebook survey indicating that she did not believe in God. The story also reports that she commented in an atheist online discussion forum. Her suggestion that "taxpayers have a right to their opinions" and "these beliefs may change" did not convince the school where she worked to rehire her.

Fired for Saying Work is Boring

A teenager working in Clacton, Essex, was fired for posting that work was boring on her Facebook page. The Telegraph.co.uk reports that her employers were not impressed with her defense that all administrative work is boring, and it would have gotten more interesting.

Fired for Inappropriate Jokes

The Courthousenews.com reports the city of West Allis, Wisconsin, fired a police and fire department dispatcher. The 21-year veteran dispatcher commented on her Facebook page that she was addicted to "vicodin, adderall, and quality marijuana." The report goes on to explain that drug tests were negative, and the employee claims she had been joking and included "ha" in her post. The city noted, "Making stupid jokes on Facebook, where the line between public and private communications is admittedly blurred, calls into question the good judgment and common sense of the grievant, and her resulting ability to perform her job."

Stand Out Via Facebook

If a target company maintains an active page, visit frequently and comment often. Your best bet is to demonstrate your interest and passion for its brand, and don't hesitate to offer suggestions and advice related to your expertise.

A few Don'ts to keep in mind:

- Don't post questions that you could easily answer via your own research. Use questions to inquire about opinions or suggestions unique to the people responding on the company's career page.
- Don't forget to build your own brand by sharing what you know on the company's Facebook page. You may get noticed!
- Don't make your work and content information private on Facebook. If an employer is impressed with you, it should be easy to contact you online.

Kerry Noone is the former Senior Marketing Manager at Sodexo, a food and facilities management company with employees worldwide. I questioned her about her company's Facebook recruiting approach and for advice for job seekers.

I have been on several Facebook company recruiting sites, and have seen a lot of job seekers asking things that they could easily find out. How can candidates leverage the opportunity to interact on Facebook?

"If you look at the Sodexo Careers Facebook page, you will see candidates who ask if there are "open jobs in Raleigh, NC " (as an example) and our response is always the same. We provide them with a direct link where they can search open positions at Sodexo, and we offer to connect them with the right recruiter if they decide to apply for a job. It is encouraging when candidates proactively post on their walls that they have applied for jobs and ask for help connecting with the right recruiters.

These candidates obviously have taken time to read past conversations on our Facebook page. These candidates are also more likely going to come to an interview prepared, because they invested the time to learn more about the company culture, mission, and values.

You will also notice on our page that there are many Sodexo recruiters responding to candidates, and not just me as the voice of Sodexo careers. This is not by accident. Our goal is to be appropriately responsive. If a student is interested in our internship program, the manager who leads our internship program will respond to the comment on the wall. Similarly, if a registered dietitian is interested in a position at Sodexo, someone on our clinical recruiting team will respond."

I don't see a lot of brand building or networking on the part of job seekers. Do job seekers tend to use this for networking? If so, can you comment on how it might help a candidate? In general, what tips and suggestions do you have to help job seekers take advantage of the opportunity to connect on Facebook?

continued from page 235

"My advice to candidates is to take advantage of the personal branding opportunities that social networking sites like Facebook provide. By communicating your personal brand with consistency, and including links to other online profiles, like LinkedIn, Twitter, and a Google profile, you will be more likely to catch the attention of recruiters and hiring managers who will recognize you as a strong candidate.

After you have thoroughly completed your profile, you are in a better position to search for companies, people, and professional groups, to connect with and build your professional network. Once you have connected, spend time reading the discussions on their Facebook wall.

When you are ready to contribute to the discussions, be sure the information is relevant. You can learn a lot about a company by reading the discussions on their Facebook wall, including the company's culture and hiring process, and who the key decisions makers are. You never know who you are going to connect with and who will be able to help you get hired, so don't be afraid to reach out and make personal connections.

Trish Freshwater is a great example of a person we hired through Twitter and LinkedIn. Trish found a job she wanted to apply for at Sodexo through www.indeed.com, and she spent time researching the company and connecting with current employees on our many different social networks."

It's impressive on your site how many replies to direct questions the job seekers get. Is this a main reason for having the Facebook page? What do you see as the biggest advantage—for the job seeker and the recruiter—for having Facebook as a recruiting platform?

"One of our social media goals is to improve our candidate experience, because we know that a positive candidate experience will have a direct impact on our brand. We want candidates to learn more about our company culture, and part of our company culture is to care about our past, present, and future employees.

One way we achieve this is by being responsive. We address every wall post or discussion question, because we want potential candidates to know there are real people ready to help them in

continued from page 236

their Sodexo job search. We've also made a conscious decision to allow virtually any discussion, positive or negative, as long as it isn't offensive and is related to the culture and experience of working for Sodexo.

If we are not able to answer a question or comment from a candidate, we make sure they are in contact with the appropriate person at Sodexo. As I mentioned, this is a team effort. Our recruiters are responding to their candidates and making personal connections. In turn, our candidates are reaching out to let us know how much they appreciate the access to our recruiters, and how much easier they have found the hiring process with us to be."

Do you (or your colleagues) have any advice for people regarding using Facebook successfully? Of course, clean up your profile, etc., but what about groups to join or ways to use it for searching that are not always published?

"Social networking is mutually beneficial for employers and candidates. It allows both parties time to get to know each other. In addition to improving the candidate experience, it allows the employer an opportunity to share with candidates their culture, and it allows the candidate to connect with real people who can answer their questions.

The easier we make it for candidates to connect with us through social networking sites, the more successful we will be with our social recruiting. Like many companies, Sodexo has a complete social media strategy, which also includes multiple opportunities for a candidate to connect with our recruiters.

We want candidates to reach out to us, which is one of the reasons we created a 'Network With Us' page on our career site. On this page, candidates will find a growing list of 18 social spaces where they can connect with Sodexo recruiters, including Facebook, LinkedIn, Twitter, YouTube, and more. In addition to making the best use of your profile with a consistent and up-to-date personal brand, I recommend taking full advantage of the access a company provides through social networking sites."

WE USE FACEBOOK TO SOURCE HIRES

Raj Singh is director of global staffing at Intersil (www.intersil.com), an international company that designs and manufactures analog integrated circuits. He is also the co-founder of myJoblinx (www.facebook.com/myJoblinx), an application to help companies connect with job seekers via Facebook. Raj explains that at Intersil they have interviewed several people who contacted them first via Facebook.

This is Raj's advice for people who want to gain attention via a company's Facebook site:

If you're an active job seeker willing to publicly announce your search, Raj suggests that "before you apply for a position, go to the company's Facebook wall and engage with the company. You can say you are looking for a job. But be specific. For example:

> Hello! I am a _____, and I am very interested in the _____ position (req # 1234). Is it possible to speak to someone about this opportunity before I apply?

Raj explains, "By doing that, you distinguish yourself from the majority of people, who will just apply online and go into the database. If a recruiter is alerted about your interest, he or she can actually look for your application, instead of waiting for it to appear in a database search." He also says, "Be sure to be specific with your post. Anyone who does this on the Intersil Facebook page will receive a reply from a recruiter."

If you are a passive job seeker and do not want to announce your intentions to find a new job, Raj suggests a more subtle approach. For example, comment on something posted on the company's page. He remembered one such commentor from a couple of years ago. The person responded to an announcement of a new part for a chip being produced for handheld displays. He said:

> This seems to be a pretty good solution for backlighting issues. Have you ever looked at part #_____ produced by _____. Note: the other part was built by a competitor.

Raj noted, "We were so intrigued that this person was so interested in a very detailed aspect of our work, recruiters looked him up and reached out to ask him to interview. While he was not hired, in other circumstances, he could have landed a job."

Advertise on Facebook

Have you ever considered advertising that you want a job?

Marian Schembari, currently social media manager at Couch-surfing, once ran a Facebook ad campaign that landed her a job as a book publicist. She explains:

> *"It taught me to think outside the box, to be determined, and how to network. I also made a ton of friends and started a blog that is still going strong today, and [the ad is] the whole reason behind my current business."*

Marian labels the campaign, which cost less than $100, a "raging success." She explains on her blog, http://marianlibrarian.com, that she focused on being as targeted as possible when writing her ads. She states:

> *"People are more receptive if they see the name of their employer in big letters in the ad. It's super easy to target them, and the results are much better! If you can't target companies, target the type of industry you want to work in, not the job title, as that can be limiting, and people aren't as drawn to notice an ad with a job title they don't have."*

Marian identified several publishing companies and their employees, including HarperCollins, Random House, Penguin, Rodale, and Macmillan, as recipients of her message. Her ad linked to her website, which provided her resume, references, and work portfolio. She encourages others to create a complete online presence, including work samples, a blog, quotes from employers, and any applicable multimedia. Directing people to a LinkedIn profile is an option, but she does not believe it would carry the same impact as a fully fleshed out, personalized online profile picture: AD: http://marianlibrarian.com/2009/08/13/the-ad/

Marian raves:

"At least one person from every publisher I focused on e-mailed me, to tell me they passed my resume on to HR, to say that they wanted to meet, or even just to say they liked my idea."

Marian and her Facebook campaign have been featured in many publications, including: *Real Simple* magazine, ABCNews.com, Bankrate, and HarperStudio's website, where Debbie Stier, Associate Publisher and Director of Digital Marketing, wrote about Marian:

"The publishing industry desperately needs people with these skills: creative, innovative, risk takers who know how to work the tools of the Internet and aren't afraid to use them."

Marian offers the following tips for anyone considering advertising for a job on Facebook:

- Follow up with everyone who contacts you! Make sure to respond promptly to whatever e-mail they send, and connect with them on LinkedIn and Twitter if you can. This keeps you and your job search fresh in their minds—and that's the most important part of this strategy.
- Remember that while the ads get you noticed, they won't do the hard work for you. You need to be qualified, and have the chops to back up your work. So make sure your website is amazing, you're personable in e-mails, and you have a little patience!
- Job seekers should expect a lot of e-mails saying, "I like your idea! So creative! Not hiring, but I wanted to reach out." This is fine. You've made a contact at a company you want to work for. Make friends! Ask their advice on your resume. Ask if they know any similar companies who are hiring. See if they do informational interviews. Don't stop with just that one e-mail. These ads essentially buy access to relationships,

and you need to really cultivate those for the ads to do their job properly.

Ian Greenleigh, social media manager for Bazarvoice.com who blogs at daretocomment.com, is another former job seeker who landed his job as a result of advertising on Facebook. Unlike Marian, he did not target particular organizations in his ads. Instead, he shared the fact that he had been nominated for an award in his ad, in order to attract interest.

He explained that he ran two campaigns; one saying, "I want to work for you," which garnered 274 clicks from 309,000 impressions (views) at a cost of $125, and another ad asking, "Need sharp talent?," which earned 80 clicks from 168,000 views and cost $50. He received a constant stream of feedback during the month or so that he ran his ads, receiving at least one comment on the blog he linked from the ad or a message every day of the campaign (see his ad, Figure 11.2.).

Ian offers the following advice to job seekers:

> *"It's important to demonstrate that you have the skills you say you have. For me, I was using social media to demonstrate that I would be a good fit for a job in social media. You can use this type of 'social proof' for any job that requires you to show leadership, or to be creative or innovative.*
>
> *It's not important if other job seekers use this technique; people you are targeting probably have not seen an ad like this, so it is likely to get their attention. If you can pair the campaign with a blog, to discuss the process and mention specific company names, it helps attract attention and provides a great place to share additional information about you, as well as engage in two-way conversations with people who have advice or suggestions to help with your search."*

Do you think placing some ads might be a good idea for you? Scroll to the bottom of your Facebook profile and click on

"Advertising." Facebook provides all of the information you need, as well as a webinar about how to optimize your campaign.

Applications and Productivity Tools

Consider taking advantage of some of the following tools:

- **SimplyHired.com**, a job search engine and recruitment advertising network, allows you to easily leverage your Facebook contacts and identify potential job opportunities at companies where your friends work. SimplyHired notes the following:

    "Users who log in with Facebook are able to discover jobs based on their current or previous work titles, locations, interests, and their friends' companies on SimplyHired.com. From the search results page, job seekers will be able to browse friends' companies and search for job openings. This changes job searching from a passive to an active process, by suggesting relevant jobs and helping users tap their friends, to get an inside track on a job."

- **BeKnown**, owned by Monster.com, allows you to create a professional profile and maintain professional contacts on Facebook, yet keep those activities separate from the more social activities that might be happening on your main profile. It is similar in many ways to LinkedIn, but it's a network you build via your Facebook contacts.

- **BranchOut.com**, which offers a news feed and messaging platform designed specifically for career-related activities, allows you to expand your personal connections in Facebook into a professional network.

- **Glassdoor's Inside Connections** helps you identify connections that could link you to jobs by highlighting when you have people in your networks who work at the places where you're interested in applying.

- **FreshTransition.com** organizes every part of your job search, tells you about jobs that fit your needs, reminds you of everything you need to do, and connects to your social networks to suggest specific people who may be able to help with your networking.
- **JackalopeJobs.com** is a platform for jobseekers that allows you to search for relevant jobs, reach out to relevant connections, and stay organized. It helps pull job openings and ranks them relevant to your network via Facebook or LinkedIn profiles.
- **CareerSonar.com** helps candidates discover the most promising job opportunities in their social and professional networks. The social job discovery service lets job seekers easily find their most relevant opportunities: those to which they have strong inside connections who can push their resumes to the top of the stacks.

Things to Remember

I once wrote a blog post suggesting that job seekers take a lesson from my local Target store during back-to-school shopping season. They were marketing deli meat and cheese, but all of the shoppers were in the back of the store picking up notebooks, binders, and pencils. How did they respond? They brought a deli cart full of samples to the school supply section, in an effort to attract customers.

My blog post advised job seekers to take note and "be where they are," referring to employers. When you are in the market for a job, you need to make sure that you put yourself where employers will find you. Facebook, while not intended to be a professional network, is as good a place as any to be where they are. It dwarfs the other networks in size, and provides opportunities to interact that are not available via other networks.

Especially when you are looking for work, you need to take some precautions to ensure that your Facebook profile works in your favor:

- Allow your "Work and Education" and "About You" content (including your bio, where you work or have worked, and information about your educational background) to be available to non-friends. Share your contact information as well. This allows people who are searching for individuals with your expertise to find you. Facebook's social graph search makes it even more important to provide this information as public.
- Recognize that everything in your profile may potentially be public; take precautions and do not share information you don't want everyone to know.
- Connect with friends who are likely to maintain a high level of professionalism and will not post anything inappropriate on your wall. Block users who don't fit your professional standards via "Privacy Settings."
- Post updates that provide useful information and make a point to share updates about your job search, so your Facebook community will know you are looking for opportunities if you are publically looking for work. (If your job search is private, you should not use status updates to alert your network). It's okay to say you are looking for a job in your status and in your profile. Keep people posted, but don't expect that subtle hints will win you a referral.
- Find groups to join and network with people regarding professional and personal interests. Don't be afraid to comment, and share ideas and expertise on peoples' walls and in group discussions. Ask questions. Expand the number of people who have an interest in you.
- Recognize that hiring managers at many companies are spending a lot of time, money, and effort to create presences on Facebook to interact with applicants. Demonstrate why you are a strong candidate via updates on their pages.
- Keep your controversial beliefs to yourself or risk alienating someone who may otherwise hire you (unless you would not

want to work with someone who does not appreciate your beliefs, in which case, take your chances).

- Keep an eye out for applications and productivity tools that use Facebook to help connect you with potential opportunities.

When you create a professional and focused Facebook profile, you open up a world of new prospects.

How Using Google+ Can Fuel Your Job Search

Google+ is the network most job seekers ignore. In some ways, it is similar to Facebook because it allows you to follow people's updates, write lengthy posts, and share links with your network. It also mimics Twitter; you do not need an introduction or permission to follow someone on this open network. Instead of "friends," like on Facebook, Google+ allows users to create "circles" of contacts. Circles are good for two reasons: they allow you to digest information from specific groups you select to follow, and to push selected content out to targeted audiences.

Much like Twitter, Google+ can help you open doors to communicate with key contacts and influencers. The immediate usefulness of Google+ depends on your industry and how many people you can locate who are actively spending time there.

In the long run, however, due to Google's search algorithms, having a presence there, connecting with appropriate contacts, and making a point to communicate about your expertise via the network may make it easier for people to find you and see what you offer professionally. There's no doubt this network has the potential to help you advance your goals and to be found, especially if you allow your posts to be "public." In doing so, you use Google+ to broadcast your information to an exponential audience. Google indexes these posts and makes them more accessible via search to people in your network. (Google refers to this as "search plus your world.")

Your Google+ Personal Profile

It's easy to create a Google+ account if you already use Gmail or any other Google product (such as YouTube). If you have an account, sign in and click on the +You tab on the top of your screen. If you don't already use a Google product, go to https://plus.google.com and start out by creating your public profile.

Whether you need to create it from scratch or update your public profile, first impressions count. Use your real name and allow Google+ to personalize your +1s. As Google explains, "+1 personalization on non-Google sites allows Google to tailor content and ads to you across the Web, based on your Google profile, +1 activity, and social connections."

It's important to write a complete, targeted, and optimized profile. Review and revise it until you clearly articulate your value. These are the sections you need to fill in:

Your Tagline

Choose something short and sweet that describes you. When people scroll over your profile picture in Google+, they will see either your tagline or a part of your tagline, depending on how long it is. For a graphic designer, for example:

Bringing visuals to life from paper napkin drawing to final print production.

Introduction

Consider repurposing your LinkedIn bio (your summary) on this social network. Target your audience, and incorporate keywords you want people to use when they are searching for you, which will "teach" Google search about your areas of expertise.

Within your personal profile, you have the following categories to complete:

Bragging Rights

Keep it professional here. It's tempting to add something funny or sarcastic, such as "survived raising teenage children" or "learned to avoid traffic in L.A." Instead, incorporate awards or professional accolades to help raise your reputation or credibility. For example:

Won Stevie Award for Sales & Marketing, 2013.

Earned "Competitive Manuscript Award" from the American Accounting Association, 2013.

Recognized as Manager of the Year, [organization name], 2013.

Occupation

You could simply include your job title here or add some appropriate flair or humor. For example:

- Making your design dreams come true.
- Resourceful artist and designer . . . passionate about sharing ideas!
- Designer by day. Designer by night.

Employment

Google+ showcases your recent employment when people visit your Google+ page—this information appears under your name and is the first thing people will see when they navigate to your page on Google+. Instead of just listing your title or company, expand your business' description to include accolades or useful information:

Diamond International, Director of Human Resources, SPHR. President, SHRM of Oakland County. Creating HR processes from scratch.

Westfield Marriott, Banquet Manager. Creating unique, themed, special occasions to meet all budgets.

Be sure to fill out this section completely, including all of your past jobs, as it can help employers who are searching for candidates to decide if you are a qualified fit.

> Your employment shows up when someone visits your profile on Google+, so it's important to make sure you list more than just your title! Listing a non-descript title, such as "vice president" or "manager," won't help someone want to learn more about you! Try out the "view as" button next to the "edit profile" button to experience how your profile looks to other people.

Occupation

You could simply include your job title here or add some flair or humor. For example:

- The Mad Scientist of Online Recruiting.
- Resourceful marketing blogger . . . passionate about sharing ideas!
- Writer by day. Writer by night.

Education

Complete the education section to match your LinkedIn profile.

Remaining Sections

Make sure to fill in everything that makes sense in the rest of the categories. Do not feel compelled to list your relationship status, but do include links to your other online profiles and if you contribute to other online sites, be sure to list them in your profile.

Photos

Be sure to include a photo for your Google+ —ideally, you'll use the same professional avatar as you do on your other social networks.

Google+ also has a "banner-like" photo—similar to the timeline photo on your Facebook profile. You can create a photo (it needs to meet their specified size) using any number of tools.

Using Google+

Once you get the hang of it, Google+ is very easy to use. Explore the icons behind the Home tab of your Google+ screen to do everything you need to do.

- **Events.** You never know what events may be scheduled for your area or a place you plan to visit.
- **Photos.** You have an option to use Google+ applications to store your photos.
- **Communities.** This is a really useful function of Google+— it's almost like LinkedIn's Groups. You can discover communities in any number of topics, or you can start your own community and lead discussions. Ideally, the best communities will have frequent and active discussions and a lot of interactions.
- **People.** The "People" tab is where you can find people to add to your circles. You can choose people to follow by putting them in circles, and people will add you to their circles. The great thing is that you can easily segment the people you follow and designate messages targeted to those groups. For example, you could have a circle of "colleagues," and you can easily see what they are sharing with their circles. At the same time, you can have more targeted or niche groups, for example, "local colleagues" or "networking contacts I've met in person." No one knows what circle they are in, they only know you've added them to your circles.

You can see what people share (and they see what you share) in real time, or they can scroll through their streams of information at their leisure.

- **Hangouts.** A hangout is a free video chat with up to nine other people. You can chat face-to-face, host online meetings, and broadcast your results with the world via YouTube.

> When you log into a Google product, you'll see a red number at the top, on the right side of your screen. It shows you what is going on in your community. Click on it to see what you can learn there.

How to Find People on Google+

There are a lot of different ways to identify people to follow on Google+.

You can go to Google and enter: {site:plus.google.com google}. Then include a keyword to help locate others in your field. For example: {site:plus.google.com google nurse}. Don't include the {   }s in your search.

- **http://findpeopleonplus.com:** Indexes Google profiles. You can search by any keyword.
- **www.gpeep.com**: You can register on this service to help other people find you.
- **www.recommendedusers.com:** Suggests people in niche topics to circle.

What to Say in Google+ Updates

Luckily, learning what to say on Google+ isn't much different from learning what to say on Twitter or Facebook. While you have more space to detail your opinions and expertise, you should use the same guidelines outlined in the Twitter and Facebook chapters to post on Google+.

How to Push Content to Targeted Audiences

If you are looking for a job as a store manager, for instance, you may create circles (groups of contacts within Google+) of people who work in these types of environments. Once you establish a circle, you can post an update and designate it to go only to your selected audience. For example:

> *It looks like green is the hot color for spring. Here are some places where you can pick up a little splash of color for your wardrobe [link].*

A job seeker looking for a financial-planner role may create circles of other financial planners or people who share content about what is happening in the profession. Using Google+, he can easily follow what people in that circle post or provide content targeted to that group:

> *Have you seen the latest data on new home sales? Sales inching up—what does it mean for consumers? My take: [link]*

> *Investing in bonds may not be a bad plan for younger clients. See what the Wall Street Journal is saying on page 1 today: [link]*

More Sample G+ Updates: Social Worker

Dorlee M (+Dorlee M) is an MSW clinical social worker with an MBA (in marketing, from her former career). She uses Google+ to network, learn about new developments in the mental health and career/leadership areas, and promote her social work career-development blog, www.dorleem.com.

Offering resources to followers

Great #psychology #mentalhealth sources: Some of these #twitter feeds you'll be familiar with, but some of them may be new to you . . . [links]

Important article on how the new normal is turbulence and how "we need to honour the past but we need to know how to learn from the future." #innovation #leadership [links]

Are you looking for good study guide tools to help you pass the #LMSW [link] exam?

Providing advice from her expertise

To help you cultivate your capacity to keep on going:

1. *Make sure your goals are utterly aligned with what's important to you.*
2. *Be gentle with yourself.*
3. *Be mindful . . . #resilience #worklife.*

Linking to posts that followers might enjoy

The amazing power of #meditation . . .

Sample G+ Updates: Fashion Coach

Ayo Fashola is a certified style coach™ and wardrobe consultant. She uses Google+ to build connections, foster relationships, and share resources relating to her background and experience as they relate to her target audiences. She highlights posts relevant to women entrepreneurs between the ages of 40 and 55 years old.

Providing links to useful or fun resources

How to Dress 10lbs Slimmer!!! [link]

How To: Flirty Lashes and a Sexy Pout [link to demo video]

Do you shy away from wearing color? Does color SCARE you? Do you want to wear more color in fun, fresh ways, but are not quite sure where to begin? Here is something to get your color education moving in the right direction. This knowledge can be applied to how you dress.

Offering inspirational advice

Becoming a woman full of confidence, beauty, grace, and charm comes from nurturing, cultivating, and developing your spiritual center. It comes from recognizing that you are one with life and life is one with you. It comes from recognizing that no matter how bad, or shameful, or guilty you feel about the past, every morning that you wake up is an opportunity to forgive yourself and start fresh. An opportunity to start anew and begin again.

Expressing gratitude while reminding readers of her expertise

Highly looking forward to being in Dallas next week and getting into some closets. I feel so grateful to all my clients that believe in me and support me in my vision, path, and mission, and most importantly allow me the JOY to play and express my passions in the best possible way. Thank you! Thank you! Thank you!

Sample G+ Updates: Librarian

Luke Rosenberger (+LukeRosenberger) is director of library technology and historical collections at a health science university library and a bilingual virtual reference librarian. He showcases his expertise:

Providing links to useful resources

Don't miss this—you'll thank me. This is 5 minutes of pure awesome digital storytelling that my colleague +David Hale created for ignite dc #8, which was last night (http://ignite-dc.com).

Showcasing industry news

This is going to have enormous implications. Enormous. I'm encouraged by ACU's involvement in this, because of their very-well-planned and well-researched "ACU Connected" effort, which has been going since fall 2008 (http://www.acu.edu/technology/mobilelearning/). But this is going to affect the entire McAllen community in dramatic and unexpected ways. [link to students moving from ABCs to apps]

Offering details about upcoming events

I'd encourage all my nearby colleagues who are interested in emerging technologies, education, and community outreach to consider an exciting new kind of professional development opportunity coming up at the end of this month. ActionCamp San Antonio is a chance for innovators from the local education and nonprofit communities to come together, share, and learn from each other about strategies, technology tools, and experiences.

Sharing links to resources quoting him

I was a little nervous about being interviewed for this story, but I think it came out pretty well in the end. [link to Getting Schooled on Social Media, MySanAntonio.com]

Letting People Know You Are Mentioning Them

If you use Facebook, you may be familiar with "tagging" someone in a post by putting the @ symbol before his or her name, alerting the person of the mention. Similarly, on Google+, you can tag someone in a post by adding + or @ before a person's name. For example:

Just read +MiriamSalpeter's newest post. Have you thought about how to be generous online? [link]

+1

Google+ encourages you to offer blog posts and Google+ updates your vote of confidence by clicking on the +1 button. You can +1 posts from within Google+, and many blogs make it easy to +1 their posts directly from their sites, too. This is another way to communicate online and to show appreciation. Don't hesitate to +1 anything you appreciate, but keep in mind that Google will index and may showcase your choices for others when they are searching online. Don't be casual when you offer a +1, and don't +1 anything you don't want everyone to know you read and liked.

Other Ways to Communicate on Google+

Google+ is evolving, and the ways you'll be able to communicate and interact with potential colleagues, mentors, and new contacts will continue to change. You can use Hangouts (a video tool), Communities (like Groups on LinkedIn), Chats, and Games to touch base and expand your circle of friends. Keep in mind—whenever you are using an online tool, you have an opportunity to see or be seen by potential employers. (For example, some savvy recruiters search game forums to help identify potential hires for technology areas.) Communicate clearly, concisely, and with the intent to impress no matter where you spend time online.

Things to Remember

As with any strategy, give Google+ some time to work. It's possible you'll connect with a great contact in your first week of using it, but it is more likely that you will need to spend time lurking and reading, and then posting and commenting, many times before you connect with the perfect person. Remember, all it takes is one great contact to change your job search for the better; Google+ has the potential to introduce you to the one person you need to know, and it offers opportunities to make it easier for people who are looking for someone *like* you to *find* you. It's a win-win!

13 The Benefits of Blogging

With millions of blogs currently online, you have probably read many without even knowing it. A blog is different from a Web page—it allows two-way communication (assuming comments are enabled), and also tends to be updated frequently, compared to a static website. There are many blogging platforms, which allow almost anyone the ability to easily create and launch a blog, even with little technical expertise (including Wordpress.com, Blogger.com, and Typepad.com). You don't need to know HTML or how to build a website from scratch to create and run a blog, but you do need to learn a few technical tricks to post and publish. (I'll describe some of the technical aspects in the next chapter.)

Creating a blog to showcase your knowledge in a subject area is probably the best way to control search results for your name, and to ensure that people looking for someone with your expertise will be able to find you through search engines. To create and run a blog that will propel your career, you need to have a clear understanding of what you offer and how to market it. If you use the tips and tricks in Chapter 4 to help you identify what you want people to know about you, it will be much easier to move forward with a blog that serves as a platform to develop your personal brand.

Blogging May Advance Your Career

Many recognized industry professionals agree that blogging will advance your career. Penelope Trunk, the founder of three startups—most recently, Brazen Careerist (http://www.brazencareerist.com), explains some of the many reasons to consider blogging:

- **You will force yourself to specialize.** The act of picking a topic and sticking with it is good for you, because specializing is good for your career. After all, you can't be known for something if you are not specializing in something. Once you are known for something, you have a lot more leverage to get the kind of work you want to be doing.
- **You will let people know you have good ideas**. One of the biggest complaints people have about their work is that no one listens to their ideas. Everyone wants to be a creative thinker, but not everyone feels like that sort of work is open to them. With a blog, you can show people your creative thinking. Got a lot of great ideas? Good, because there are a lot of days in the week for you to include them on your blog.
- **You will show passion and commitment**. There is a lot of evidence to show that we have a proclivity toward hiring people we like. If you are a blogger, and post at regular intervals, you don't need to tell people about your passion and commitment—it's right there on the page for key people to see.
- **Blogging helps you move up quickly.** To escape the entry-level grind, you can either pay your dues and spend time

working your way up the ladder, or you can establish yourself as an expert by launching a blog. High-level jobs are for people who specialize, and hiring managers look for specialists online. "Decision-makers respect Google karma," writes Tim Bray, director of Web technologies for Sun Microsystems—on his own blog, of course.

- **Blogging creates a network.** A blogger puts himself out in the world as someone who is interesting and engaging—just the type of person everyone wants to meet. "A blog increases your network because a blog is about introducing yourself and sharing information," says Kaputa.
- **Blogging can get you a job.** Dervala Hanley writes a quirky literary blog that got her a job at Stone Yamashita Partners, a consulting firm. Hanley told me that the firm was attracted to her ability to put her business experience into personal terms on her blog.
- **Blogging is great training.** To really get attention for your blog, you're going to have to create daily entries for a while. Post daily for at least a few months to get rolling, and then three or four times a week after that.
- **Blogging makes self-employment easier.** You can't make it on your own unless you are good at selling yourself. One of the most cost-effective and efficient ways of marketing yourself is with a blog. When someone searches for your product or service online, make sure your blog comes up first. Curt Rosengren, a career coach, periodically Googles "career passion"—keywords that he thinks are most important to his business—just to make sure that his blog, Occupational Adventure, comes up high on the list. He estimates that his blog generates at least half of his coaching business.
- **Blogging provides opportunities and could be your big break.** Building brands, changing careers, launching a business—these endeavors are much easier once you've established yourself online. According to Rosengren:

"My blog is a foundation. I'm building an awareness that I can leverage to do other fun things with my future, such as product development or public speaking."

Penelope explains, a blog gives you a leg up when you meet someone new. Dylan Tweney, a freelance writer, told me that his blog, the Tweney Review, gives him instant legitimacy with clients. Visually creative types can blog beyond just text. Mark Fearing, who has a cartoon blog, states:

"Cartooning and illustration are very crowded fields. My blog has gotten me more notice than any other publicity tool I've used. Plus, the blog gives me a way to have a new conversation with potential clients about other work."

A CAREER BLOGGING SUCCESS STORY

Ben Eubanks, a human resources professional for a nonprofit human services organization in Huntsville, Alabama, and creator of upstartHR.com, explains how blogging propelled his career:

"Blogging is one of the most valuable and least used personal branding tools. We hear all the time about the value of Twitter, LinkedIn, and other tools for building and sharing a personal brand. But one of the least explored is the blog. At one time, blogs were ridiculed and ignored because they were uncommon, used for personal rants/raves, or just plain useless.

Today, blogs are a major branding tool used by organizations such as Harvard Business Review, CNN, Zappos, and other global entities. Those companies use blogs to share important news that is relevant and timely for their customers. I have good news: you can do the same with your own blog.

I started blogging when I began looking for a job in my chosen field. Since then, I've had more success and opportunity to develop professionally than most people do in a dozen years! Because of

continued from page 262

my blog, I have done the following:

- *Interacted daily with VP/director level pros in my field*
- *Cofounded a conference that drew attendees from around the world*
- *Written an eBook targeted toward my industry's certification exam*
- *Created and solidified dozens of partnerships with other blogs and businesses*
- *Established myself as an expert in my niche, both locally and nationally*

Not everyone can have that same measure of success, but what if you achieved even half of that? What sort of impact would it have on your job search and long-term career development? Job coaches tell you to pay attention to Google results for your own name, and that having a good reputation online can carry over to real life. What better way to impress future employers than with a blog about your profession?

I promise you this—my resume has a lot of different info about positions I've held, but the one that I'm most proud of is the section on blogging and my online footprint. The only cost of this sort of venture? Time and effort."

Ben's reminder that authoring a blog takes time and effort is an important consideration. Assuming that you have strong writing skills and an interest in using technology, creating and maintaining your own personal blog could provide a terrific return on your time and effort. Having a blog offers terrific networking opportunities, and a sturdy platform for your job search or entrepreneurial efforts.

Demonstrate Your Expertise

There is no doubt that blogging will help demonstrate your expertise to a broad audience. Jessica Miller-Merrell, SPHR (www.blogging4jobs.com),

BLOGGING IS GOOD FOR ENTREPRENEURS/ BUSINESS OWNERS

Kristen Fischer (www.kristenfischer.com) is a copywriter and author. She explains how her blogs (www.ramenrentresumes.com and http://creativelyselfemployed.blogspot.com) impact her business:

"I have two blogs, one for each of my books: Ramen Noodles, Rent and Resumes: An After-College Guide to Life *and* Creatively Self-Employed: How Writers and Artists Deal with Career Ups and Downs. *These blogs enable me to offer fresh content to my readers, and hopefully, if they haven't purchased the book already, they will.*

I think blogs are a great way to continuously connect with readers and establish yourself as a leader in your niche. Keeping up with a blog is a lot of work, and sometimes I don't have the time to post the top-quality content I would like. Nevertheless, I enjoy keeping the blogs and connecting with my audiences."

is known as @Blogging4Jobs on Twitter and is a Human Resource Consultant and New Media Strategist with her company, Xceptional HR.

Jessica has used creative online strategies such as blogging, chat forums, and text messaging in her human resources roles for over 12 years. She explains:

"Several years ago, I was looking for a way to fill open positions for a Fortune 500 company, where I worked as a Human Resource Director, while also defining my brand and differentiating myself from other human resource and recruiting professionals. Blogging was the answer.

Developing a blog provides a central connection point, to help visitors, potential clients, and employers learn more about you, your interests, and who influences you, beyond the traditional resume or LinkedIn profile. A blog also allows you to provide a consistent and controlled message about you and your personal brand.

Being a blogger is not easy; it takes commitment, initiative, and effort. However, there are several potential benefits:

- **Relationships.** *I've developed relationships with new friends and colleagues as a result of a popular blog post, and landed new clients and business because someone visited my blog to learn more about me.*
- **Media Access.** *I am able to interview companies with whom I want to do business or learn more about. Job seekers can use their blogs as entrees to interview people from targeted companies, as a form of informational interview. I'm also able to attend conferences and events, often at no cost, with special access.*
- **Developmental and Leadership Experiences.** *Growing professionally within an organization may be difficult, especially in an economy that is more focused on cost cutting than training and development. Your blog can help fill that gap by putting you in touch with industry leaders and information, at little or no cost."*

Things to Consider Before Beginning a Blog

If you are thinking about starting your own blog, consider the following before you get started.

How Much Time Do You Have?

Writing regular, quality content is one of the most important indicators of a successful blog. Assess your time commitment and ability to maintain the blog. It is difficult to determine exactly how long it will take; your time investment depends on your writing skills, knowledge of your topic, the final product you want to produce, how much effort you put into perfecting it, whether or not you include special touches (such as adding photos), and how you will market your product.

I would estimate that setting up a blog could take between 5 and 15 hours, including learning time, selecting the right templates, and teaching yourself to navigate the back end of the blog. This is a one-time investment; once you set everything up, you just need to write posts, respond to comments, market the blog, and keep it up to date technically.

On a weekly basis, assuming you blog at least two to three times, budget at least seven hours per week to maintain a professional blog. This includes the time you will spend planning, writing, and publishing your posts, as well as time promoting your blog, by commenting on other sites and social networking platforms (such as Twitter or LinkedIn), and responding to comments you receive.

You may consider blogging on someone else's site first, to decide if it is a good fit for you. In Chapter 4, I listed a number of choices for posting articles without having your own blog. For example, I mentioned that Examiner.com is an outlet that welcomes people to sign on as regular bloggers who write about a specific niche topic.

Another idea before you start your own blog—use the information in this book to find blogs of interest and build relationships with those bloggers by commenting on their sites and sharing their links via other social media sites. If you are an expert and write well, some bloggers will welcome a guest post from you. In select cases, you may have an opportunity to contribute frequently.

What to Write About

Typical professional blogs provide readers with an ongoing series of articles (known as posts) that have a common theme. According to *ProBlogger* (Wiley, 2008), by Darren Rouse and Chris Garrett, niche blogs are more successful. For example, a teacher may create a blog that shares information about new developments in the education field. A photographer may create a blog to showcase her pictures. Someone looking for a job as a legal assistant may write a blog that captures his knowledge about that industry.

Writing a niche blog allows the author to target a specific audience. The actual content and length of your posts depends upon your professional goals and writing style, and may change over time. Identify a niche topic related to your career goals, and write a blog that provides readers information about that topic.

Maybe you are thinking about starting your own business? If so, write a blog that will attract potential customers and position you as a subject matter expert. While writing a personal blog about your interest and expertise in *Star Wars*, for example, may be a lot of fun, and could certainly expand your network, unless it links to a professional goal (for example, you write science-fiction screenplays), it is not very likely to propel your career.

On the other hand, if you are an expert in healthcare reform and create a blog that provides your opinions regarding the subject, it is likely that you will be able to use it as a platform to advance your brand and potentially become known as a go-to expert.

BLOGGING YOUR WAY TO A CAREER

Katherine Simmons is CEO of NETSHARE (http://netshare.com), an online career community with job listings and resources for senior managers earning $100,000 or more per year. She counsels members regarding career strategies and harnessing the Web for career advancement.

Katherine agrees that blogging is an excellent way to propel a job hunt forward. This is her advice regarding how to leverage a blog during a job hunt:

"Most job seekers make the mistake of targeting a job or title rather than a company. Something that I have learned over the years is that fit is everything; you need to target the company you want to work for, not the job. Once you have identified the ideal employer, you can get them to talk to you by talking about them.

continued from page 265

This is a new networking strategy that a number of my career-coaching friends are starting to advocate. Most companies monitor their online brand, so if you start writing about your target company in an industry blog, chances are, they will find you, at least to follow your web posts.

A blog is also a great tool to demonstrate your expertise and industry knowledge. And you can use the blog posts to introduce yourself to executives inside the company, using e-mail or social media outreach, to ask, "Did you see my latest blog post about your company? Care to comment?" It's a great way to start an online dialogue.

Consider the case of Walt Feigenson, a lifelong computer professional who started counseling executives on personal branding, social networking, and getting started with their own blogs. As part of his own personal branding strategy, Walt maintains his own blog, Wally's Follies, and posts articles on a wide variety of topics relating to building an online presence.

The founder of a natural beverage company, B&R Liquid Adventures, found one of Walt's articles through a Google search, commented on it, and then read through Walt's blog—and liked what he read. He approached Walt and made him an offer to join the start-up, as Chief of New Media, to help promote a new kind of Kombucha fermented tea.

As Walt writes on his blog, 'I've never worked in consumer packaged goods, and I'd never tasted Kombucha before—and if you knew me, you'd know I'm not a health food nut. But I do know marketing, and I've been participating in Web 2.0, whatever that is, for some time.' Clearly, Walt's blog demonstrated that he knows his subject, and was able to attract the attention of the right company, who needed his skills.

You can hone this blogging strategy by targeting companies you are interested in, rather than trolling the Web for opportunities. Here's how it works:

- **Research your target company.** Assess the company's special challenges, examine likely new product segments, assess its competitive position, perform your SWOT analysis, etc.

continued from page 268

- **Write your blog post.** *Offer your expert opinion about the path you see the company taking. Your opinions can be complimentary and supportive, or may offer insights into the potential downside to the company's strategy. Your blog entries do not have to be long, but they should be thoughtful and articulate.*
- **Create awareness for your blog.** *Use your social media network and contacts to promote blog interest, and to make sure your blog entries get the attention of the hiring managers at your target companies. E-mail the CEO or the department manager at your target company, reference the blog, and ask for his or her thoughts.*

Your blog will get attention and should open some doors. The objective of the blogging exercise is to begin the dialogue that may lead to a job offer. Providing blog entries for comment provides an opening to start talking with senior staff. Granted, the dialogue may not always result in an interview, but it is certain to get you noticed, which is a great first step."

A Blog—the Hub of Your Social Media Presence

Many people refer to their blogs as the *hub*, or center, of their social networking activity. It's a good place to connect various profiles, and to provide links to other places where you provide advice, information, or content.

Once you know what you have to offer, writing regular posts to your blog about topics you hope to become known for will:

- Help connect you to a community of colleagues, experts, and potential mentors.
- Provide opportunities to expand your network, instigate two-way communication, and meet new people from around the world.

269

- Help you further define your message and potentially become known as a subject matter expert.
- Provide a 3-D portfolio of your work.
- Influence how Google and other search engines index your name, and what people find when they search for you.

Connecting With Colleagues and Mentors

Just as you wouldn't become a caterer before preparing and serving food to your friends and family for practice, you do not want to start a blog without taking some time to see what other people are writing, and how the blogosphere for your community interacts. Chris Brogan, author and President of New Marketing Labs, suggests you "grow bigger ears," by listening first. In Chapter 2, I suggest several places to look for blogs to read in your niche. My favorite (and one that Chris also recommends) is Alltop.com. It indexes many blogs in various topics. Use several keywords to search and you are bound to find a group of blogs to start your reading/listening tour.

Ways to Get Bloggers' Attention

Once you find a group of bloggers whose work you enjoy, consider using these strategies for connecting with them and their readers:

- Reading and commenting on the blogs you enjoy helps build rapport with influential people in your field. Not only will you land on their radar screens, it is possible that you will earn opportunities to guest post on some of the sites where you build strong relationships. As previously mentioned, when I launched my blog I spent as much time reading and commenting on other blogs as I did writing my own blog. I still invest as much time as possible reading and tweeting links to my colleagues' blog posts, and the relationships I built early on still support my blog and career today. But just saying "nice post!" doesn't count as a comment; you should respond to something specific on the post—either agree or disagree—and do so politely. You may even use the opportunity to respond on your own blog, so your comment can include a link to your post, with a more in-depth reply. Most bloggers appreciate a well-written and thoughtful comment.

- Once you comment, be sure to check back to see if you engaged anyone. It's possible to extend your reach and connect with various people on one blog; take advantage of the opportunity to befriend or connect with other commentators via online conversations.

- If you strike up an exchange with someone, be sure to check if he or she has a blog and a Twitter account. Always keep an eye out for new opportunities to connect and extend your network.

- Since blogging takes a lot of effort, you may not be surprised to learn that blogging communities tend to be very close. Once you demonstrate your willingness to collaborate and your interest in joining a blogging community, it is likely that the community will welcome you and appreciate your contributions. Recognizing your status as a newcomer and making a concerted effort to ingratiate yourself will help smooth the way for potential mentorships and friendships.

- Write about bloggers you admire and link to their posts. Many bloggers have a Google alert set for their names and also monitor their back links (when someone links back to their posts).

- Use other social networks to help promote the bloggers you appreciate. Retweet their posts or send out your own tweets promoting their blogs (be sure you include their Twitter names in the tweets so they are likely to notice your efforts). Use LinkedIn, Facebook, and Google+ to share their posts. Be sure to use the tagging features in each network. For example, by including the @ symbol before their names. In Google+, use the + sign before the person's name.

To help encourage comments on your blog, try asking for comments. One thing I learned from reading marketing experts' blogs is that people like you to tell them what to do next. So, if you are selling something, you need to ask people to buy it. If you want comments on your blog, ask people for their opinions.

For example, at the end of a post, ask, "What do you think? Share your ideas in the comments section." Or, "I welcome your thoughts. Please feel free to comment to continue the conversation."

In addition to replying to comments via your blog, send an e-mail message to commentators. Most blog sites require anyone who comments to leave an e-mail address. People who reach out are hoping to make a connection with you, so you enhance your reputation when you extend that personal connection.

Expand Your Network Via Two-Way Communication

Once you connect with selected bloggers and have begun to build an online understanding (I would hesitate to call it a relationship just yet), commented on other blogs, and received comments on your own posts, it's a good idea to reach out via e-mail, to let bloggers/mentors know you appreciate their efforts.

Don't be shy about asking for information specific to your situation if relevant, and be sure to keep in touch with your new contact—don't just move on to a new target once you exchange e-mails. Continue to support his or her goals, and it is likely that you'll receive the same in return.

USING MY BLOG TO CONNECT

Kate Davids, who specializes in online marketing and promotional events, blogs at http://katetheprofessional.wordpress.com. She explains how her blog has been a great support tool:

"My blog gives me an excuse to speak with professionals from all over the world, including John Antonios (@JohnAntonios), who lives in Beirut, and Karima-Catherine (@karimacatherine), who lives in Canada.

continued from page 272

My blog always comes up in job interviews. Interviewers are always impressed I have a blog. Currently, I work at a Facebook application company. I met the man who hired me through Twitter, but he asked me if I would be interested in a position because of my blog. He tweeted me: ' . . . I'm a big [name of company I used to work for] fan. Your blog implies that you're job hunting. Is that the case, or did you just not update the copy? :)'

I then said I was still looking, got an interview, and got a job. This job is helping me earn a little money over the summer and provides experience in the field. The blog has also come up with my school. I wrote about how difficult it is to get a loan, mentioning my school name, and the next time my recruiter spoke to me; he mentioned my blog and began trying to help me."

Define Your Message—Become a Subject Matter Expert

Malcolm Gladwell suggests in his book *Outliers* (Little, Brown and Company, 2008) that you need 10,000 hours of practice to be an expert at something. That may or may not be true, but there is no doubt that focusing on your goals, and writing about topics related to your niche on a regular basis, will improve your ability to engage with people on those topics. Having a blog forces you to focus on a specialty, to see what other people are saying, and to learn even more—so you can keep ahead of the crowd.

If you know your topic, write well, and follow the suggestions in this book, you have an opportunity to become well known in your industry.

A Personal Website—Your Portfolio and Social Resume

Job seekers may not be accustomed to the idea of attracting employers whom they have not contacted themselves. Creating a site that

A BLOG AS AN AVENUE TO A BRAND-NEW CAREER

The best example I know of someone who has used a blog to help define his brand, leverage his expertise, and create opportunities for himself is Dan Schawbel, Managing Partner of Millennial Branding, LLC and author of *Promote Yourself* (St. Martin's Press, 2013).

Dan explains:

"My first blog was called Driven-to-Succeed, which was a career development guide for college students. I created it on what is now called Google Blogger. I used the blog to share what I learned when I was looking for a job, and offered advice about how students can prepare for the real world before graduating college.

The challenge was that no one commented on the blog, and very few people would answer my e-mails because no one had heard of me. It wasn't until I read Tom Peters' famous 'Brand Called You' article that my entire world changed. I realized that I shared Tom's beliefs, and that I could become the Gen-Y spokesperson for personal branding—because I had been living it all along.

Since there weren't any other people my age talking about personal branding, I claimed the niche immediately via a new blog named the 'Personal Branding Blog,' hosted at Wordpress.com. I posted on it between 10 and 12 times a week.

I drew on my marketing knowledge to propel the blog's content, but I also kept up-to-date with the latest social media, personal branding, and career development techniques, research, examples, and ideas, by subscribing to other blogs and news sources.

I wrote advice posts, linked to other relevant blogs, started games, reviewed career books, and interviewed industry experts. Aside from writing and publishing a high volume of content each week on the blog, I aggressively commented on any blog that mentioned the words 'personal branding.' I also e-mailed industry experts, to align myself with people who were already influential in the personal branding arena.

Eventually, after almost two years of using Wordpress to host my blog, I made an investment and moved the blog to my own domain name, personalbrandingblog.com. This was an important step; it gave me more control and allowed me to begin to host ads on the site, which lets me generate revenue.

continued from page 274

> *By that time, I had gained a large following and a lot of notoriety as a result of my blog, including becoming an AdAge top 40 marketing blog. Careerbuilder.com listed it as a top blog in 2008 and 2009, and it's syndicated by several media sites, including Reuters and Forbes. I also achieved my goal of landing a book deal as a result of the work I had put in building the blog.*
>
> *PersonalBrandingBlog.com now attracts over 100,000 visitors per month, and I was able to attract expert contributors to share regular guest posts while I spend my time marketing the blog to attract new visitors and to constantly build the brand. I was able to leave my day job to focus on my own business—all as a result of my work and the growth of the blog. My best advice to new bloggers is to start small, never give up, and believe in your product and yourself."*

serves as your online hub and social resume is a great way to draw potential hiring managers to you.

Success depends on being found, and, more often than not, being found depends on search engines such as Google. You may have heard of options for creating an online presence and landing page, such as About.me, Vizify.com, Rebelmouse.com, or Flavors.me. While they allow jobseekers to share customized information, they are not optimized for search and less likely to attract employers. A LinkedIn profile, and professional platforms on other sites, such as Twitter, Google+, and Facebook, share your message, but there is no better way to control Google results for your name than to own the URL for {yourname}.com and to run an active blog on that site (learn how to optimize the blog for search engines in the next chapter).

Your social resume should incorporate an easy way to contact you, your resume (use Scribed, www.scribd.com, to upload your resume and share it via your site), a biography or an "About" page, work samples, career highlights, endorsements, and links to your other social networks, such as LinkedIn and professional Twitter and Facebook profiles. If you are in a creative profession, you might consider links to Pinterest, Instagram, or Flickr or other portfolios of your work online. Other potential categories include: credentials, distinctions, honors, awards, press/media, case studies, consulting, newsletters, news and events, volunteer projects, a demo reel, art portfolio, sample projects, a wiki, speaking events, photos, associations, clubs, and technical competencies. A blog site that serves as your social media hub and social resume may also include multimedia options, including professional YouTube videos and audio.

When you create links on your site to describe your skills, specific experience, and accomplishments in-depth, the site helps bring your resume to life, and also provides a multidimensional experience for the reader (go to http://kenrevenaugh.com to see an example of a social resume by Ken Revenaugh, which ties in the key factors covered here).

A Different "Social Resume"

CareerCloud.com is a site that bills itself as a social resume, but it is more like the various sites mentioned that allow you to curate your information than the type of social resume I would suggest you have. CareerCloud is a great option to gather and connect your professional, online identity. It includes data from LinkedIn, which gives it a very professional feel. However, I still suggest owning a website in your own name for the best results.

FROM THE OTHER SIDE OF THE HIRING DESK— IMPORTANCE OF AN ONLINE RESUME

Andrea Santiago, veteran recruiter, career columnist, and guide to health careers for About.com, explains the importance of having an online resume:

"A key component of your online presence and job search campaign is your online resume. Even if you are not actively seeking a new job, you should always have at least a basic outline of your professional background displayed somewhere online.

continued from page 276

LinkedIn.com is just one way you can post a digital resume, at no cost. Your blog and company website are also great places to maintain a digital resume or bio that showcases your experience and qualifications.

Maintaining an online resume is a great way for you to be discovered by recruiters as well, and sometimes jobs will even come to you without you needing to apply. Typically, if a recruiter identifies you online as a potential candidate, that means your qualifications are a strong fit for the job the recruiter is representing.

As a veteran recruiter, I've identified candidates online, as a hiring manager and as a third-party recruiter representing searches for client corporations. One of the first things recruiters or hiring managers do when working on a new search is to look online, via search engines and online networking sites. This is particularly true of smaller companies, where hiring managers may try to avoid spending hundreds of dollars on job board postings by identifying a few potential candidates online. I've also been approached for numerous business opportunities based on my online profile, including jobs, freelance work, and speaking engagements, so I know first-hand that online resumes are extremely valuable for career advancement.

Additionally, digital, or online resumes help promote your personal brand. When someone searches your name on a search engine, for example, your online resume will often appear in search results. This enables you to exercise control over your brand and online presence.

Online resumes are easy to update and keep current. Additionally, you can insert a link to your online resume into your e-mail signature line, on your Facebook page, or anywhere your contacts can see it. Online resumes are a simple way to increase your visibility, which will increase your odds of finding a job.

If used and placed properly, your online resume may be a more important job search tool than your traditional resume. The traditional version may become more of a formality that you will use to follow up with someone after they have viewed your online resume."

Things to Remember

Job seekers, careerists, and entrepreneurs who follow the suggestions in this chapter will be a giant step ahead of their peers. With little to no start-up costs for a very basic blog, and without very much technical knowledge, you have the opportunity to create a respected and magnetic presence that:

- Expands your circle of influence and lets you engage in two-way communication with colleagues and mentors in your field from around the world.
- Demonstrates your expertise, passion, and abilities, and helps you become known as an expert.
- Defines your message and improves your writing and communication skills.
- Creates a hub for your work, and a place where people have the opportunity to dig deeper into your portfolio.
- Influences what Google and other search engines know about you and helps define what people will find when they search for you online.

In the next chapter, I describe some of the technical aspects of blogging, and share details and advice to help you get up and running quickly.

14 Getting Started with Your Blog

I f you are ready to launch your own website to host a blog, there are a few things you need to decide. Some of the information in this chapter is on the technical side, but don't let it scare you. It can be challenging to get started, but once you know what you are doing, the rewards should be worth the effort. Remember, there are currently millions of blogs. If that many people can create a blog, so can you!

Where Will Your Blog Live?

You need a host for your blog. I like to think of this as where the blog *lives* (although that is not a technical way to describe it). There are several things to think about when you decide where to host your blog. For example, do you want to set up, install, and maintain the back end of your blog yourself, or will you need help?

A Hosted Site

If you think that you will need help maintaining your blog, then you will want to consider a hosted blog site. Think of this as the equivalent of going to a party, where you don't need to do the cooking or cleaning—someone else takes care of everything, you just need to show up. There are many options for setting up a blog, and some are as simple as completing a brief signup process. Before I share some suggestions and recommendations, here are some pros and cons to using a hosted site.

Advantages to a Hosted Site

- You don't need a lot of technical knowledge to get started. Reading and following the instructions in this chapter will be all you need to know to start publishing.
- It is cheap or free to launch. You do not have to contact a third party to reserve a domain (URL), and you do not need to pay for monthly hosting. All you need to do is blog!
- You won't need to worry about updating your software to stay current. Your host handles everything for you. There is no upkeep as far as the backend goes. This can be very freeing if you are not a techie and don't want to worry about if a new version of the software that keeps your blog running will interfere with your design.
- Search engine optimization (SEO) is built into these sites. You will benefit from the boost this provides, and the search engines should index your posts—making them easier for people to find without you having to do anything.

Disadvantages to a Hosted Site

- Usually, the URL of your hosted blog will have the host's name in it. For example, if Wordpress hosts your blog, the URL may be http://www.johnsmith.wordpress.com. On WordPress.com, you can use a custom domain for your blog (such as yourname.com) instead of the default address you get when you sign up (yourname.wordpress.com). This is called Domain Mapping, and it's a paid upgrade.

- You have fewer options regarding design and templates to use than with a self-hosted blog. It is much less customizable than a self-hosted site, and you cannot install plugins that extend functionality.

- The host may include ads on your site to reimburse them for their costs. If you wind up having a popular blog, someone else (your host) will be earning money from your efforts.

- You don't totally own the blog, and may not be allowed to include ads that could give you residual income. You are required to function under the host's policies.

- If you decide to move to a self-hosted blog later, you may encounter upgrading challenges and lose some momentum with your Google rankings.

A Self-Hosted Site

If you are willing to take on an additional challenge, and if you are pretty sure that writing a blog is a long-term professional goal for you, you may wish to consider a self-hosted site. Keeping with our previous analogy, self hosting a site is the equivalent of you throwing a party. Anything that goes wrong is up to you to fix, and you do all of the work!

Advantages to a Self-Hosted Site

Among the advantages of hosting your blog is that you own and control everything, and can adapt it to suit your needs.

- If you wish to include revenue-generating ads, you are free to do so.

- A self-hosted blog has a URL that you choose—it does not include a hosting company's name in it.

Disadvantages to a Self-Hosted Site

- It is more complicated to get this type of blog up and running. There are more steps, and it requires a bit more technical knowledge (you may wish to hire someone to set it up for you).
- You need to reserve your URL, and you need to maintain the blog's backend, to prevent security concerns such as hackers who may find their way into your blog and do damage to your site or content.
- It is not free to host your own blog. Even though you are self hosting, you still need to pay a company to let your blog *live* on its servers (this is also referred to as hosting, so even a self hosted blog still needs a host!). You will have to cover costs for the domain name (typically no more than $10 per year) and monthly costs. Depending on what company you choose to host your site, costs may range from $5 to $6 per month with a large company, to around $50 or more monthly to host with a boutique firm that provides more personalized services.
- You are more likely to run into some hosting issues. Sometimes, a software upgrade will cause problems with your design. Some companies may have unexpected downtime on their servers, meaning that people will not be able to reach your site at that time. When you discover these issues, it will be up to you to troubleshoot with the host company to fix the problem.

Select a Platform

If you decide the pros outweigh the cons and want to start your blog on a hosted site, your next step is to choose a host. Some common sites include Wordpress, TypePad, Blogger and Squarespace. Microblogging platforms, such as Tumblr.com, and Plurk.com, are also possibilities. Of these, microblogging platforms, Tumblr has the best reputation for search engine optimization. However, I would recommend not relying on a microblog to build your main website.

Other Options

Of course, there are many more options for creating a website. If you'd prefer a low-impact online option, you may want to try these tools to help you put up a professional online presence extremely quickly with little effort.

http://www.weebly.com/features.html
http://www.wix.com/
http://www.doyoubuzz.com/us/
http://brandyourself.com/
http://www.webs.com/
http://carbonmade.com/
http://flavors.me/
http://about.me
http://Zerply.com
http://www.rebelmouse.com
http://www.careercloud.com

Blogging is a personal experience, and choosing a platform that works for you will depend on what feels comfortable. You may want to try different platforms before you choose. However, my personal recommendation (and what I have always used) is Wordpress. An advantage of Wordpress not mentioned above is that you can start on a free (hosted) platform, Wordpress.com, and later move to a self-hosted platform on your own site.

Dan Schawbel mentioned in his story in Chapter 13 that he made this move, from PersonalBrandingBlog.Wordpress.com to his personal URL: PersonalBrandingBlog.com. I did the same thing. When I started blogging, I set up my blog at KeppieCareers.Wordpress.com, but then migrated it to KeppieCareers.com. If you do this—start at one domain, and then move to another—you will lose some traction in your Google rankings and other blog rankings. However, the advantage of using Wordpress.com is that you can pay a small fee (less than $15 per year as of this writing) to have your posts redirected, so people who find them on Google will land on the site they are seeking instead of a dead page.

Wordpress is the blog platform of choice for many well-known bloggers. Pam Slim, author of *Escape from Cubicle Nation* (the book and the blog), advises her readers not to worry about creating a perfect blog, but she does make one caveat:

> *"Please create your first site on Wordpress. It can grow and flex with you, and there are thousands of talented designers who can help you with it."*

There are many self-proclaimed geeks who work in Wordpress, and, as mentioned, there is a huge online community available to answer questions and help other bloggers. There are also many free tools and templates developed and frequent updates. While some believe that Wordpress is a little more complicated to use than some other platforms, it makes up for it in flexibility and options, allowing your blog to grow into a more involved, self-hosted blog. In this chapter I will go over the main things you need to know to get started, and I provide additional resources in the Appendix for getting started with Wordpress.

Secure a URL

Even though you will not require a URL if you decide to have a hosted blog, it is a good idea to secure one. Why? Because the name you may want could be taken later on if you decide to self-host. It is very easy to secure a URL, and should only cost around $10 or so per year.

Your first step is to test the URL you want to use, to see if it is already taken. I would suggest that the first URL you purchase be [YourName].com. For example, I own www.MiriamSalpeter.com.

Depending on your business or industry, you may wish to consider using other keywords in your URL, which may help people find your blog when using search engines. Obviously, if you are starting a business, it is a good idea to own your business name's domain. For example, my blog's domain is my business name: http://www.KeppieCareers.com.

When you choose your domain, be sure to think about your brand and target audience. If you are using this site for professional reasons, don't give it a name that is tongue-in-cheek. You will probably want to choose a .com domain, but if that is not available, try .net and .org as alternate choices.

In *ProBlogger* (Wiley, 2008), by Darren Rouse and Chris Garrett, they point out that some people include hyphens in their domain name, most likely to land domains they want when similar names without hyphens are not available. Darren and Chris explain that hyphens may make it difficult for people to remember the domain, and suggest that "there is a perception that hyphens are spammy" (although, there are certainly successful sites that use hyphens in their name, such as www.job-hunt.org). They also remind readers to consider the legal implications of a domain name, and to avoid using trademarked names. Some other considerations include:

- You may want to reserve many domains. For example, if you have the .com, you may wish to own the .net and .org as well. You do not need to host all of them on a site, but owning them will prevent anyone from using them, as long as you renew the domains.
- If your name has a common misspelling, you may wish to own both.
- If there are plural versions of your name, you may wish to reserve those as well.
- How does your domain name look when it is on the screen? Think about whether or not it is difficult to read, or if it includes a word that many people misspell, making it harder

to find your domain. Most importantly, make sure it doesn't spell anything with an embarrassing result.

IndependentSources.com made the following list of unfortunate domain names:

- A site called Who Represents, where you can find the name of the agent who represents a celebrity. Their domain name is www.whorepresents.com.
- Experts Exchange, a knowledge base where programmers can exchange advice and views, can be found at www.expertsexchange.com.
- The Mole Station Native Nursery, based in New South Wales, can be found at www.molestationnursery.com.
- If you're looking for computer software, there's always www.ipanywhere.com.
- Then, of course, there is the art designer website, www.speedofart.com.
- Want to holiday in Lake Tahoe? Try their brochure website at www.gotahoe.com.

All joking aside, your domain name is important. While it is not expensive or difficult to reserve, it is crucial. Ask your trusted friends for their opinions, carefully review the available choices, and pick one (or more than one) that makes the most sense for you.

To secure your URL, visit a domain registrar, such as Godaddy (www.godaddy.com) or Bluehost (www.bluehost.com). Note that you will only *require* a domain name if you self-host, but I recommend everyone follow these steps to reserve their domain name, so no one else has the chance to reserve it.

When you reserve your domain, find out if the company will remind you before it expires. Some of the larger companies will e-mail you a reminder, but I have heard of bloggers who find their blogs inactive as a result of not renewing their domains, and who never received any notification. Regardless, it is up to you to keep track of your domains, so be sure to make a note of renewal dates.

If you decide to self-host, many companies will be able to simultaneously set up a hosting account for you as well. In fact, GoDaddy.com is able to load Wordpress into a hosted site for as little as $10 per month.

Building Your Blog

If you have a lot of technical expertise, I would suggest you consider a self-hosted blog using Wordpress.org. Wordpress.org is Wordpress' software, which you can download to maintain your own blog. Wordpress.com is the site that allows anyone to easily set up a blog site in minutes.

I have many friends and colleagues who have moved to that solution after hosting their blog with other service providers. You might as well start where you will probably want to finish! If you are less technically inclined, I still believe that Wordpress.com is a very good solution.

There are several other resources specifically dedicated to blog building that I list in the Resources section of this book, but some start-up directions are provided here.

Signing Up for a Hosted Wordpress.com Blog

This is probably the easiest thing you will do. Go to http://wordpress.com and follow the button to "Get Started." All you need is a username and password. On the next screen, you will choose a domain name. For example, if I choose Miriam Salpeter as my username, the blog's name will be MiriamSalpeter.wordpress.com. You can change this later, but it is a good idea to choose something you like. As noted you have several options, either for a free or paid blog.

Once you confirm your e-mail address, you will sign into your blog and land on the dashboard page. The dashboard is the backend of your blog—you are the only one who sees it, and it controls everything people see when they visit your blog.

Settings

Start by fixing your settings to the right time zone, and be sure your blog title reads exactly as you wish. The proper time zone is important; if you ever schedule posts to go live at a future date or time; you need the blog to be set to the correct time.

Appearance

Consider choosing a simple, uncluttered template that does not distract from your message. Bells and whistles may be fun to incorporate, but be sure you keep focused on the reason for your blog—to provide an easy way for people to find out about you and to learn about your expertise. It is easy to become overwhelmed with design options, but don't let it stop you from getting your blog up and running. You can always change the design later and add information or options for your readers.

Click on "Themes" in your dashboard, and play around until you find something that you like. Don't worry too much about the other options in the Appearance section of the dashboard. You can focus on widgets and extras once you actually have your blog up and running.

Pages

Follow the link to "Pages," and then "Add New," to create important links on your blog, including an About page with your bio and information that makes your qualifications clear. It's important to provide a way to contact you, so include a Contact page in your navigation bar. Also consider using www.scribd.com to include your resume, or incorporate it directly onto a dedicated Resume page to make it easy to find.

Your pages will appear as navigation bars on your site. Because these pages are prominent on your site, they provide the easiest way for readers to learn more about you.

Writing Your Blog Posts

Technical and design details are important—you need to have a solid foundation to build your blog, and an aesthetically pleasing, easy-to-navigate site that will help people learn all about you. However, the content on your site is the most important thing, and you should spend the most time considering what you want to say and how.

Click on "Posts," and then "Add New," to compose a blog submission.

The first time you see the "Add Post" dashboard, it may seem complicated; but don't worry, just roll the mouse over each button to learn what it does. Add a title at the top and start typing your blog in the posting field.

If you are copying and pasting a document you wrote in Word or another program, don't just copy it into your blog. Instead, click either the "Paste From Word" or "Paste as Plain Text" button (on the second row of your dashboard, above the blog text). Next, copy the text and then insert it into your blog. This helps prevent formatting problems.

The other important button to know is the one that looks like a link of a chain, the Insert-Edit Link. This tool allows you to insert a link to another site or post. Linking is a great way to build relationships with other bloggers, as they will be notified of incoming links and may then follow up to see who is mentioning them. To activate this link, all you need to do is highlight some text that you have written, which you want to be in the link to a new post. When you highlight text, you will be able to select the chain/linking tool and insert the URL of the link you want to use. It is a simple, yet important aspect of blogging.

Once you have several posts, you may even consider cross-linking posts within your own blog (for example, you may want to refer to yesterday's or last week's post). Be sure to provide a link to encourage people to visit more than one page. For example, you may want to provide a link to your resume page at the end of some posts. Use the linking tool liberally to direct people through your blog.

Categories

On the right side of your dashboard, you have a place to create "Categories." Use this carefully—you don't want too many categories. Think of the umbrella topics that relate to the different areas in which you plan to write, and make those your categories. You can add a new category at any time.

Post Tags

This is an important tool, and is located on the right side of the "Post" dashboard. Tags are one way that Google and other search engines figure out what your post is about Using tags gives you a lot of say in how your post will be categorized. If there are certain words that you want people to use to find you (for example, "career coach" are keywords I would use), use those words to tag every post. Additionally, include your name in every post's tags. If you have a business, use that name as well.

Publish

Once you have written, categorized, and tagged your post, it is time to publish. You have several options: publish it immediately or schedule it for the future. After you publish, congratulations—you are a blogger!

Your Voice and Authenticity

There are many approaches to blog writing, and there is no one right tone, voice, and perspective. Use the information in this book to identify your target market, and provide useful, topical, and timely information that will appeal to that audience.

Sometimes, it is useful and appropriate to insert a personal voice in your blog. Some people refer to this as being authentic. In other words, let your readers know the real you—provide them your viewpoint and share your mistakes along with your successes. Most blogs incorporate some aspect of the writer's viewpoint. How much to share depends on you, your industry, and your goals for your blog.

One very successful blog in the human resources arena effectively incorporates personal perspective with topical information. Sharlyn Lauby, a Senior Professional in Human Resources who has been recognized by the Society for Human Resource Management, is president of ITM Group, Inc. (www.itmgroupinc.com), an employee training and organizational consulting firm. Sharlyn launched her blog, HR Bartender (www.hrbartender.com), in 2008, to provide a friendly place to discuss everyday workplace issues. The blog, with its unique blend of personal and professional information, is recognized as one of the top blogs in the industry. Sharlyn answered the following questions about creating a successful blog:

How and why did you decide to be HR Bartender?

"I decided to write a blog as a way to interact with current and prospective clients. I didn't want to solely rely on an electronic newsletter, which sometimes gets deleted before it is opened.

The HR Bartender name comes from my days in corporate human resources. I always thought people wanted me to be like a friendly neighborhood bartender—someone who knows their name, will listen to their stories and problems, and help them reach a solution. It is meant to be casual and comfortable, as if we were talking over drinks and nachos after work. The name also plays very nicely into my foodie status."

What reactions do you get from clients/prospective clients? How does it impact your business?

"I have really fabulous clients. Many of them read HR Bartender and leave comments. When I call and/or visit them, they will mention something they have read on the blog or that they forwarded a post to their boss, which is nice.

I do tell prospective clients up front about the blog (it is included in my proposals). HR Bartender gives them a sense of how I think and view human resources. The HR Bartender logo is on my business card—it's a great conversation starter!"

How does social media help you stand out?

"The HR Bartender name and logo are pretty catchy, if I may say so myself. And human resources pros get the bartender analogy. So, there are many things I can do to leverage it.

For example, I started sending out tweets on Friday afternoons about Happy Hour, referencing bartender blogs and recipes. Frankly, I wasn't really sure if anyone was reading them. Then, right before a long holiday weekend, I started getting questions about whether I was going to tweet Happy Hour early because of the holiday. That's just one fun example, but it emphasizes the fact that people do pay attention to what you say, and appreciate a personal spin."

Post Length

How long should your posts be? This is another question that depends on you, your topic, and your audience. Conventional wisdom suggests that online readers have very short attention spans. If you believe your audience would not be willing to digest a long post, you should consider writing short blogs. If your audience typically reads highly technical, lengthy research papers, a longer blog post probably won't faze them.

Personally, I have written blog posts of varying lengths, but I do try to keep posts to about 750-800 words. If my post is longer than that, I consider breaking it into two parts. Generally speaking, I'd suggest posts of at least 250 and no more than 1,000 words.

After reading some of your favorite blogs, you'll have a good baseline to follow. If everyone else in your industry writes long posts, assume people will read your long posts, too. However, you may be able to distinguish yourself by writing shorter, more succinct posts.

Make Your Posts Scannable and Add Photos

Beyond the length of your posts, it is a good idea to use bullet points or numbers as often as possible, as well as paragraph breaks. It is difficult to read long chunks of text on the screen. Help your readers by breaking things up. Once you identify several blogs you enjoy reading, make a point to note how the author sets up his or her text.

Adding photos can be another good way to spice up your blog (in Wordpress, there is an icon on the top part of your post toolbar, next to "Upload/Insert"). However, if you are not a photographer, you will need good sources of quality pictures. Here are some ideas:

- **http://www.pachd.com/:** free of charge, but you need to give credit to the artist.
- **http://www.morguefile.com/:** they have free images.
- **http://www.flickr.com/:** click on "Advanced Search" and select "Creative Commons Commercial." You do need to give credit for these images in the blog, but the artist allows you to use them for free. Be sure you do not inadvertently use a protected picture.

How Often to Post

If you plan to use your blog as a networking device and expect to attract readers, it is a good idea to post relatively frequently, especially when you first start. The blogs that attract the most readers post at least once a day, but that may be overly taxing for most new bloggers.

I would suggest posting new, quality content at least three times per week to start.

One reason for this is that you want Google to recognize that your site has frequent updates. Adding new content regularly will help trigger the search engine to crawl and categorize your site. It's also important to post consistently if you want people to recognize you as an expert. Let's face it, posting one blog a week about your topic does not necessarily indicate that you know that much about what you are writing. Blogging often invites interaction and sets you up as a subject matter expert in your niche.

Getting Ideas for Your Blog

I think that one of the most difficult parts of blogging (once you set everything up and learn the technical ins and outs) is thinking of things to write. Here are some ideas to get you started. Some will resonate more than others, depending on what your blog is about:

- **Comment on the news of the day.** Even if your blog is not specifically about a topic that everyone is talking about, if you think about it, you may be able to come up with a relevant post in response. For example, career bloggers might make an analogy between job seekers and a sports team that came from behind to win. Be creative, and you may be surprised by how many topical posts you are able to write. Another advantage is that you can tag the post with keywords that people are searching, which may win you some new traffic.
- **Read other blogs and respond via your own blog.** When I first started blogging, I spent a lot of time commenting on other blogs. Sometimes, I used my comments to spawn my own blog post.
- **What should people know about your area of expertise?** For example, if you are a teacher, focus on some aspects of

the profession that you enjoy and share your ideas about them. Maybe you believe in a certain type of curriculum; write about it. If your expertise is in sales, you may want to write about whether or not relationship selling is dead. If you are a librarian, focus on what libraries offer their patrons. It's a good idea to think in terms of themes. Maybe every Monday, you write about a particular topic or area, and every Wednesday you choose a different focus, etc.

- **Review books.** You may be surprised to learn that there are many people who offer to send you books in your niche topic area if you review them on your blog. If this interests you, make a point to read books relevant to your blog and post reviews. Reading the books should give you lots of ideas for additional blog posts as well.

- **Use titles with numbers and lists.** Blog readers typically love these. For example: "5 Ways to Improve Your Sales," or "10 Steps to Earning the Money You Deserve." These types of titles are sometimes referred to as "link bait," as people are more likely to find and share your post, therefore linking to it. So, write some lists!

- **Answer a question.** It isn't difficult to find questions. Look at Quora.com to inspire some ideas, or invite people to ask you questions via your social networks that you will respond to on your blog. For better search engine optimization, consider titling your post using a question people may ask Google. For example: "How to earn more money" or "How to find a job." What questions are people searching for that you can answer?

- **Interview someone.** Once you have your blog up and running (or even before you have an audience), think about people you would like to learn more about and request an interview. Depending on the person, it is a good idea to have various ways to handle the interview. Some people will respond to some e-mailed questions, others will make time to share information with you via phone or Skype (a free software that allows you to make call or conduct video interviews via the Internet).

- **Have one post per week that links to blog posts others wrote that you enjoyed.** This is a great way to get the attention of other bloggers; mention their name in your post, link to their blogs, and be sure to tag their names for that blog. Many bloggers will have a Google alert set, and will find the post via the incoming link or alert.

- **If you use Twitter, consider sharing your tweets in a post.** If you provided great advice or even retweeted links via your Twitter account, you might as well get some extra use from it. You can incorporate live tweets using Twitter.com. Click on "Expand" under the tweet you want to share, choose "More," and "Embed Tweet." Twitter will provide a code to include in your blog post. In your blog, add the code in the HTML mode. Use Storify.com to showcase conversations or chats from twitter.

- **Ask for guest posts.** Once you have already established your blog, you may want to invite guests to post. This can be a great way to grow your traffic, as those bloggers may alert their readers about the post on your blog, or create a redirect page with an intro and a link to the post on your site. I once invited colleagues to respond to a question, and posted their replies in a series of posts. It's always a good idea to build relationships with other bloggers and cross-promote.

- **Once you are an established member of a blogging community, ask bloggers if they would accept a guest post on their blog.** This is a tricky thing, as bloggers may be very proprietary about what goes on their site. Build a relationship with the blogger first via comments and links, and learn if the blogger accepts guest posts.

- **Do you have non-proprietary presentations you may be able to share?** Use Slideshare and incorporate the presentation as the main focus of a post.

- **Share a conversation about a client or a story about a situation you encountered.** This can be especially effective if you are able to illustrate a lesson you learned. Just be sure to protect the identities of all involved.
- **Consider incorporating a video post or using audio.** Video blogging (vlogging) has become popular, and some people enjoy the opportunity to watch what you have to say instead of just reading it. Upload a video to YouTube and you can easily embed it in your blog.

Measuring Traffic—and How to Increase It

If you use a hosted Wordpress blog, you have some analytics under "Dashboard," and "Blog Stats." If you have a self-hosted setup, you may use a program like Google Analytics to track your traffic. You can Google, "How to add Google Analytics to my blog" to find instructions. Or, follow up with available forums; Wordpress has a very active forum for questions and answers.

What if you find out that no one is reading your blog? It's like having a party and nobody comes. Don't despair. First of all, remember that one of the reasons that you created your blog is so people who Google your name find your body of work and expertise. If you are following directions regarding tagging your posts, and focusing on how you can share your expertise, you are achieving part of your goal.

But having regular visitors would be the icing on the cake. If you use the various techniques mentioned throughout this book to grow your online community, you will be well on your way to growing your blog traffic. Here are some reminders and ideas to help you increase your traffic and visibility:

- Start a LinkedIn group or a Google+ community specifically targeted for the population you'd like to reach with your blog. As a list owner, you can automatically feed your blog's content to group members who might click through to read more.

- Don't forget to actively comment on targeted blogs. Find your niche blogs, and focus on a few that have large, active communities (you can tell by reviewing the number of comments). Connecting with communities will attract visitors.

- Build a community of friends online. One idea is for you to select some people you admire and write some posts about them. It is even better if they have active Twitter accounts. This helps make a strong connection. Promoting others is a very good way to help people notice you.

- Read a big, popular blog in your niche and respond to his or her post via your blog and link back.

- Write "link love" posts each week, where you recommend and link to other blogs.

- Consider mixing it up by posting some video blogs. Some people really like watching videos, and if you have a presence on YouTube, you expose your ideas and brand to a new, very large search engine.

- Be sure you are using LinkedIn, Twitter, Google+ and Facebook to cross-promote your posts. Share links, and as you grow your communities you will find that people will click through to your blog.

- Spend time on Google's keywords analytics, and use popular words to tag appropriate posts: www.Google.com/AdWords.

- Consider submitting your blog to some directories. Google {directories to submit your blog} and follow the links that are most current. Consider including your blog in some of the directories listed.

- Don't forget to try guest posting or hosting guest posts. I don't suggest this until you are up and running, though. You don't want to confuse your readers about who authors your blog and who is the authority.

- Find group blogs and places to post that already have a lot of traffic. Posting some of your content there could help attract an audience; however, this is no guarantee. Also, be aware that cross-posting a lot of the same content may impact how Google and other search engines index and rank your site.

- Jim Stroud, who produces social media content, trains recruiters, and speaks on a variety of subjects, suggests submitting the URL of your social resume to Google, Yahoo, and Bing, to insure that recruiters and others can find it.

Optimize Search Engine Traffic

Nick Reese, founder of Microbrand Media, is an affiliate marketer whose livelihood depends in part on ranking well in major search engines (www.nicholasreese.com). He explains:

"Search engines are the librarians of today's world. You ask them a question and they will help you find an answer. Just like how a librarian relies on the title of a book, search engines rely heavily on the title of your web pages to determine what each page is about.

When setting up your WordPress blog, you will want to pay special attention to each page's title tag. Customizing each page's title tag isn't hard, but this extra degree of customization will help your pages rank higher, and help you get found more easily. Here are a few guidelines to writing your title tags:

- *Keep them under 70 characters, including spaces.*
- *Include the keywords you want to rank for as far to the left as possible.*
- *Make your title tags easy to read and understand.*

Simple search engine optimization options, such as customizing your title tag, are available in many premium themes. If you choose a free theme that does not have these options, I recommend using a plug-in, such as 'SEO Ultimate,' which can be installed via the plug-in area within WordPress.

Another important way to increase traffic is to take advantage of search engine optimization (SEO). While it sounds fancy, all this really means is that you want to do what you can to appeal to search engine traffic. In the blogging community, there is a bit of controversy about SEO blogging. Some people believe that if you provide quality content, that is the most important thing you can do to increase your search results."

Controlling Your Online Presence

Willie Jackson (http://williejackson.com), a technology professional currently serving as senior marketer and engineer at W3 EDGE, knows a thing about having an online presence. He reminds us of the following:

"One of the most effective steps a web-savvy and forward thinking job seeker can take is to take control of their web presence."

We know that recruiters and hiring managers are Googling candidates. Are you prepared? When is the last time you Googled yourself? Willie offers the following advice to help prospective employers or clients find the information you want them to know:

"When someone searches for you online, you want to have a helpful set of results on your Search Engine Results Page (SERP), results that reflect your qualifications. The last thing you want to show people is results that look unprofessional, unprepared, and irresponsible. While not everyone has drunken Facebook pictures and radical political views to hide, it's always a good idea to polish everything within your control.

So, the next question is obvious: How do we take control of our search results? The goal is to 'rank' for our name, so when people Google us, they find what we want to show them. There are a few simple steps we can take to do this:

- *Register yourname.com (or some permutation, even if it includes a middle initial) and set up a simple website there.*

- *Point all your social profiles (Facebook, LinkedIn, Twitter, Google+, Plaxo, etc.) to yourname.com.*
- *Consider a service like qalias.com to supplement your SEO goals.*

We want to rank for our name and also give people a place to link when they mention us online. So {yourname.com} will be a place that lists your professional qualifications, shares a bit of your personality, shows that you're proactive about managing your online presence, and introduces you to the online world.

Search engines work by providing people with quality, relevant information about their query. If you focus on the goal of 'teaching' search engines that who you are should be associated with yourname. com, you can see how important it is to link to this site. Every link to your site reinforces the impression you are trying to give search engines. The more people and sites linking to you using your name as 'anchor text,' the clickable words on a webpage in a link that take visitors to a new location, the better.

Services like Qalias (http://www.qalias.com) provide an additional boost, since they're built with SEO in mind. Many social profiles perform very poorly in terms of SEO, so we want to supplement out efforts with additional services if we have a common name or want to push some unflattering results off the first page of search results for our name.

Need an example?

A friend of mine shares a name with people who have some pretty awful search results—criminals and someone who has committed suicide. My friend suspected that these search results might be harming him, as he was having a very hard time finding a job despite his excellent qualifications. Sure enough, he landed an interview with a company that took one look at him before saying, 'Oh great! You're not the killer.'

Can you imagine?

My friend enlisted me to help him take control of his web presence. We set him up with a personal website built on WordPress, and published a post relevant to his field. He linked all of his social profiles to this site and within a few weeks, he was the top search result for his name. I'm pleased to report that he found gainful employment shortly after this, and has been thrilled with the results of these efforts.

Another lesson we can draw from this is how our personal website (or blog) can be used to demonstrate a deep subject matter expertise, beyond what a resume or cover letter can show. If you can demonstrate experience, become respected for your thoughts in a particular field, and have control of your web presence, it's likely that job offers will find you instead of you having to search for them."

Additional Tips

Connect Your Social Media Profiles

Make a point to connect your various social networks with your blog. You can provide direct links from your blog to your social media accounts by following these directions. Only link to your professional networks that you would want potential employers to find.

LinkedIn

- On the LinkedIn home page, click on "Edit My Profile."
- Go to Linkedin.com/profile/profile-badges.
- Choose your favorite button and copy the code.
- In your Wordpress blog's dashboard, go to "Appearances," then "Widgets."
- Select the *Text* widget, and drag it to the side panel.

Copy and paste the code you captured on LinkedIn and save changes.

Facebook Badges

- Sign into your Facebook profile.
- To create a badge, navigate to http://www.facebook.com/badges.
- Select a badge you like (you may even edit the badge).
- Select the type of site where you will use the badge, and copy and paste the code into a Text widget on your blog.

Twitter

- Log into Twitter.
- Go to http://twitter.com/goodies/widgets.
- Select "Create new" and pick one you like; then copy the code.
- In your Wordpress blog's dashboard, go to "Appearances," then "Widgets."
- Select the *Text* widget, and drag it to the side panel.
- Copy and paste the code you captured on Twitter and save changes.

Google+

- Log into your Google+ account and go to www.gplus-widget.com. Select Get Widget.

Search for Your Content

Once you begin to share content online, you may want to conduct regular searches to see if anyone is "borrowing" your words or "scraping" your blog for their own purposes. In addition to setting Google alerts for your name, you can do a Google search for any phrase in your blog, to see if anyone is replicating it. If you do happen to find someone replicating your blog, it is up to you to decide what to do about it. Some people ignore it, others forcefully work to find the owner of the offending site and demand that their content be removed.

Blogging as a Job

If you really like blogging, you can even find a job doing it! Problogger (http://jobs.problogger.net/) has a blogging job board. Just Google {blogging, jobs} for links to various paid opportunities to write about a topic.

Things to Remember

Blogging is the best way to build your brand and to share your expertise. If you follow the suggestions in this chapter, you will be able to get started with your own blog. In this chapter I explained:

- Advantages and disadvantages of having a hosted or self-hosted blog.
- How to secure a URL/domain name (and why it is important), regardless of your choice for your blog.
- Resources for creating a blog or website, and walked you through getting started on Wordpress (my recommended blogging platform).
- How to think about your blog's voice, as well as what to think about with regard to post length, how often to post, visual considerations, how to generate ideas for your blog, and how to increase your blog traffic.
- Expert details to help you increase your search engine optimization, control your rank for your name, and measure and increase your traffic.

- How to link to your other social networks, how to find out if someone else is using your online content, and how to find a job blogging.

As a self-professed non-techie, take my word for it—you can do this if you are willing to put some effort into it. If you need help getting started beyond the information here, use Google to find answers to almost everything you need to know, and post questions on LinkedIn or Twitter. While this may not be the easiest thing you will ever do, the potential payoff is well worth your time and effort.

More Tools to Extend Your Reach and Reputation

Job seekers who do not take advantage of social media tools are missing valuable opportunities to connect. However, not every network is well suited to every job seeker. Trying to participate in each platform is the equivalent of standing at a street corner and handing out invitations to a dinner party, in the hopes of having a group of people you want to feed show up at your table. It is possible, but highly unlikely. Which networks you should join depends on your unique skills and goals.

This chapter provides information and details about networks job seekers may not have considered leveraging for job search. I hope highlighting these opportunities will also remind you that there are many ways to take advantage of online tools. You do not necessarily need to conform to one particular set of networks or strategies. Learn about what is out there, decide for yourself where your skills are best served, and use the most effective approach for you.

Microblogs

I've written at length about Twitter, but there are several other services you may use to get the feel of writing and sharing information if you are not ready to commit to a blog. Tumblr, Postrous, and Plurk are not the best tools to develop an identity online; they do not provide the search engine optimization results or the unlimited design options that a blog platform such as Wordpress offers. However, they are relatively easy to use and make good training grounds for budding bloggers.

Tumblr

Tumblr's site (www.tumblr.com) explains it "lets you effortlessly share anything. Post text, photos, quotes, links, music, and videos, from your browser, phone, desktop, email, or wherever you happen to be. You can customize everything, from colors, to your theme's HTML." You can also share your posts to Twitter and Facebook and reblog, which allows you to pass along information you find on other sites.

Plurk

According to Wikipedia, Plurk (www.plurk.com) is "a free social networking and micro-blogging service that allows users to send updates (known as plurks) through short messages or links, which can be up to 210 text characters in length." The network indicates all of the updates of interest to you on your timeline, and you may respond by instant messaging or text messaging. Wikipedia points out that over 35% of Plurk's traffic comes from Taiwan.

More Social Networking Tools

Although LinkedIn, Facebook, Google+ and Twitter get the most press, there are many other social networks that may be useful for some job seekers. This is far from a comprehensive list, but it is a good review of some potentially useful sites you may not have heard of.

Pinterest

If your expertise relates to anything best highlighted visually, such as an interior or fashion designer, an architect, chef, or artist, Pinterest will be a great tool for you. For people in service industries and for those who don't have obvious visuals to share, Pinterest can be more challenging to implement. However, if you are creative, you can figure out how to leverage this popular tool. (Even accountants can use Pinterest with some effort!)

How to Use Pinterest

You may want to think of Pinterest primarily as a sharing platform more than a social networking tool, but there are "social" aspects to this network that allow you to "pin" information you like on virtual pinboards. (You can have public boards that others can see and access as well as some private boards.) Pinterest is different from most of the other big networks we cover because it is very focused on visuals—you pin pictures, which then link to a URL for more information.

What's the social part of Pinterest? While you can follow, "like," and add discussions to pins, you may connect with people who can connect you with job opportunities by drawing attention to the actual items you share, or "pin." Like other social networks, it provides a mechanism to connect with people who share your interests.

Like Twitter and Google+, Pinterest is an open network, which means you don't have to follow someone to see what they share—you can just visit their boards. It is simple to use, just click and re-pin, like, or tweet a link to a pin!

Create and Share Pins

You can share links to videos, books, infographics, quotes or sayings, photographs, even blog posts or articles. Name your Pinterest boards; be sure you give some thought to how you name them so they align with your business and contain appropriate keywords whenever possible. Use your imagination and creativity as you build your visual content, but don't be afraid to lift ideas from other active pinners.

For example, you could name a board "Top Up-and-Coming Photographers," or share your "Favorite Images of All Time" or even "Websites that Rock." For the less visual business, you could name one of your boards, "Tools that Get me Through" or "Go-To Technical Resources."

Pinterest allows you to create community boards and invite multiple pinners to contribute to it. This is another way to build partnerships and communities.

Find New Contacts on Pinterest

You can use Pinterest to grow your network by searching Pinterest for keywords, such as "fashion designers" if you are looking for a job in that field. You can search by pins, boards, or people. You'll find contacts who post using keywords related to your interests.

Once you find boards, you can "follow" either all or certain boards cultivated by people who interest you. You should repin, share, and comment on the boards, which can result in new contacts and possible business partnerships.

Be sure to share content on your own boards, such as pins that you've liked from other people's boards, or add your own visually engaging content, which may include photos of your designs (fashion, furniture, food, events you attend or host, books relevant to your industry, photos of people you respect in your field, videos, infographics (visual representations of information), and quotes.

CREATE YOUR OWN VISUAL CONTENT

Did you know you can create your own infographics? Try Visual.ly, Easel.ly, and google.com/publicdata/directory to produce aesthetic, sharable content on Pinterest. You may find your information going viral!

You can also create a visual in a PowerPoint slide, save it as a JPEG, and share it to Pinterest or other networks.

Be careful not to use images that are copyrighted or protected. Always list the image owner and the person who said the quote.

A NOTE REGARDING PINTEREST

When you re-pin (or share) from Pinterest, click through to the original source to ensure you don't link to content disguised as something else. Always pay attention to the pinner and consider their reputation and authority. There has been a buzz about copyright infringement issues on Pinterest. For example, is it okay for someone to pin something that they did not create or develop? Pinterest claims they are protected in the same way YouTube is when people share video content. Always credit the original source of material you do not create. Pinterest is taking steps to monitor pins to ensure linking to the original source and there is a clear definition of their copyright policy on their site.

A Question and Answer Site: Quora.com (http://www.quora.com/)

Quora calls itself "A continually improving collection of questions and answers created, edited, and organized by everyone who uses it." Their goal? "To have each question page become the best possible resource for someone who wants to know about the question."

Executive recruiter Harry Urschel of eExecutives Search Professions (his blog is: http://www.thewisejobsearch.com) believes that Quora is unique because if you ask a high-level question regarding engineering, you are likely to receive a response from a chief engineer at Motorola or Intel. I noticed a member asking a technical marketing question that Ramit Sethi, a New York Times bestselling author of *I Will Teach You to be Rich* answered.

How does a site like this help you? In general, it follows the same principle as other social media sites: sharing information and advice in your subject matter area helps you raise your profile. When you answer questions with good information and people begin to turn to you for advice, your digital footprint (how many people know about you online) increases. When more people know about you, your network grows and this improves your chances for learning about (and being recommended for) opportunities—both jobs and entrepreneurial ventures.

As someone who has been using Quora since early in its tenure, Douglas Kling, Director of Recruiting at HUNTER Technical Resources explained:

"The format allows for interactive discussion amongst subject matter experts on an ever-growing variety of topics. But, it also levels the playing field between the known experts and the unknown experts. The platform allows heretofore unknown experts in a specific space to increase their digital footprint based on the actual quality of the information they provide."

Tools to Measure Influence

Klout.com

This site purports to measure a person's online authority, via assigning a number between 1 and 100 to represent social media influence. To see a score, you need to sign in and connect your various social networks. Klout notes, "The science behind the score examines more than 400 variables on multiple social networks beyond your number of followers and friends. It looks at who is engaging with your content and who they are sharing it with."

The average Klout Score is 40. Klout explains, "Your score is determined over a large period of time, and is not necessarily representative of your number of followers and friends." In addition, Klout notes that the score, which is from 0 (least influential) to 100 (most influential) reflects influence, not activity. In other words, it doesn't measure how busy you are on social media (how many posts you have, or how many updates). What matters is how many people pay attention to you and what you say. As you may imagine, any tool attempting to assign a score indicating influence is going to meet resistance, and many people accuse people who have high scores of gaming the system. The best way to raise your score is to share good information that interests people and inspires them to pass it along.

Kred.com

This is another measuring tool (less discussed) that claims to evaluate both influence and outreach. Their site notes, "Kred scores reflect Trust and Generosity, the foundations of strong relationships." They explain that "influence is the ability to inspire action." It is scored on a 1,000 point scale and based on how often you are retweeted, replied to, mentioned, and followed on Twitter. If you connect your Facebook account, Kred will give you influence points when people engage with you on your wall via posts, mentions, likes, shares, and event invitations.

Outreach, according to Kred, "reflects generosity in engaging with others and helping them spread their message." The highest outreach score so far is 12, and it is measured by your retweets, replies, and mentions of others. On Facebook, you get outreach points for interactions on your wall and other walls registered with Kred.

Plaxo

Plaxo (www.plaxo.com) is a social network that helps you keep all of your contacts' information in one place, and is accessible online. Plaxo allows you to share photos, videos, and reviews, as well as content from Flickr, YouTube, Digg and other stream sites. You may also keep an address book and a calendar through Plaxo, which syncs with Yahoo, Google Mail, Outlook, Mac, and others. Here are some user thoughts regarding Plaxo:

> "I have found that if I need an e-mail address for a particular executive I can find it most often on Plaxo—more so than on LinkedIn, where I need to be connected to a person in order to have their contact information. As a recruiter, I find Plaxo very helpful in that sense. It often saves me quite a bit of time, and saves me the hassle of having to hire a researcher."
>
> —N.B., Search Consultant

"Plaxo is a great Rolodex site!"

—WALLACE JACKSON, Multimedia Producer
and i3D Programmer for Acrobat 3D PDF,
JavaFX, Mobile & Virtual Worlds

"Plaxo has moved from its spam-like original to an essential tie-up between your address book, LI, and itself, to make sure that you have the right contact details of every contact up to date. I don't use its social networking facilities much, as compared to Facebook."

—IAN MCALLISTER, Recruiter, Professional CV Writer

"I occasionally use Plaxo; it's good for keeping addresses, details, etc."

—MICHAEL WARE, Interim Finance Manager at Oriel Services Ltd.

Ryze

Ryze (http://ryze.com) explains that "members get a free networking-oriented home page and can send messages to other members. They can also join special networks related to their industry, interests, or location. More than 1,000 organizations host networks on Ryze, to help their members interact with each other and grow their organizations . . . you can message other members, join networks, view member home pages, and much more, for free." They also have a paid service that lets you conduct advanced searches for a few dollars per month. Here are some thoughts from Ryze users:

"I looked into Ryze and they only have 120,000 users right now, so I don't know if that would be an effective use of time."

—BRUCE BIXLAR Creative Retail Buyer |Experienced
Manager|Social Media & LinkedIn Profile Writer|[LION]
"Delivering More than Expected"

"Ryze I think is a classical second comer option, and trying to integrate the best of the rest ends up like the committee designed a camel as a solution to the next horse."

—IAN MCALLISTER, Recruiter, Professional CV Writer

Naymz

Naymz (www.naymz.com) is a free service that touts itself as a "one-of-a-kind network that helps you manage and measure your social reputation." It uses peer assesssments and connects to other social networks.

Ning

Ning (http://about.ning.com) is a platform for creating your own social network. It accommodates features such as photos, videos, forums, events, etc., which you customize. You can join via a customizable profile page, and then will be able to message and friend other users.

Ben Eubanks, a human resources professional for a nonprofit human services organization in Huntsville, Alabama, and creator of upstartHR.com, maintained a Ning network to help share updates and give people a sense of community. He explains:

"It's a great promotion to say there's a private forum just for customers to share ideas. Ning is for reaching out and building a network of people within a specific area of focus. It requires a lot of time for moderation, content creation/sharing, networking for growth, etc.

With the new pricing plans, Ning is no longer free, even for small, personal network creators. The text chat feature was one of the best functions, but it's now only available under one of the higher-tiered pricing plans. I use my own network for connecting and communicating with customers; I also share videos and special private content only available to people who have purchased my eBook.

Ning networks are not good for taking the place of Facebook, Twitter, and LinkedIn connections and communications; people can use LinkedIn groups (or Facebook groups) to do the same thing as a Ning network, without the cost."

Hubpages

HubPages (http://hubpages.com) bills itself as a website designed around sharing advertising revenue for high quality, user-generated content. Users write and publish posts and may be compensated via Google's AdSense, which manages a revenue split with writers. If you search Google, you may find many HubPages as search results.

Squidoo

Founded by Seth Godin, bestselling author, entrepreneur, and marketer, Squidoo (www.squidoo.com) is a community website that allows users to create pages (called lenses) for subjects of interest. This is another easy option for creating online content without doing too much work.

Ezine

Another place to share your expertise and potentially extend your brand, Ezine (http://ezinearticles.com) explains that it "serves millions of unique visitors monthly, has over 100,000+ RSS feeds plus 700+ email alert lists, designed to announce every new article posted to over 100,000 permission-based members/publishers." Visit their site to learn more about how to submit your expert articles and take advantage of their distribution system.

Tools to Connect Popular Social Networks and Email

Wouldn't it be great to be able to have immediate access to online information about people who email you, right from your inbox?

ACCOMPLISHING PAGE-ONE SEARCH RESULTS

As an IT manager and director at the same company for over 21 years, until it closed, Oliver Schmid realized that he needed to try something new to contradict the prejudice that his skills must be somewhat limited and one-sided. He began to turn to social media channels.

Oliver discovered Twitter, and used it to ask for and collect advice about self marketing. He concluded that he needed to demonstrate his skills and expertise to a broad audience, and began to blog about everything and anything IT related. He explains:

> "I eventually realized that I had portrayed myself as a 'jack-of-all-trades, master-of-none,' which is really not what I had intended; it occurred to me that I had to specialize more. I went back to the drawing board, wrote down my accomplishments over the last 6 to 10 years, and created my resume on Wordpress.
>
> I concluded that my success was really in evaluating current business processes and procedures, my ability to envision possible improvements, and how to make things better and more cost effective for an organization. I saved my last company millions and improved operations.
>
> I wanted to be on page one in search results for these accomplishments, and was looking into other ways on how to spread the word. I decided to create a blog (http://outsource4success.wordpress.com) in my area of expertise, and published various articles.
>
> Eventually, I discovered Ezine Articles and began to repost my articles there. Bang! All of sudden—almost overnight—I was on page one of all Google and Bing searches for Oliver Schmid."

A former colleague found Oliver on Google and recommended him for a freelance position with a Norwegian technology company, which turned into a long-term contract arrangement. He said that without Twitter, and his other efforts to get his name out there, he probably would not have found the job:

> "They weren't looking for me—they just spotted me online and it worked out. I would recommend anyone—in a job search or not—to build an online reputation. It can really be the difference between getting a job or just looking."

With applications and plugins for your Gmail or other mail services, you can. Check out these applications (also available on desk or laptops) to make it easier to identify and keep track of people who email you:

Rapportive's site (http://rapportive.com/about) explains, "Rapportive shows you everything about your contacts right inside your inbox. You can immediately see what people look like, where they're based, and what they do. You can establish rapport by mentioning shared interests. You can grow your network by connecting on LinkedIn, Twitter, Facebook and more. And you can record thoughts for later by leaving notes. Imagine relationship management built into your email. For free."

Xobni's website (https://www.xobni.com/about/) notes that these services "automatically find all the people with whom you've ever exchanged emails, calls, or SMS messages. They instantly provide a full view of each contact, complete with their photo, job title, company details, and email history — as well as updates from LinkedIn, Facebook and Twitter. Xobni is available for Outlook and BlackBerry. Smartr Inbox is available for Gmail. Smartr Contacts is available for Android and iPhone."

Social Bookmarking and News Sites

Jacob Share is a job search expert who created the award-winning JobMob® (http://jobmob.co.il/).

Jacob notes that when focusing on social networking, bigger is not better; rather, it is important to emphasize "having the right kinds of people in your network—the people who are more capable of helping you reach your goals."

Jacob identified several potential results from using sites such as Reddit, Digg, and StumbleUpon, which he refers to as:

". . . social bookmarking networks, since they grow as users 'bookmark' (save) websites to them. Saved bookmarks are public by

default, which means that bookmarking a website is a way to share that website with other people in your network.

Other people refer to these websites as 'social news networks' because any bookmarks you save are shared as news to your contacts, who can then share that news with their interested contacts, and so on. Either term is fine and you'll see them both all over the Web."

Jacob suggests the following potential advantages to engaging on these sites:

- **Learning:** As social bookmarking sites, people are constantly saving their favorite links from around the web on each and every topic, including job searching and in your industry. There are also many links about companies you may be targeting.
- **Networking:** Each of these sites lets you meet and network with other users around a topic, such as what's hot in your profession, or a specific article/news item.
- **Personal branding:** By regularly finding, organizing, and sharing quality links, especially around a specific topic such as your domain of expertise, people will gradually notice and think of you when they have a question about that topic.
- **Job leads:** Some of these sites have job boards catering to their user communities; recruiters looking for experts about specific topics and industries may use all of them.
- **Traffic:** If you have your own professional website, being an active social bookmarker can earn your site massive amounts of visitors. In fact, the most-respected and influential users of these communities, called power users, can often make a living off of envious companies who aim to copy their traffic-building success.

Spending some time on social media networks like these is not at all like sending your resume to a company and hoping for the best. The more you use them intelligently, the more benefits there are.

USING NETWORKING AND BOOKMARKING SITES TO YOUR ADVANTAGE

Here are Jacob Share's suggestions for using social bookmarking and social news sites to help propel your career plans.

Reddit (www.reddit.com)

- **Jobs page:** Hiring announcements are made on their blog, at http://blog.reddit.com/.
- **Typical user:** American male, smart, very tech savvy/geeky, young, sarcastic, who would love to work in a startup if they aren't already.
- **Effective usage tip:** If you have anything in common with the typical Reddit user, join Reddit and start bookmarking links that the community will like. More importantly early on, visit other people's submissions, vote them up (you like) or down (you don't like), and get involved by leaving insightful comments in the article discussions, especially those started by power users with similar backgrounds to your own (i.e., the power users who are most likely to like you).

Digg (www.digg.com)

- **Typical user:** Web savvy, tech savvy, young, likes gadgets, design, Apple, science, and comedy.
- **Effective usage tip:** If you're interested in the topics that Digg focuses on, join Digg. Digg includes the following aspect, similar to Twitter: You can create a My News page, which automatically pulls in the articles that have been "dugg" by the people you follow, so choose people who you'd like to learn from and/or network with.
- **Effective usage tip #2:** Digg has posted an Employees page at http://about.digg.com/team. Each digger has an account on Digg, which you can see by clicking on their avatar. Sometimes, the next best thing to networking with power users of a website is to network with the people who build and maintain it.

continued from page 320

StumbleUpon (www.stumbleupon.com)

- **Jobs page:** http://www.stumbleupon.com/jobs/.
- **Typical user:** Appreciates effort and originality, such as amazing art work, long articles, and creative thinking.
- **Best feature for job seekers:** Its career planning channel at www.stumbleupon.com/discover/career-planning/, which includes some of the most popular and useful articles on the Web about job search and careers.
- **Effective usage tip:** Join StumbleUpon with the intention of focusing on your industry, and then regularly Stumble (discover and thumb up) relevant articles. The more focused you are, the better. For example, I joined StumbleUpon by creating my JobMob profile at http://jobmob.stumbleupon.com/, and I almost exclusively bookmark job search-related articles there (over 2,000 likes). Then, look for other Stumblers (site members) who also Stumbled relevant articles, and build a network of like-minded contacts.

Jacob also explains:

"Each of the social networks described here has a voting mechanism for users to promote their favorite websites. This is the easiest way to share links with everyone else and not just people in your network, because the votes are public, i.e. anyone can see who voted for each article.

Digg, the website most well-known for making content popular this way, lets people click a button to vote for an article they liked, which is called digging that article, and its votes are called diggs.

Reddit and StumbleUpon both let users vote 'up' or 'thumb up' links they liked and vote 'down' or 'thumb down' links they didn't like."

Find Niche Social Networks

Jacob suggests, "As good as the social networks covered in this chapter are, they still might be too big and general for your job searching and online networking needs. To decide if a network is worth your time, look for a "what's popular" page, and use that as a measure of the audience's tastes. Any statistics on that page might also give you an idea of how many people are really active on the site, and dates should indicate if the site's audience is still active. You don't want to waste your time on a website whose best days are behind it.

Also leverage your existing networks to find out if there are even better sites that you don't yet know about. Ask your contacts where they spend most of their time online, and you might discover some valuable places. In fact, the best way to do this is to ask your contacts what their favorite network is for professional purposes, or you can try asking where they would prefer you to meet up with them online.

Check out Traffikd's list of social media and social networking sites. This web directory lists over 500 social networks by category, and there are currently over 30 categories, so there's a good chance you can find at least one niche network worth diving into on a regular basis."

YouTube

With 800 million unique users per month, people watch over 4 billion hours of video every month on YouTube. Video sharing is something you may want to consider. Video resumes have gotten a lot of press in the last few years, and some believe that having a video presence is important for job seekers to demonstrate their expertise. Since creating and sharing videos is not difficult (all you need is a basic device to record and upload to YouTube), most everyone can access this medium. Depending on your skills, using video to share your expertise may be a good avenue to grow your online brand if:

- You enjoy being on camera and have equipment that creates a quality final product.
- You can sit and speak without fidgeting or creating other visual distractions.
- You are creative enough for your industry and can produce a product that represents the best of what you have to offer.

Unfortunately, the most well-known video resumes are those that go viral (become popular) for the wrong reasons and become embarrassments for their creators. If you are good on camera and enjoy this medium, experiment with video blogs to share your expertise and consider adding a video resume to your online portfolio.

Here are some other tips from Loic Le Meur, founder of the Twitter software application Seesmic:

- Don't think, just shoot.
- Interview others—(You can use your phone).
- Add a "subscribe to this channel" button at the beginning of all of your videos. It takes 20 seconds to do this with YouTube annotations.
- Transcribe your videos to get more search visibility.
- Add a simple "Watch the next video" button at the end of each video.
- Starting a YouTube video description with a link to whatever you want to promote is a good way to get traffic from YouTube to your site, since YouTube standard annotations don't let you do that—you need to buy advertising if you want to link from a YouTube video to a non-YouTube URL which isn't a YouTube content.
- Respond to comments.
- Create short videos.
- Post often.
- Create one or many YouTube channels.

Katrina Kibben, Social Media Consultant (http://katrinakibben. wordpress.com/), explains that the easiest way to attract people to view your YouTube video is to transcribe the content into the video description verbatim. She explains:

> *"The description I am referring to is available for editing after you upload the video (not the description that is shown while the upload is processing). There is no character limit so feel free to include all of the content available.*
>
> *"When you transcribe these videos, you earn search traffic to your YouTube channel by making it easy for search engines to "read" your content. Plus, with the new annotation tools and custom backgrounds, you can showcase your brand while the videos are viewed."*
>
> *She warns, "Now remember, one video will not drive millions of hits to your YouTube channel or to your website. Create a series of quick 30- 45 second videos on a certain topic then create a playlist of those videos with a keyword relevant title. "*

Audio Sites

Podcasting and audio content has become another popular way to share expertise. One easy way to enter this forum is use BlogTalkRadio (http://www.blogtalkradio.com). All you need is a computer and a phone to create audio content to share online.

WHAT SKILLS DO YOU NEED FOR RADIO?

If you like to talk and think this might be a good medium for you, review these tips from Maggie Mistal (www.maggiemistal.com), career change consultant and well-known radio personality:

- **A true passion for radio**—*I have never met a successful host who didn't love radio. It's a great medium for great conversation.*

continued from page 324

I listened to talk radio for years before becoming a host. Once you start hosting a show, you even look at life differently—everything becomes fodder for radio. If you have a conversation, read an article, or react to a story, you start to think in terms of what would make for great radio conversation.

- **Creativity and authentic passion**—*To consistently come up with compelling topics it takes a lot of creativity and passion for your show. I have heard some people say that radio can be "like a beast that needs constant feeding." Unfortunately if you get that attitude, I think it's going to be hard to come up with topics. I look at radio as a chance to share my message of "soul search, research, and job search" in new and different ways, so that people really get it. I share my own advice and stories, I have guests on my show like Martha Stewart and Deepak Chopra to share their advice on following your passion, and I take listener calls to help them apply the soul search, research, and job search message in their own situations. I am constantly looking for new ways to get my message across through my show, and I never get bored.*

WHAT ARE THE KEY MECHANICS OF RADIO HOSTING?

Maggie explains:

- **Hosting skills**—*Valuable skills include opening/closing, resetting, managing the clock, managing guests, keeping the show moving at the right pace, eliciting callers, managing callers (respectful but not so polite you let them take over), and the ability to make listeners feel like you're "inviting them into your living room."*
- **Content expertise**—*This includes sharing information and answering callers' questions in a quick, yet relevant and useful way.*
- **Education and entertainment ability**—*This includes comedic abilities and an ability to share information in a fun and compelling way.*
- **Presence**—*The ability to stay focused and engaged in a seemingly one-sided conversation, and the ability to present without audience feedback, are key.*

continued from page 325

WHAT SHOULD SOMEONE THINKING ABOUT CREADING AN ONLINE SHOW CONSIDER?

- **Soul search**—*What is the philosophy behind your show? What is your mission and purpose with it? What is at the core of your message and why are you sending it? What audience do you want to attract? What are you trying to say, and what's the best way to convey that message?*
- **Length**—*How long do you need to provide useful information but leave them wanting more?*
- **Format**—*This depends on your topic and mission. Are you taking calls or is it you and your guests (or some combination)? Remember, it takes time to build a caller base because most people like to listen versus actually call in. If you're going to have guests, you need to add that into your planning time. I find it takes about four hours of prep for every one hour of airtime.*
- **Sponsors**—*As you build popularity, you might want to approach organizations that would benefit from advertising on your show and gaining access to your listeners.*

In terms of format, again it depends on your mission, but to elicit callers Maggie suggests:

- *Open with a compelling topic and share your own related anecdote.*
- *Ask for calls from listeners.*
- *Expound on the topic and tie each guest into the topic.*
- *Reset the show often, by saying who you are, what the show is about, today's topic, etc.*
- *Interview guests.*
- *Have a signature show close.*

ANY DO'S AND DON'TS FOR PREPARING?

- *Prepare bullet points in advance of what you are going to say. Do not read verbatim; speak conversationally.*
- *Before going on air, take a few minutes to stretch out your chest, shoulders, neck and face. It will also help you relax.*
- *Don't staple your papers together or rattle them while recording; microphones pick up a lot and you don't want anything to distract listeners from your message.*

continued from page 326

- *Focus on what the audience wants to hear, not just what you want to say.*
- *Remember that people often listen to radio while doing other activities, so keep your points simple and have examples that illustrate what you're trying to convey.*
- *Speak clearly and slowly.*
- *Remember to breathe.*
- *Drink only room temperature or warm liquids. Cold liquids will tighten your vocal chords and distort the normal sound of your voice.*
- *If you forget what you were going to say, it's okay. Rather than freeze up, look to your bulleted list for guidance.*
- *Don't talk over others. It's distracting to the listener.*

WHAT ARE SOME GOOD TECHNIQUES FOR GETTING THE MOST OUT OF YOUR GUESTS?

- *Prepare for your guests (i.e., read or at least deeply skim their book, ask the guest to provide the top five bullet points on his/her topic, etc.).*
- *Ask yourself what your audience will benefit from hearing this person talk about? Ask pointed questions to get concrete answers. It helps to listen to talk show hosts and take notes on how they interview guests. Incorporate what you like from their styles.*
- *Give topic and/or sample questions ahead of time to your guest, but don't talk too much before the show; it takes the spontaneity away from the actual interview.*
- *Weave in your guest's bio throughout the interview, rather than presenting it all up front.*

DO YOU HAVE ADVICE FOR A SHOW WITHOUT GUESTS? IS IT POSSIBLE TO BE ENGAGING ALONE ON RADIO?

- *Care deeply and speak passionately about your topic.*
- *Have real life examples.*
- *Ask for listeners' reactions.*
- *Use your radio voice—love the sound of your voice on air; it may take some getting used to hearing yourself but you have to like the sound and have fun with it.*

Slideshare and Scribd

Slideshare (http://www.slideshare.net; more than 60 million monthly visitors) and Scribd (http://www.scribd.com; 90 million readers per month) are two options many job seekers often do not consider to share their information and expertise.

If you are considering authoring an eBook or the equivalent of a white paper about a topic in your area of expertise, Scribd is a good place to share it. Slideshare has become very popular as a place to share presentations and to think about presentations creatively. In fact, some people have used Slideshare to create resumes, which they then publicize via LinkedIn, their blogs, or just on Slideshare's search engine.

Writing and design skills are useful for these mediums. If you are creative, you may be able to attract attention by offering job search documents that most people do not offer.

For ideas about how to create a Slideshare resume, take a look at Chris Ferdinandi's example at www.slideshare.net/cferdinandi/resumesm.

FourSquare

FourSquare (http://foursquare.com) is a geo-location based service that merges your offline and online worlds. Marketers use these geo-location services to push information about products and services through Twitter and Facebook, and individuals use them to connect on the move with friends and engage in game-like interactions. Savvy recruiters use it, too.

Once you have downloaded the application to your smart phone, you can use FourSquare to win the mayorships of locations by checking in (being in the places and using their geo-enabled devices to connect with the system).

If you are comfortable announcing your location to a select community (or to everyone), you can also use geo-location services as a job search/networking tool.

Jill McFarland, marketing director and blogger (http://www.jill
mightknowjack.blogspot.com), points out some important aspects
of geo-location via location-based services (LBS):

- **Community**—LBS combines online and real life interactions. When you check in, you can see what your friends are
  doing and get recommendations; through layering, you can
  see a city through the eyes of a trusted source.
- **Gaming**—Many users of LBS begin because they are drawn in
  by the gaming aspect. They want to say that they are the mayor
  or score the most points for checking in to various locales.
  FourSquare appears to have the lead in LBS right now because
  it is more of a game experience than other LBS services.

How can you apply gaming and geo-location to a career search?
Meghan M. Biro, founder of TalentCulture (www.talentculture.com)
and a globally recognized recruitment expert, suggests:

*"Know all the players in a target company—and that includes know-
ing where they are. Most job searchers have a wish list of companies
they are targeting. Go one step further and scout out the key players
at target companies on Twitter, LinkedIn, Facebook, and Google+.*

*If you are diligent and a good researcher, you may also find
great networking contacts on FourSquare. Observe what they say,
what articles they link to, where they go, and who they follow.
You'll get a sense of who they are, what they value, what their
comfort zone is, and what they think about."*

Some recruiters are already thinking about how to use geo-
location tools. Andy Headworth, who advises companies on how to
use social media as a recruitment tool and blogs at www.sironasays.com,
explains how he uses FourSquare to identify candidates:

*"Enter {"at companyname" 4sq–jobs} on http://search.twitter.
com site, or, alternatively you can use Google; to search for*

{site:twitter.com "at companyname" 4sq–jobs}. This will find anyone who has checked in to a company, so they will likely be employees of that company, interview attendees, or people attending meetings there."

Using LBS could help you connect with a savvy recruiter.

Determine How to Connect

With information about the key players at your target companies who are using LBS in hand, devise strategies to connect with them. Meghan advises:

"Use traditional networking to connect, then take it to the next step by requesting connections via FourSquare. If you frequent the same locations, this may be a perfect connecting point.

Always initiate appropriate follow-up, research, and prep for inter-views, thinking about the value you could bring to an organization and expressing it in a compelling way—give yourself every advantage."

With LBS, especially the ones that are game-based, Meghan notes that you will have to make good choices about how to network with your targets, even though you have less-than-complete information. When you're trying to win a job opportunity, you seldom have per-fect information; but you can make better choices by using LBS to observe the actions of the people who are involved in hiring. Meghan explains:

"Winning a new job requires you to step out of your comfort zone to win. Using LBS as a job-seeking tool could be stepping out of your comfort zone. It's scary, but it's in your self-interest to give yourself every strategic advantage.

Sometimes where you are is who you are—like when you're the mayor of your coffee shop. Sometimes you need to move to a new location. Sometimes you have to decide to shake things up to win.

It is possible to network your way to new connections that can support your job search. Sign into FourSquare today and try it out."

Things to Remember

Alexandra Levit, business and workplace author and speaker, clearly articulates the value of participating in these and other networking opportunities:

"Social media enable an exponentially larger network, reaching potential contacts through blogging, posting YouTube videos, and tweeting. And instead of talking about your career change among your small group of friends, you now have the power to reach those friends' friends' friends.

Online networking also saves time and is much more convenient. Instead of commuting to a hotel and spending two days in a suit just so you could meet one or two valuable contacts, you can have dozens of conversations and lay the foundation for meaningful one-on-one relationships in the course of a few hours.

Every study on the power of social networking illustrates that people who share useful content have the most success in terms of building relationships.

Don't feel it's necessary to be a member of every hot new network; save time by evaluating your purpose for having a presence on each one you participate in. Differentiate between personal and professional networks, and communicate your boundaries to your contacts. Use them to establish contact with individuals you might not have the opportunity to meet otherwise. Avoid asking for a job directly or assuming you have a close relationship with someone immediately just because you have followed them online. These things take time, and several interactions.

My advice? Evaluate your skills and interests, and assess what networks work the best for you. Don't be afraid to start small. For example, use existing online sites such as Ezine to post content, or contribute posts to niche sites if you don't think you are well suited to writing a blog. If you hate yourself on camera, don't feel compelled to post a YouTube resume; but if you have a great voice, focus on an audio online presence.

Authenticity—being who you are—is a constant topic in the blogosphere. If you figure out who you are and what you have to offer, and evaluate the best ways to share what you want people to know about you, you will be able to take advantage of the social web—to expand your reputation and attract opportunities you may have never thought possible.

Nothing happens before you start. Pick a network and sign up. And be sure to ping me to let me know you are online!

GLOSSARY

Alltop.com: a magazine rack of blogs, this site categorizes numerous topics and provides easy access to blogs in your targeted niche.

Applicant tracking system: computerized systems that most large and mid-sized companies use to electronically review applicants' resumes.

Blog: a type of website that includes information, commentary, opinions, and advice about a topic or topics. Some people maintain personal blogs, which resemble diaries. Other blogs are professional in nature, wherein writers share expertise about a subject area. There are also corporate blogs, which are aimed at connecting with customers. Blogs may include writing, video, graphics, and audio elements.

Blog host: a company that provides space on their servers and equipment to store your blog, usually for a fee.

Blogroll: a list of blogs that a blog owner recommends and posts on his or her own blog. Not very popular, but you will sometimes see people use blogrolls.

Connector: people in a community who know large numbers of people and who are in the habit of making introductions. The term was popularized by Malcolm Gladwell, in his book *The Tipping Point*.

Digital footprint: the impact an individual or company has online, measured by how easy it is to find information via search.

Doppelganger: someone who shares your name.

Encore career: a career that provides purpose, passion, and a paycheck. Promoted, with resources for those seeking encore careers, via http://www.encore.org.

Facebook: A social networking website. It allows users to add friends and send them messages, and update their personal profiles, to notify friends about themselves. Additionally, users can join various groups and networks.

#FollowFriday or #FF: a Twitter tradition. Users send names of people they recommend following via Twitter, using this hashtag on Fridays. Some people include specific reasons for the recommendation and/or additional hashtags, to suggest why people should follow.

Geolocation: the geographic location of an object, such as a cell phone (and the person holding it).

Google alert: a tool that tracks subjects or keywords, and sends e-mail alerts when it indexes something relevant. Go to www.google.com/alerts to set up alerts.

Group (LinkedIn): an interactive option on LinkedIn that provides users with opportunities to connect via common interests, which may be personal or professional. Leading or managing a group may provide opportunities for networking beyond simply participating.

Hashtag: designated by the # symbol, it is a way to identify or *tag* a topic or event on Twitter. Attaching the # makes events or anything mentioned on Twitter easier to search.

Hosted/self hosted: a choice blog owners make; have a hosted blog that resides on a company's server or self host, which involves taking responsibility for setting up and managing the blog site's back end.

Invitations (LinkedIn): inviting others to join your network or accepting their invitation. When a contact accepts an invitation, you will be in each others' first-level contacts. This is free. LinkedIn allots 3,000 invitations to each member, and invitations others send to you do not count against this total. There is no cost to issue or accept invitations.

Introductions (LinkedIn): requesting that contacts introduce you to one of their first- or second-level contacts. which sets off a chain of communication from you, to your contact, to the target contact, or to another intermediary contact, and then to the target contact. These are also free, and, with a free LinkedIn account, you have five of these to use at any time.

inMails (LinkedIn): sending an e-mail-like communication directly to someone not in your first-level network, through the LinkedIn communication channel.

Informational meeting: an informal meeting with someone; this provides an opportunity to share your expertise and insights from your research, and a chance to ask specific questions about a company, field, person, etc.

Keywords: the important terms that are more relevant to you. The words you want people to use to find you; how you describe yourself.

LinkedIn: an online professional networking site that allows users to connect and share information, resources, and job postings.

LIONs: LinkedIn Open Networkers. These are people who announce their interest in connecting with anyone on LinkedIn.

Live Tweeting: Live tweeting is when conference attendees forward notes and tidbits of information from speaker sessions via Twitter to people who are following them.

Microblogging: Twitter, Tumblr, Posterous.com, and Plurk.com. Erick Schonfeld suggested on TechCrunch that microblogs are "designed for quick hits but can support photos, themes, and other more blog-like features."

Networking: making contact with people for the purpose of sharing information and advice; often relates to job hunting, but is not something that only active job seekers should do. Can happen online (via social networks) or in person.

Passive job seeker: people who may be open to considering a new job, but are not actively engaged in sending out resumes and researching new opportunities.

Pull job search strategy: job seekers who actively engage online and via appropriate social networks, who can expect that opportunities, including jobs, may actually find them (via their networks), without them needing to apply. This ideal version of job hunting is possible when people make a point to share information and advice, and demonstrate their subject matter expertise.

Push job search strategy: the old-fashioned job search approach, which involves sending resumes to apply for advertised jobs.

Skype: a technology that allows both audio and video conversations via computer.

StumbleUpon.com: a website that uses a ratings system to create a collaborative opinion about a website's value.

Technorati.com: founded as the first blog search engine, Technorati.com indexes millions of blog posts and has become a source for the top emerging stories, opinions, photos, and videos. Technorati.com tracks the authority and influence of blogs, and indexes who and what is most popular in the blogosphere.

Twitter: a service that allows users to send and read messages, known as *tweets*. Tweets are short posts of up to 140 characters, displayed on the author's profile page and viewable to anyone electing to follow them. Tweets often include a URL linking to additional information. This type of messaging and sharing of information in brief spurts is known as *microblogging*.

Twit pitch: a short description that explains your value proposition. In a Twitter bio, this pitch is 160 characters maximum. More generally, it refers to a brief explanation of an individual's accomplishments and skills.

Quora: a collection of questions and answers created, edited, and organized by everyone who uses it. Quora's goal is for each question page to become the best possible resource to answer each question.

Vlogging: this refers to videos that are posted on blogs.

RESOURCES ▶

Blogs and Blogging

Bedord, Jean. *I've Got a Domain Name. Now What?* (Happy About, 2008).

Butow, Eric and Bollwitt, Rebecca. *Blogging to Drive Business: Create and Maintain Valuable Customer Connections.* (Pearson Education, Inc., 2010).

Garner, Susannah and Birley, Shane. *Blogging For Dummies.* (Wiley, 2010).

Gunelius, Susan. *Blogging All-In-One For Dummies.* (Wiley, 2010).

Hussey, Tris. *Create Your Own Blog: 6 Easy Projects to Start Blogging Like a Pro.* (Sams, 2010).

Rosenberg, Scott. *Say Everything: How Blogging Began, What It's Becoming, and Why It Matters.* (Broadway, 2009).

Rouse, Darren and Garrett, Chris. *ProBlogger.* (Wiley, 2008).

Tomasi, Chuck. *Sams Teach Yourself WordPress in 10 Minutes.* (Sams, 2010).

Entrepreneurs

Goodman, Michelle. *My So-Called Freelance Life: How to Survive and Thrive as a Creative Professional for Hire.* (Seal Press, 2008)

Goodman, Michelle. *The Anti 9-to-5 Guide: Practical Career Advice for Women Who Think Outside the Cube.* (Seal Press, 2007)

Israel, Shel. *Twitterville: How Businesses Can Thrive in the New Global Neighborhoods.* (Portfolio, 2009)

Lacy, Kyle. *Twitter Marketing For Dummies.* (Wiley, 2010)

Levinson, Jay Conrad, et al. *Guerilla Marketing for Job Hunters 2.0* (Wiley, 2009)

Peneberg, Adam L. *Viral Loop: From Facebook to Twitter, How Today's Smartest Businesses Grown Themselves.* (Hyperion, 2009)

Percival, Sean. *MySpace Marketing: Creating a Social Network to Boom Your Business.* (Que, 2009)

Shih, Clara. *The Facebook Era: Tapping Online Social Networks to Build Better Products, Reach New Audiences and Sell More Stuff.* (Prentice Hall, 2009)

Slim, Pamela. *Escape from Cubicle Nation* (Portfolio Hardcover, 2009).

Facebook

Kraynak, Joe and Belicove, Mikal E. *The Complete Idiot's Guide to Facebook.* (Alpha, 2010)

Pearlman, Leah and Abram, Carolyn. *Facebook For Dummies (2nd Edition).* (Wiley, 2009).

Vanderveer, Emily A. *Facebook: The Missing Manual.* (Pogue Press, 2011).

LinkedIn

Alba, Jason. *I'm on LinkedIn—Now What? A Guide to Getting the Most Out of LinkedIn.* (Happy About, 2009)

Schaffer, Neal. *Windmill Networking: Understanding, Leveraging and Maximizing LinkedIn: An Unofficial, Step-by-Step Guide to Creating and Implementing Your LinkedIn Brand—Social Networking in a Web 2.0 World.* (Book Surge Publishing, 2009).

Vermeiren, Jan. *How to Really Use LinkedIn.* (Book Surge Publishing, 2009).

Howes, Lewis and Agin, Frank. *LinkedWorking: Generating Success on the World's Largest Professional Networking Website.* (Four Eighteen Enterprises, 2009)

Personal Branding

Arruda, William and Dixon, Kirsten, *Career Distinction.* (Wiley, 2007).

Schawbel, Dan. *Me 2.0, Revised and Updated Edition: 4 Steps to Building Your Future.* (Kaplan, 2010)

Schawbel, Dan. *Promote Yourself.* (St. Martin's, 2013)

Miscellaneous

Alboher, Marci. *One Person/Multiple Careers: How the Slash Effect Can Work for You.* (Warner Business Books, 2007)

Brogan, Chris and Smith, Julien. *Trust Agents: Using the Web to Build Influence, Improve Reputation and Earn Trust.* (2009)

Ferrazzi, Keith. *Who's Got Your Back?* (Broadway Books, 2009)

Gladwell, Malcolm. *Outliers.* (Little, Brown and Company, 2008) and *The Tipping Point* (Little Brown, 2000)

Hansen, Katharine. *Tell Me About Yourself: Storytelling to Get Jobs and Propel Your Career.* (JIST Works, 2009)

Mandell, Lisa Johnson. *Career Comeback.* (Hanchette Book Group, 2010)

Levinson, Jay Conrad and David Perry's very helpful book *Guerrilla Marketing for Job Hunters 2.0* (Wiley, 2009).

Multiple Applications

Crompton, Diane and Sautter, Ellen. *Find a Job Through Social Networking* (JIST Works, 2010).

Fertik, Michael and Thompson, David. *Wild West 2.0: How to Protect and Restore Your Online Reputation on the Untamed Social Frontier.* (AMACOM, 2010)

Kelsey, Todd. *Social Networking Spaces: From Facebook to Twitter and Everything in Between* (Apress, 2010)

Schepp, Brad and Debra. *How to Find a Job On LinkedIn, Facebook, MySpace, Twitter and Other Social Networks.* (McGraw-Hill, 2010)

Twitter

Fitton, Laura. *Twitter for Dummies.* (Wiley, 2009)

Israel, Shel. *Twitterville: How Business Can Thrive in the New Global Neighborhoods.* (Penguin, 2009)

Makice, Kevin. *Twitter API: Up and Running* (O'Reilly Media, 2009)

McFedries, Paul. *Twitter: Tips, Tricks and Tweets.* (Wiley, 2009)

Morris, Tee. *Sams Teach Yourself Twitter in 10 Minutes.* (Pearson Education, Inc., 2010)

O'Reilly, Tom. *The Twitter Book.* (O'Reilly Media, 2009)

Sagolla, Dom. *140 Characters: A Style Guide for the Short Form.* (Wiley, 2009)

Whitcomb, Susan Britton, Bryan, Chandlee and Dib, Deb. *The Twitter Job Search Guide.* (JIST Works, 2010)

Job Search Resources

www.job-hunt.org

www.quintcareers.com

www.rileyguide.com

www.jobsearch.about.com

Sites Providing Company Information

www.ebosswatch.com

www.glassdoor.com

www.hoovers.com

www.referenceusa.com

www.vault.com

www.wetfeet.com

Recruiter Directories/Staffing Associations

www.headhuntersdirectory.com

www.i-recruit.com

www.recruitersdirectory.com

www.searchfirm.com

Job Boards

AIRS job board directory –
www.airsdirectory.com/mc/forms_jobboard.guid

AllStarJobs.com – www.allstarjobs.com

CareerCast.com – www.careercast.com/jobs

Idealist.org – www.idealist.org

Indeed – www.indeed.com

JobBoardReviews.com – www.jobboardreviews.com

Job-hunt.org – www.job-hunt.org/jobs/states.shtml

Jobtarget.com – www.jobtarget.com

Linkup.com – www.linkup.com

RileyGuide.com – www.rileyguide.com/jobs.html

Simply Hired – www.simplyhired.com

SnagAJob.com – www.snagajob.com

USAJobs.com – www.usajobs.gov

LinkedIn.com – click on Jobs tab

Twitter as a Source for Job Descriptions

@jobshouts – www.jobshouts.com

@TweetMyJOBS – www.tweetmyjobs.com

@twitjobsearch – www.twitjobsearch.com

Deep Web Search Tools/Meta Search Engines

www.pipl.com

www.polymeta.com

Personal Branding

360° Reach Personal Brand Assessment – www.reachcc.com/ 360reach

Dan Schawbel – www.personalbrandingblog.com

Reach Personal Branding – www.reachcc.com

Student Branding – www.studentbranding.com

Keyword Tools

Google AdWords – https://adwords.google.com/select/KeywordToolExternal

Tag Crowd – www.tagcrowd.com

Wordle – www.wordle.net

Resources to Research Non-Profit Careers

CommonGood Careers – www.commongoodcareers.com (@cgcareers)

Dowser – www.dowser.org (@dowserdotorg)

Encore.org – www.encore.org

Idealist – www.idealist.org (@idealist)

Nonprofit Professionals Advisory Group – @gassnerotting

Steve Joiner – @IdealistSteve

Tools to Help Monitor and Defend Your Reputation

DefendMyName.com – www.defendmyname.com

DoneReputationManagement.com – www.donereputationmanagement.com

Google Alerts – www.google.com/alerts

SalesForceMarketingCloud.com – salesforcemarketingcloud.com

Reputationdefender.com – www.reputationdefender.com

ScoutLabs.com – www.scoutlabs.com

SocialMention.com – www.socialmention.com

TweetBeep.com – www.tweetbeep.com

Resources to Find Blogs to Read

Alltop.com – www.alltop.com

Google blog search – www.blogsearch.google.com

Google alerts – www.google.com/alerts

Technorati.com – www.technorati.com

StumbleUpon.com – www.stumbleupon.com

Resources for Creating A Blog

Blogger – www.blogger.com/start

Movable Type – www.movabletype.com

Typepad – www.typepad.com

Wordpress – www.wordpress.com/ or www.wordpress.org

Additional Easy Blog Site Creation

www.about.me

www.brandyourself.com

www.carbonmade.com

www.doyoubuzz.com/us

www.flavors.me

www.rebelmouse.com

www.weebly.com/features.html

www.wix.com

www.webs.com

Options to Create Online Resumes

Author's note: these will vary in results depending on your target and the site's SEO at the time you use their tools. I recommend a Wordpress blog as the top way to showcase your online resume.

www.careercloud.com

www.doyoubuzz.com/us

www.jobspice.com/home

www.jobrary.com

www.krop.com/creativedatabase

Sample Social Resume

www.kenrevenaugh.com

Secure a Blog Host and Register a Domain

Bluehost – www.bluehost.com

Godaddy – www.godaddy.com

Places to find Photos for Blogs

www.flickr.com

www.morguefile.com

www.pachd.com

Create Content Without Your Own Blog

Review books on Amazon.com

www.examiner.com – Examiner.com

www.ezinearticles.com – Ezine

www.google.com/profiles – set up a Google Profile

www.helium.com – Helium

www.hubpages.com – HubPages

www.ning.com – Ning

www.shine.yahoo.com – Shine

www.squidoo.com – Squidoo

www.workitmom.com – WorkIt Mom

LinkedIn Resources

Job Seeker Premium on LinkedIn – www.linkedin.com/jobseeker

LinkedIn's blog – blog.linkedin.com

Track News About Twitter

Mashable – www.mashable.com

Twitter Applications

Hootsuite – hootsuite.com

TweetDeck – www.tweetdeck.com

Twitter Client – www.twitter.com

Twitter Directories and Search

Advanced Search on Twitter – search.twitter.com

FollowerWonk (search for Twitter Bios) – www.followerwonk.com

Justtweetit – www.justtweetit.com

Receive updates of tweets on any keyword – www.twilert.com

Twellow.com (Twitter Yellow Pages) – www.twellow.com

Tweepz (search for words, names, and hashtags) www.tweepz.com

Twitter terms directory –
support.twitter.com/groups/31-twitter-basics/topics/104-welcome-to-twitter-support/articles/166337-the-twitter-glossary

Wefollow – www.wefollow.com

Twibes.com – list of Twitter groups

Location Based Search

Local Tweeps – www.localtweeps.com

NearbyTweets.com – www.nearbytweets.com

Twellowhood – www.twellow.com/twellowhood

Tweepz.com

Lists on Twitter

www.twibes.com

www.wefollow.com

Follow/Following Managers

www.doesfollow.com

www.justunfollow.com

www.manageflitter.com

Evaluate Twitter Influence

Klout – www.klout.com

Kred – www.Kred.com

TweetStats – www.tweetstats.com

Twittercounter – www.twittercounter.com

Twitalyzer – www.twitalyzer.com

URL Shorteners

Bit.Ly

tinyurl.com

ow.ly

General Twitter Resources

Track hashtags – www.hashtags.org

Tweetake (allows you to back up your Twitter followers, favorites, direct messages, friends, and tweets) – www.tweetake.com

Bufferapp.com – to post and schedule updates.

OneCube.com's Smart Stream – to engage in Twitter chats and follow hashtags

Google's Twitter Timeline

For fun stats, try Tweetstats – www.tweetstats.com

Tips, Tools, Tactics & Strategies for Twitter – www.tweettrainer.com

Monitor Twitter's status – status.twitter.com

Blog about Twitter run by Darren Rouse/ProBlogger – www.twitip.com

Identify Twitter trends – www.whatthetrend.com

Blogging Resources

Art of blog – www.artofblog.com

Build a better blog – www.buildabetterblog.com

Copywriting tips – www.copyblogger.com

How to make my blog – www.howtomakemyblog.com

ProBlogger – www.problogger.net

Problogger's Blogging Job Board – www.jobs.problogger.net

Pushing social – www.pushingsocial.com

Facebook

BranchOut – http://branchout.com/

Be known – beknown.com

Claim your name – Log into your account and visit www.facebook.com/username

Facebook Fan Page – www.facebook.com/pages (click the "Create a Page" button)

Informational Article – applicant.com/facebook-as-a-job-search-tool

Jibe.com – www.jibe.com

Search Engine Optimization Tools

Google AdWords – www.Google.com/AdWords

Qalias – www.qalias.com

Submit your blog to search engines

www.google.com/addurl/

www.search.yahoo.com/info/submit.html

www.bing.com/webmaster/SubmitSitePage.aspx

Online Resources to Investigate

Audio – Blogtalk Radio www.blogtalkradio.com

Digg – www.digg.com

Ezine – www.ezinearticles.com

Flickr – www.flickr.com

FourSquare – www.foursquare.com

Hubpages.com – www.hubpages.com

Instagram – www.instagram.com

Naymz – www.naymz.com

Ning – www.about.ning.com

Plaxo – www.plaxo.com

Plurk – www.plurk.com

Reddit – www.reddit.com

Ryze – www.ryze.com

Scribd – www.scribd.com

Slideshare – www.slideshare.net

Squidoo.com – www.squidoo.com

StumbleUpon – www.stumbleupon.com

Traffikd's List of Social Media and Social Networking Sites – traffikd.com/social-media-websites

Tumblr – www.tumblr.com

YouTube – www.youtube.com

Career and Social Media Advice from Book Contributors

www.threshold-consulting.com – Walter Akana

www.jibberjobber.com/blog – Jason Alba

www.careertrend.net/blog – Jacqui Barrett-Poindexter

www.talentculture.com – Talent Culture/Meghan Biro

www.brazencareerist.com – Brazen Careerist

www.onthejob.45things.com – Anita Bruzzese

www.write-solution.com – Dawn Bugni

www.careerealism.com – Careerealism/JT O'Donnell

www.bestfitforward.com – Chandlee Bryan

www.comerecommended.com – Come Recommended

www.yoursocialmediastrategist.com – Diane Crompton

www.mnheadhunter.com – Paul DeBettignies

www.cornonthejob.com – Rich DeMatteo

www.upstarthr.com – Ben Eubanks

www.blog.fishdogs.com – Craig Fisher

www.blueskyresumes.com/blog – Louise Fletcher

www.executiveresumebranding.com – Meg Guiseppi

www.blog.sironaconsulting.com – Andy Headworth

www.girlmeetsgeek.com – Kate-Madonna Hindes

www.topmargin.com – Gayle Howard

www.hrbartender.com – HR Bartender/Sharlyn Lauby

www.heatherhuhman.com – Heather Huhman

www.jobmob.co.il – Job Mob/Jacob Share

www.jobwhiz.com – JobWhiz/Debra Feldman

www.job-hunt.org – Susan Joyce/Job-Hunt.org

www.exclusive-executive-resumes.com/blog – Erin Kennedy

http://katrinakibben.com/ – Katrina Kibben

www.alexandralevit.typepad.com – Alexandra Levit

www.jefflipschultz.wordpress.com – Jeff Lipschultz

www.blogging4jobs.com – Jessica Miller-Merrell

www.maggiemistal.com – Maggie Mistal

www.careersherpa.net – Hannah Morgan

www.careerrocketeer.com – Chris Perry

www.lindseypollak.com/blog – Lindsey Pollak

www.employaid.com – Barbara Poole/Employaid

www.karlaporter.com – Karla Porter

www.ramergroup.com – Mike Ramer

www.chameleonresumes.com – Lisa Rangel

www.recruitinganimal.com – Recruiting Animal

http://blog.resumebear.com— Resume Bear

www.fasttracktools.com – Fast Track Tools/Ken Revenaugh

www.sitalruparelia.com – Sital Ruparelia

www.secretsofthejobhunt.com – Secrets of the Job Hunt/Chris Russell

http://www.careersolvers.com/ – Barbara Safani

www.keppiecareers.com – Keppie Careers/Miriam Salpeter

www.healthcareers.about.com – Andrea Santiago

www.workforceconnection.net – Anita Santiago

www.marianlibrarian.com – Marian Schembari

www.smartblogs.com/leadership – Smart Blog on Workforce

www.netshare.com – Katherine Simmons/NETSHARE

www.escapefromcubiclenation.com – Escape from Cubicle Nation/ Pam Slim

www.inflexionadvisors.com/blog – Mark Stelzner/Inflexion Advisors

www.jimstroud.com – Jim Stroud

www.careerfolk.com – Donna Sweidan

www.blog.penelopetrunk.com – Penelope Trunk

www.timsstrategy.com – Tim Tyrell-Smith

www.eexecutives.net/select – Harry Urschel

www.radicalrecruit.wordpress.com – Geoff Webb

Other Book Contributors

www.leahsgotit.blogspot.com – Leah Barr

www.writingonpurpose.com – Teresa Basich

www.linkedin.com/in/beckybenishek – Becky Benishek

www.thesalesmatrix.com – David Benjamin

www.chasinggoodness.com – Robyn Cobb

katetheprofessional.wordpress.com – Kate Davids

www.cfo2grow.com – Samuel Dergel/CFO2Grow

www.tastidlite.com – Tasti-D-Lite/B.J. Emerson, Social Technology Officer

www.kristenfischer.com – Kristen Fischer

www.lauragainor.com – Laura Gainor

www.alexisgrant.com – Alexis Grant

www.daretocomment.com – Ian Greenleigh

www.linkedin.com/in/alisunhernandez – Alisun Hernandez (@SunnyinSyracuse)

www.williejackson.com – Willie Jackson

www.loiclemeur.com – Loic LeMeur

www.shanemac.me – Shane Mac

www.thoughtmechanics.com – Barry Maurice/Thought Mechanics

www.au.linkedin.com/in/noelpatterson – Noel Patterson

www.pizzeriaventi-atlanta.com – Pizzeria Venti in Atlanta

www.twentyorsomething.com – Susan Pogorzelski

www.sueannereed.com – Sue Anne Reed

www.nicholasreese.com – Nick Reese

www.linkedin.com/in/ellensautter – Ellen Sautter

www.olivers14.wordpress.com – Oliver Schmid

www.ripplesinreality.blogspot.com – Saranya Thirumoolan

www.linkedin.com/in/rekhathomas – Rekha Thomas

www.brettvanderwater.com – Brett Vanderwater

Tweets (and Twitter Users) to Emulate

Twitter can be a terrific resource for people in any industry. The following Twitter users tweet about different topics, but all use Twitter, in part, to illustrate their expertise in their fields. Take a look at the sample professional tweets taken from their Twitter streams as examples of how you may want to consider sharing information and connecting with others in your field.

S. Collier Ward, R.A., LEED A.P. is a consulting architect and author. He authors a blog, an architect's resource for professional blogging at http://www.buildingcontent.highercontent.com. He tweets **@Collier1960**.

He retweets other posts that may interest his followers:

RT @usgbc: milestone: There is now 1 billion square feet of #LEED-certified space worldwide! http://ow.ly/38Yht

RT ArchiDame—The number of women in architecture falls again feature in @architectsjournal kindly quoting me—http://bit.ly/a8juNn

Some messages directly connect with others who have an interest in his topic (via including their @ name):

@INFILLnc & @bobborson Thanks for adding to & promoting the Architectural Bloggers Daily last night. I appreciate it. http://bit.ly/9yXaSt

He shares content he created and invites comments. Note how Collier uses hashtags to attract people in his field:

Please check out the new look at Building Content, critiques welcome http://www.buildingcontent.highercontent.com #BlogChat #Architectural

#Architects, here the latest at Building Content, "Art Imitating Life" http://www.buildingcontent.highercontent.com/art-imitating-life.html

Ed Cabellon is the Director of the Campus Center at Bridgewater State University in Massachusetts. He blogs at http://edcabellon.com/ and tweets **@edcabellon**.

He shares advice and information about using social media in higher education, indicating he is aware of this issue and connected to people who also write about it:

RT @mikefixs: RT @TweetSmarter: 100 Inspiring Ways to Use #SocialMedia In the Classroom: http://j.mp/9BPH8G #RIT

He lets everyone know that he presents about this topic:

Headed over to present to the women of @dphieBSU on Social Media :-) I'm really getting good at this topic ;-) #bsulife

He shares articles of interest to his colleagues. Note the use of hashtags to attract attention:

Nice post on the @The_SA_Blog by @joeginese: "You've Just Been VolunTold" http://ow.ly/37Tav #sachat #highered

He offers a direct answer to a question in his area of interest:

@joeginese Foursquare for Universities is a great place to start: http://ow.ly/36rE6
#sachat Pro Mentors and #sagrad students: Be on the lookout for an email tonight or tomorrow with your pairing :-) Have a blast!

Marsha Collier is author of the "For Dummies" series of books on eBay, and e-commerce, and Social Media Spokesperson at The Collier Company, Inc. Her most recent book is *The Ultimate Online Customer Service Guide: How to Connect with your Customers to Sell More*! Learn more and connect with her via www.marshacollier.com. She tweets **@marshacollier**.

She comments and retweets about her field:

Well put RT @ty_sullivan Look @ every customer that walks through your door as your rent. Because they are! Engage. Welcome. Keep. #custserv

She lets people know when and where she will be speaking and what conferences she attends. Note how Marsha directly connects by including @ names in her tweets:

@JessicaNorthey I will be speaking on Weds in Montreal at @ webcomMT, it opens free to the public at 3pm http://bit.ly/b8K91B
    Webcom-Montréal International will explore how Web 2.0 can reboot business: I'll be there w @armano, will we see you? http://post.ly/1Cbey

She shares what other people are saying about her work:

"Excellent Resource for All Ages" TY @JulieSpira for the review of my Facebook & Twitter For Seniors Book http://amzn.to/9hoD7h

She offers comments without a link relevant to her followers:

When preparing your presentations. Realize its as much HOW you present, as what you're saying
Desirre Andrews is the founder of Preparing For Birth, and a doula and childbirth educator. Her website is http://prepforbirth. com/ and she tweets @preparing4birth.

She advertises classes she is teaching:

Winter class session begins January 3rd. Our new class location is Active Chiropractic Wellness Center in Colorado . . . http://fb.me/NvH3koND

She mentions where she will be presenting:

Final touches and printing out handouts for the @CAPPAnet working training in New Orleans this week coming week.

Comments on relevant topics without a link:

The postpartum mother needs to be honored and cared for. Normal, life event still requires healing, energy conservation & support.

Shares links to information she knows will be useful for her community:

It is important that the birthing mother's support partner or team really is on board with what she wants and . . . http://fb.me/ IdTCrF9F

She interacts directly with her followers and shares professional advice:

@marfmom so the cardio appt went well? Drink loads of fluids today and rest before NST/BPP. Norm for a dip in fluid above 5 is good

NOTES

NOTES